LIVING BIOGRAPHIES OF
Famous Men

LIVING BIOGRAPHIES OF
Famous Men

By HENRY THOMAS AND
DANA LEE THOMAS

Illustrations by
GORDON ROSS

Blue Ribbon Books
GARDEN CITY, NEW YORK

CL
PRINTED IN THE UNITED STATES OF AMERICA

Contents and Illustrations

CONTENTS

Introduction

like Kemal, Ataturk and Sun Yat-sen, state leaders like Disraeli and Churchill, and all-round lovers of living and striving like Benvenuto Cellini.

A group as varied as this has but one thing—that subtle essence of personality, that "fame of heroic thought, or deed," which the ones call fame. If

Franklin "either write things worth reading, or do things worth writing."

I<small>T HAS BEEN</small> the purpose of this series to bring to life as comprehensive an assemblage as possible of the outstanding personalities in history. In each of the previous volumes, these personalities have been grouped together according to their pursuits or professions. For example, one of the volumes has been devoted to Great Philosophers; another to Great Composers; still another, to Famous Rulers. And so on, through the entire series.

In this volume, however, we have found it advisable to supplement the general plan of the series with a somewhat different arrangement. Instead of grouping a number of men under a *single category*, we have here included the men who have not fitted into any of the *former categories*.

Because of the greater flexibility of this arrangement, we are able in this volume to present a wider horizon and a more diversified spectacle in the adventure of human life. Thus, we have here soldiers like Alexander and Bolivar, explorers like Marco Polo and Columbus, musicians like Paderewski and Caruso, dramatists like Shakespeare and Goethe and Bernard Shaw, revolutionists like Karl Marx and Garibaldi, state builders

INTRODUCTION

like Kemal Ataturk and Sun Yat-sen, state leaders like Disraeli and Churchill, and all-round lovers of living and striving like Benvenuto Cellini.

A group as varied as human endeavor. Yet they all have one thing in common—that subtle essence of personality, that "perfume of heroic thought or deed" which the poets call fame. "If you would be famous after you are dead," said Benjamin Franklin, "either write things worth reading or do things worth writing."

H. T.
D. L. T.

ALEXANDER THE GREAT

Important Dates in Life of Alexander the Great

B.C.

356—Born at Pella.

343—Became pupil of Aristotle.

340—Quelled (at the age of 16) uprising of hill tribes on Macedonian border.

336—Became king of Macedonia.

335—S u b j u g a t e d Greece.

334-32—Conquered Asia Minor.

332-31—Conquered Egypt.

331—Invaded Persia.

328—Reached the borders of Hindu Kush.

328-26—Invaded the outposts of India.

326-23—Consolidated his conquests in Asia.

323—Died.

Alexander the Great

356 B.C.—323 B.C.

HE WAS the savage heir to a savage throne. His father's banquets, writes the historian Athenaeus, "were, because of their riotousness and their violence, veritable workshops of war." King Philip corrupted everybody who came into contact with him. "Even if a man was not a ruffian upon his arrival," observes another ancient historian, Theopompus, "he soon became one under King Philip's life and habits." It was the ambition of Philip to turn the entire world into his private hunting ground.

Like father, like son. When he was only fourteen, Alexander acted as regent of Macedonia (modern Bulgaria) in the absence of Philip who had marched away upon one of his military campaigns. A delegation of Persian noblemen came to visit the young prince. They brought with them a royal gift—the stick and the ball used by the Persian king when he played his favorite game of polo. Alexander picked up the gift. "This ball," he said to the Persian ambassadors, "is the world. And I am the stick that will smash it around to my heart's content."

II

THE GLORY that was Greece, the age of the great sculptors and philosophers and poets, had faded into the twilight of aggression and jealousy and bloodshed between city and city and state and state. The best men were perishing upon the battlefields, and the entire civilization of Greece was dangerously close to death.

Some of the statesmen, like the Athenian Isocrates, realized the danger. In order to save the life of their country, they advocated a United States of Greece. Their idea was excellent, but they called upon the wrong man to execute it. Philip accepted the invitation of Isocrates to weld the Greeks into a unit. He raised a Macedonian army, swept down upon the war-weary Greek peninsula, and organized all the independent Greek cities into a United States—of Greek slaves.

King Philip was a genius as an organizer of empires. Everywhere his word was law—except in his own household. His wife Olympias, the mother of Alexander, was a mystical fanatic who teetered on the border of insanity. She considered it her religious duty to make the life of Philip, whom she heartily detested, as unhappy as possible. In order to vex him, she told him that Alexander was not his son, but the offspring of a God who had come to her at night in the form of a serpent. Whatever Philip may have thought of this fairy tale, Alexander half-believed it throughout his life. Again and again he insisted that he was of divine origin.

Life in the royal palace of Macedon was a succession of rituals, dissensions and orgies. Alexander, egged on by his mother, showed no respect for Philip. At one of the royal banquets, when father and son were both stupefied with drink, Philip attempted to stab Alexander because the boy had insulted him. He was too drunk, however, to make a perfect lunge.

As Philip reeled to the ground, his son transfixed him with a *verbal* stab. "Look!" he sneered to the assembled guests. "Here is

[4]

the man who would leap from Europe into Asia. Yet when he tries to step from one couch to another, you see him sprawled out on the floor!"

III

SUCH was the atmosphere in which Alexander grew up. His father tried, indeed, to give him a good education. He hired the best tutors for Alexander. Rhetoricians, grammarians, poets, musicians, philosophers—all came to the palace and tried to tame the savage royal whelp into the semblance of a civilized man. Among his more famous tutors was Aristotle, that amazing miracle of learning who within a single head contained the knowledge of a hundred men, and who could write and talk with equal authority upon such a diversity of subjects as politics, drama, poetry, physics, medicine, psychology, history, logic, astronomy, ethics, natural history, mathematics, rhetoric, biology, and what not. But Aristotle made very little impression upon Alexander, or upon any of the other members of the royal family. Philip, Alexander and Olympias affected a superficial veneer of Greek culture. At bottom, however, they remained throughout their life an unholy trinity of barbarian wildcats. When Philip was ready to start out on his first campaign against Persia, he was assassinated—at the direct instigation, it was said, of Olympias. At his funeral Olympias insisted that the murderer should receive the same honors as the murdered king.

IV

ALEXANDER was twenty years old when Philip died. He found himself heir to a well-trained army, all equipped and ready to descend upon the Orient. The soldiers were merely waiting for a leader who possessed the imagination, the egotism, the recklessness and the skill to undertake the subjugation of the world. Alexander had all these characteristics in abundance, and to spare. He lost no time in proving his ability to all those who might have entertained any doubts about it. He quickly subdued the tribes to the north of Macedonia and then he marched upon the Greeks who, at the news of Philip's death, had tried to break away from the Macedonian yoke. He besieged the city of Thebes and captured it without any difficulty. In order to show the power of his crimson fist to the rest of the Greeks, he destroyed the entire city, put six thousand of its inhabitants to the sword, and sold thirty thousand as slaves in the public markets.

The spoils that he had captured from the city he divided among his officers. "What," asked one of them, "are you keeping for yourself?"

"My hopes," replied Alexander.

And then he proceeded to the relentless fulfilment of his hopes. He marched southward from Thebes into the other cities of Greece. Wherever he went, he was met with false flatteries and with costly gifts. The Greek rebels had learned their lesson. They proclaimed him their leader and they were ready to follow him on his expedition into the vast territories of the Orient.

His triumphant march through Greece, however, met here and there with a rebuff of a quite unexpected sort. A few of the Greeks still retained enough of their independence to tell him what they thought of him. When he arrived at Corinth he was greeted, as elsewhere, with hypocritical shouts of welcome. But he was disappointed not to see Diogenes, the Cynic, among the flatterers. Diogenes was the one man in Corinth whom he most admired and whose admiration he was most anxious to win. But the old cynic remained quietly in one of the suburbs. The pride of conquerors and the pomp of kings were matters of the utmost indifference to him. He made no attempt to see the great Macedonian procession or to meet the victorious king.

Since Diogenes refused to come to Alexander, Alexander decided to go to Diogenes. He found him lying alone in the sun. With a patronizing show of friendliness he asked Diogenes whether there was anything he could do for him. "Yes," replied the old codger. "You can do me a great favor by removing yourself from between me and the sun."

Instead of punishing him for his boldness, Alexander left him to his cynical meditations. It was not in vain that the young king had been a pupil of Aristotle. "If I were not Alexander," he observed to one of his cronies, "I would choose to be Diogenes." To which observation Diogenes, had he taken the trouble to reply, might have said, "If I were not Diogenes, I would choose to be anyone *but* Alexander."

V

ALEXANDER'S MILITARY AMBITION soon drove all philosophy and, indeed, all common sense out of his head. He was a very devil for recklessness. Where others feared to tread, Alexander rushed in. He gambled against the impossible, and he generally won out. If a river was too rapid to be crossed, Alexander crossed it. If an enemy was to be dislodged from the summit of a hill that was not to be scaled, he scaled the hill and put the enemy to flight. Obsessed with the superstitious belief that he was a son of Zeus, he felt convinced that Heaven itself was fighting on his side. And he passed this conviction on to everybody else. "Once," writes Plutarch, quoting a contemporary of Alexander as his authority, "the waves of the Pamphilian seacoast, which ordinarily came to the very edge of the cliffs, retired suddenly of their own accord to afford him passage." When he besieged the city of Tyre, the inhabitants tied down the statue of Apollo with ropes and nailed it to the pedestal, in order that the God might not be able to desert them and go over to Alexander. But, Plutarch informs us, Apollo paid no attention to the Tyrian efforts to keep him in their midst. In spite of the nails and the ropes that kept his body fastened down among the Tyrians, he fought in spirit on the side of Alexander.

With amazing rapidity Alexander conquered one Asiatic country after another. His almost incredible successes had paralyzed his enemies into a state of impotent despair. "What is the good of fighting against a warrior descended from the skies?" He was reported as being here, there and everywhere at once. Most of the armies that had been raised against him were ready to give up the struggle even before they met him on the battlefield. They were defeated not so much by Alexander, as by the very *fear* of Alexander.

He was a brilliant madman. Afflicted with the insane delusion that he was a God, he insisted upon being worshiped like a God. On one occasion, when he was struck in the thigh, he expressed amazement to see that his blood was the ordinary blood of mortals, instead of the *ichor* which was popularly supposed to be coursing through the veins of the immortal Gods. In the midst of battle he often called upon Zeus and the other divinities to come to his aid—reminding them, in case they had forgotten it, that he was their kinsman—indeed, the *greatest* of their kinsmen.

His megalomania was astounding, even to his most ardent admirers. He looked into the mirror of his own vanity—we have seen it recently in men like Hitler and Hirohito—and he saw reflected in it a visitor from Heaven walking among the pygmies of the earth. He insisted that he was the master ruler of a master race. When he departed from the borders of India after he had decided not to invade that country, he left behind him a number of bridles and helmets and other bits of armor that had been purposely manufactured several sizes too big. The Hindus must be made to believe that the Macedonians were an army of gigantic men and horses. Everything that belonged to him he considered sacred. He named a new city in Asia after his horse, and another after his dog. He was an exhibitionist of the most obnoxious type. When his army marched in triumph through Carmania, he had a banquet prepared upon a huge platform that was drawn by eight horses. He sat upon this moving platform, eating and drinking with his companions, while the parade passed through the city and the Orientals gazed with astonishment at the splendid vulgarity of the Macedonian feast.

Yet in Asia, as in Europe, there were those who saw him in his true color and his true size. On the banks of the Indus there lived a group of philosophers called the *gymnosophists* (naked wise men). Alexander sent one of his officers to the leader of these men with the message that "the Great King of Macedonia wishes to speak to you."

"But I," replied the philosopher, "do not wish to speak to the Great King of Macedonia."

"Do you dare thus to insult the Son of Zeus?"

"Tell Alexander that he is no more the son of Zeus than I am. Or tell him rather that both of us are the sons of Zeus, as are all men who are born into this world."

Whereupon Alexander's messenger resorted to bribes and threats. But the *gymnosophist* remained imperturbable. "Alexander can neither cheer me nor scare me. There is nothing I wish to gain, for I have already my philosophy; and there is nothing I fear to lose, for in taking my life Alexander will but release a precious soul from a worthless body."

"I shall advise Alexander," said the messenger haughtily, "to waste no time upon you but to go on with the conquest of the earth."

"Alexander," said the naked philosopher, "has already conquered his mortal share of the earth. Six feet."

VI

ALEXANDER'S TEMPER was as unpredictable as the New England weather. He passed from gentleness to ferocity without a moment's notice. When his troops were crossing the desert, he refused a drink brought to him by one of his soldiers. The general, he said, must suffer thirst along with the rest of the army. But when his cupbearer unintentionally offended him, he seized the poor fellow by the hair and dashed out his brains against the wall. One day, as he was sailing down the Euphrates, a gust of wind blew the royal fillet off his head and into the water. A sailor dived immediately overboard and rescued the fillet before it sank out of sight. Fearing that it might be spoiled if he dragged it through the water, the sailor placed it upon his head as he swam back toward the galley.

"Give him a silver talent for his courage," said Alexander to his steward as the sailor clambered aboard.

And then, turning to his executioner, "Have him killed for his presumption. For no man but Alexander must wear the royal fillet on his head."

Alexander was an incongruous mixture of the artist and the fiend. He read Homer when he was sober and killed his dearest friend, Clitus, in a drunken fit. His repentance over the murder when he sobered up was no less violent than his passion when he murdered him. He wept when his greatest enemy Darius, the king of Persia, died, and he executed large numbers of prisoners—having first cut off their ears and their noses—as a daily diversion. "Consistency," he said, "becomes the character of a man. But I am inconsistent because mine is the character of a God."

And when anyone questioned the godliness of his character, Alexander made short shrift of him. One of his skeptical camp-followers was the philosopher Callisthenes, a nephew of Aristotle. "The Gods," declared Callisthenes, "are justly enraged because the mortal Alexander has dared to usurp their immortal attributes." When these words were brought to Alexander's attention, he decided to put Callisthenes into "his proper place." At a banquet prepared for the occasion, Alexander arranged to pledge each guest in a cup of wine, whereupon the guest was to drain the cup, receive the kiss of friendship and prostrate himself before his "Divine King." When he pledged the name of Callisthenes, Alexander handed him the cup and then turned insolently away without the accompanying kiss. The philosopher, not to be outdone, turned with equal insolence upon his heel and strode away without the necessary obeisance.

This public demonstration of mutual hostility was tantamount to a death sentence for Callisthenes. A few days after the banquet, the philosopher was crucified on the charge of "fomenting a conspiracy against the King's life." Alexander's friends, observes

Plutarch, "are safer in the activity of his battles than in the idleness of his banquets."

Alexander was reckless of human life. One of his favorite soldiers, who had taken sick, died because he refused to follow the physician's advice. Alexander, with the logic of a madman, ordered the physician to be crucified. And then, as a further outlet to his emotion, he descended upon an unsuspecting city and slaughtered all the inhabitants—"a fitting sacrifice to the memory of my dead friend." Whenever an opposing commander fell into his hands, he cast a pair of dice to decide the man's fate. If the throw was favorable, he dismissed the prisoner with a magnanimous nod; if unfavorable, he strung him up to the nearest tree. His ingenuity in the invention of new tortures for his enemies was nothing short of amazing. Plutarch relates how once he tied down a captured officer between two trees which had been drawn together, and which were then allowed to snap back to their natural position. The violence of the rebound tore the victim in halves; and "each tree, as its branches swung aloft, carried with it a part of the bleeding corpse."

Having regaled himself with this edifying spectacle, Alexander then returned to his Homer. He always carried a de luxe edition of Homer among his most precious belongings. He liked to read the battle scenes in the *Iliad*, he said. They inspired him with a thirst for glory and a love for war.

VII

WHEN he was not fighting or reading Homer, Alexander spent his time in drinking. In his bottles, just as in his battles, this pitiable madman of Macedonia tried to be superhuman. He was not content with the excesses of ordinary mortals. He drank without stint or measure, and then he went about doing mischief like an intoxicated god. At the suggestion of a tipsy courtesan whom he was entertaining at one of his banquets, he topped off the carousals by setting fire to the palace of the Persian king. On another occasion he held a Marathon drinking contest, with a golden crown as the prize. The winner succeeded in drinking down twelve quarts of wine; but he died, together with forty-one other contestants, as a result of the debauch.

Alexander himself finally took sick at one of the orgies "which had been kept up all the night and the whole of the following day." The sickness developed into a fever, and a few days later he expired. Alexander was only 33 at the time of his death; but he had lived long enough to devastate more lands, and to inflict more mischief and murder upon the human race, than any other man in ancient history.

VIII

The sentimental historians have put a halo around the head of Alexander. They have held him up as a model of everything that is great and noble and virtuous in human life. They have called him a founder of cities, a tamer of savage races, and a builder of roads and of commerce between nation and nation.

It is sickening to see a super-brigand like Alexander thus glorified into a saint. He was not at all interested in civilization. He was interested in Alexander and in nothing else. Like a colossus, he wanted to bestride the world. Just before he died, he planned to have an entire mountain carved into a statue of himself, with his left hand holding a city of ten thousand inhabitants and with his right hand pouring a river into the sea. He suffered from a psychopathic lust for power. He built, just as he destroyed, for his own glory, and not for the sake of humanity. Historians make much of the few cities that he founded. What of the many cities that he burned down? It is foolish to maintain that through his wars he sowed the seeds of Greek culture in Asia. He merely sowed there the seeds of hatred, of revenge, and of future wars. It was the thinkers and the poets of Greece—men like Solon and Herodotus and Plato, and not the warriors like Alexander, who brought the civilization of Europe into the Orient. Alexander had no grandiose plans for the organization and the education of the world. He tamed it, just as he had tamed his wild horse Bucephalus, in order that he might saddle it with his throne and ride it to its destruction. His wars, we are told, were a boon to humanity, since they enabled him to cover the trackless wilderness of Asia with a network of roads and trading posts. But is it necessary to *kill* humanity in order to bring it together into a closer unit? Must the ways of friendship between nation and nation be paved with the skeletons of slaughtered men?

Alexander was a congenital paranoiac whose mad career set civilization back a thousand years. His name, written across the world in letters of fire and blood, spelled nothing but disaster for the human race.

MARCO POLO

Important Dates in Life of Marco Polo

1254—Born in Venice.

1271—Joined father and uncle on trip to China.

1275—Reached court of Kublai Khan.

1277—Appointed as Imperial Agent for Kublai Khan.

1295—Returned to Venice.

1298—Commanded a ship in expedition against Genoa. Defeated and taken prisoner.

1298-99—Dictated his Travels to fellow prisoner, Rustienano.

1299—Set free.

1324—Died, January 9.

Marco Polo

1254–1324

IN THE SUMMER OF 1295, three bedraggled strangers made their way through the streets of Venice. Their faces were bronzed and lined with fatigue. Their backs were bent with the heavy bundles which they carried over their shoulders. Their clothes were in tatters. The dogs barked at their heels, and the people stared. A most curious trio in that city of most curious sights; their like had never been seen before. Italian features, and Oriental manners. And their speech, too, was a peculiar mixture of Italian idiom and Oriental gibberish.

"Who are you?" asked one of the passers-by.

"We are the Polos," replied the youngest of the three—"my father Nicolo, my uncle Maffeo, and myself, Marco Polo."

The Venetian shrugged his shoulders. "The Polos? Never heard of them."

Finally the trio came to a house on the outskirts of the city. "Well," remarked the oldest with a sigh of relief, "we're home at last."

They knocked. A woman opened the door and looked at them belligerently.

"We are the Polos, returned home after our long absence."

"Returned from Hell most likely! Why, the Polos have been gone and dead these twenty-six years."

"But we *are* the Polos."

"Get along, you beggars, or I'll call the police!"

"We're not beggars. On the contrary, we've brought gifts with us."

"Gifts?"

"Yes," said the youngest, "millions of them!"

The woman, a distant relative of the Polos, admitted them reluctantly into the house. After much questioning, she became convinced that these men were not impostors. She summoned the other relatives from various parts of the city and prepared a banquet in honor of the trio "returned from the dead."

The guests are seated at the table. But the Polos have not as yet entered. They are off in their room dressing. "I wonder what strange Oriental costume they are going to put on?" remarks one of the guests—a dandy with an eye for finery.

And now the Polos make their appearance. What a dazzling display! Trailing robes of crimson satin, fold upon fold, embroidered with silver threads. "Do you like them?"

A thunder of *oh's* and *ah's* for reply.

"Then you shall have them."

They leave the room and return in a few minutes. And now they are dressed in long robes of crimson damask embroidered with cloth of gold. Their former robes of satin have been cut up into strips and are now being distributed among the guests.

They sit down to their banquet. Wines, antipasto, ravioli, more wines.

And now, before the main dishes are put on—"How would you like these *damask* cloths?"

Another frenzied chorus of delight. Again the Polos leave the room; and upon their return, they are dressed in robes of crimson velvet fastened together with diamond clasps. Once more their former garments have been cut up into strips and, in accordance with the Mongolian custom, are being divided among the guests.

And now the banquet is over. Embraces, dances, singing, more embraces and more wine. In the confusion, the Polos have again disappeared. When they come back, their crimson garments are ready for distribution. But the Polos are now dressed in the rags which they have worn upon their arrival.

"What next?"

Marco Polo orders the servants to leave the room. And then, taking a sharp knife from the table, he rips open the seams of the tatters. And, Santa Maria! What a cataract of jewels pours out before the astonished eyes of the spectators! Rubies, sapphires, emeralds, carbuncles, diamonds, cornelians, amethysts, brilliants and pearls!

"How many of these have you collected, Messer Marco Polo?"

"Millions and millions of them!"

"And you must have had many an interesting adventure in collecting them."

"Yes, I've had millions of adventures!"

Marco Polo always spoke in this extravagant manner. And soon he acquired an affectionate title among the Venetians. They nicknamed him "Marco Millions."

II

THREE YEARS after Marco Polo's return to Venice, he engaged in one of the naval battles between his native city and Genoa. He was taken prisoner by the Genoese; and, in order to while away the tedious hours of his captivity, he entertained his fellow-prisoners, as well as his captors, with the account of his travels in the Orient. A writer by the name of Rusticiano became interested in this story and gathered the material into a travel book. The *Travels of Marco Polo* marks one of the turning points in the history of human relationships. The young Venetian had started for China as a bearer of the "civilization" of the West to the "barbarians" of the East. He came back to Italy as a messenger of good will between the equally civilized races of the East and the West.

China, as Marco Polo discovered, possessed a culture as ancient and as beautiful as that of Greece or of Rome. From the Golden Rule of Confucius—"what you would not that others should do unto you, do not unto others"—to the Sacred Principle of Tai-tsung—"let no man persecute another man for his religion, for there are many ways of reaching heaven"—the Chinese sages had inspired their people with a sense of reciprocity toward one another. For almost two thousand years the "Flowery Kingdom" had enjoyed an uninterrupted march of spiritual progress. And of artistic and mental progress as well. In the first four centuries of our Christian era, the Chinese artists created some of the most lovely landscapes that have ever been painted by the hand of man. The delicate carvings, the graceful poetry and the majestic architecture produced during those four hundred years are, even today, things of undying beauty. In the sixth century the Chinese invented printing from wood blocks—almost a thousand years before the invention of printing in Europe. In the same century we find the Chinese employing coal and gas for heating purposes—a method with which the white races did not catch up until twenty-five generations later. Gunpowder, too, was known to the Chinese of the sixth century; although, being a peaceful nation, they took little advantage of this invention of accelerated murder.

From the sixth century to the thirteenth, China stood in the forefront of the world's civilized nations. And then she suffered a temporary relapse, but not for long. The Mongolians, a tribe of restless wanderers who lived in the steppes of Asia and who were related somewhat to the Huns, began to sweep over China in a series of invasions which finally embraced all the vast territory from the Pacific Ocean in the Far East to the Dnieper River in Russia. Under the impetuous leadership of Genghis Khan, the Mongol invaders in an incredibly short time acquired an empire to which the empire of Alexander was but a child's toy.

Genghis Khan had the fearlessness of Alexander, the endurance of Caesar, and the simplicity of the primitive Asiatic conquerors. Mare's meat was his favorite food, a pitched tent his palace, and a saddle his throne. He was more eager to conquer than to rule. Yet, unlike most other conquerors, he was neither vindictive nor ferocious. "Under Genghis Khan"—we are quoting H. G. Wells —"we find the completest religious toleration established across the entire breadth of Asia." Instead of imposing his barbarity upon the defeated nations, he absorbed, or rather allowed himself to become absorbed into, their superior civilization. When he conquered the Chinese people, he was in turn conquered by their culture. Unlike the Vandals who had destroyed the civilization of Rome, the Mongolians not only left the civilization of China intact, but adopted it as their own. The grandson of Genghis, Kublai Khan, owed much more to the scholarly traditions of China than he did to the customs of his own barbarian ancestors.

It was at the court of Kublai Khan that Marco Polo, and through him all Europe, became acquainted with the amazing civilization of the Orient.

III

THE mission of Marco Polo to the court of Kublai Khan was partly cultural, partly religious, and largely economic. The teachers of Europe wanted to educate China, the missionaries wanted to convert it, and the merchants wanted to do business with it. Marco Polo's family were among the merchants of Venice. His father, Nicolo Polo, and his uncle, Maffeo Polo, had spent some years as traders in the kingdom of Kublai Khan. When the Mongolian ruler heard that there were two astute European bargainers in his country, he invited them to his court. He had never seen a Christian businessman, and he was curious to know what that "strange animal" looked like.

He took a fancy to the two Venetians. Nicolo was a shrewd, dark man, "a good judge of a jewel and a good judge of a sword." His brother, Maffeo, was "a big, red-bearded man with a great eye for a horse and a great eye for a woman." Kublai Khan enjoyed their vulgarity, their cocksuredness, and their blustering good nature. He discussed business with them, and he found them very keen. He tried to discuss politics and religion with them, and he found them not so keen. He was amused at their efforts to convert him to Christianity. "It is the desire of our Pope," they told him, "to convert all the heathens to the true religion."

"And who is your Pope?"

"He is the earthly vicar of Christ, our God."

"And how does your Pope know that your God is the God of the one true religion?"

To this question the Polos had no ready answer. "We are neither teachers nor priests, but blunt businessmen."

Kublai Khan was amused, and at the same time intrigued. He told them that he might possibly be interested in their religion if he could discuss it with some people who really knew what they were talking about. He therefore suggested that they go back to the Pope and ask him to send to China a hundred teachers of Christianity, "intelligent men acquainted with the Seven Arts, able to enter into controversy, and able clearly to prove to skeptical folk like myself that the law of Confucius is inferior to the law of Christ."

Nicolo and Maffeo Polo started on their mission to Pope Clement IV. But when they arrived in Europe, they found that Clement was dead, and that there was too much dissension within the Church for the immediate election of a new Pope. Impatiently they waited for two years, and then the newly elected Pope (Gregory X) listened coldly to their plea. Instead of giving them a hundred learned men for the conversion of the Chinese, he gave them two uneducated Dominican friars. These two men possessed neither the spiritual conviction nor the physical courage for the journey. Before they had gone many days, they pretended that they were ill and begged to be sent home. "Let the Chinese,

Alexander the Great

Marco Polo

for all we care, stew in the Purgatory of their own ignorance."

Nicolo and Maffeo went on without their spiritual allies. But they had taken along with them the son of Nicolo as a possible substitute for the two Dominican friars.

Marco Polo was a likely lad of fifteen. A good head on his shoulders, and a dreamy look in his eyes. "The youngster," said Maffeo to Nicolo, "will make either a businessman or a poet."

"Maybe both," replied Nicolo.

"And he has a fine sense of religion, too. And a tongue that can hit the mark."

"He got that from his mother. We Polos are a blunt and a tongue-tied race."

Maffeo, lost in thought, kept stroking his long red beard. Finally he spoke: "Maybe the child can convert the Great Khan. Who knows?"

"At any rate," concluded Nicolo, "he will be a good help to us in our business."

IV

A JOURNEY of six years across the forests of Europe and over the mountains of Asia. Places that no white man had ever visited before. They passed beyond the peaks of Ararat, "where Noah had anchored his ark at the time of the Great Flood." And they went beyond the ruins of Babel, where the thoughts of men had been confounded because of their too many tongues. And they left behind them the haunts of dragons and the lairs of wild beasts and the habitations of wild men. And they came to the Plateau of Pamir, called "the top of the World," and from there they saw many more mountains and wastelands over which they must travel before they could arrive at the land of the Great Khan. Past the Hills of Salt and the region of Magic Fires and the Valley of the Singing Trees and the Perilous Desert where no river sang. Beyond the cavern of the Old Man of the Mountain, who bewitched the young horsemen of his country and transformed them into assassins to do his bidding. And they passed through the City of Enticing Women, where many a traveler lingered on until he was bereft of his ambition and his life. And beyond the City of Tangut, where the dead were carried out of the houses through breaches made in the walls. And then across mile after mile of pestilence and desolation and death.

And finally they came to the Great Desert. And here death threatened to put an end to Marco Polo himself. Sand-sifted air for aching lungs, and a glaring sun for fevered eyes. And one day they came to a sand-dune from which there protruded the faces of grinning skeletons—a whole caravan of men who had been shriveled to death in the desert's heat.

And it was here that Marco Polo, exhausted, lay down to die.

V

KUBLAI KHAN had a telegraph system of beating drums. And these drums informed him that three white travelers from the West were approaching his kingdom, and that one of them was mortally sick. Whereupon he sent a caravan into the desert, and brought the three travelers into Cathay, and nursed Marco Polo back into health.

And when Marco Polo opened his eyes, he found himself in the enchanted city of Xanadu, the capital of the Mongolian Empire.

"In Xanadu did Kublai Khan
    A stately pleasure dome decree,
  Where Alph, the sacred river, ran
  Through caverns measureless to man,
    Down to a sunless sea.
  So twice five miles of fertile ground
  With walls and towers were girded round:
  And there were gardens, bright with sinuous rills,
    Where blossomed many an incense-bearing tree;
  And here were forests ancient as the hills,
    Enfolding sunny spots of greenery."

And at his bedside, nursing him—so legend has it—sat Golden Balls, the daughter of Kublai Khan.

A few weeks of convalescence, seasoned with the sweetness of love—and then Marco Polo aroused himself to the mission for which he had come to China. He must convert the Great Khan.

The Khan listened to him, and thought there was much wisdom and sincerity in his speech, and became converted—not, however, to Christianity but to friendship. He took the young merchant-poet of Venice into his heart. He admitted him into the Imperial Council and dispatched him as his personal envoy to various parts of China.

The relationship between Marco Polo and Kublai Khan was of mutual advantage to two continents. For while the Chinese emperor was impressed with what he heard of Europe, the Venetian traveler was impressed with what he saw of China. Here was a country which, culturally and materially, stood on a par with every other country in the world. In the libraries of China he found books on philosophy, religion, economics, architecture, poetry, painting, music, astronomy, history, government and law. And he found that shortly before his arrival the scholars of China had compiled an Encyclopedia that covered all the above and a thousand other fields of human interest.

And, too, he found among the inhabitants the use of metals and the mining of coal, and the measuring of time by means of sand clocks and water clocks. And he noted—a thing which aroused the admiration of his mind—the use of paper money for currency; and also—a thing which stirred the admiration of his heart—the use of the spiritual currency of good will. He was delighted with "the polish, the courtesy and the respectful familiarity which distinguished their social intercourse . . . Honesty was everywhere conspicuous; their wagons and other property were secure without locks or guards; and if any of their cattle strayed, arrangements were made by which they were speedily recovered."

And he noted among the Chinese, and among their Mongolian

conquerors, the utter absence of religious intolerance. Jews, Christians, Confucians, Buddhists, Mohammedans—all were allowed to pursue unmolested their various ways to heaven, and all their places of worship were equally exempt from taxation.

And Marco Polo noted in China a system of ethics based upon a sensible foundation of enlightened selfishness: "Seek your own pleasure, but do not interfere with the pleasures of others." And he found in China the key to a profound truth—namely, that at the heart of all greatness lies simplicity. "The great man," wrote the Chinese philosopher, Mencius, "is he who never outgrows the heart of a child."

And there was something of that simplicity in the heart of Marco Polo himself. He never outgrew the wonder of a child at the magic of the world he lived in. He described with such gusto the marvels that he saw on his travels that nobody believed him. For several centuries following the publication of his *Travels*, people continued to characterize a falsehood as a "Marco Polo." Yet recent discoveries have proved that practically all of Marco Polo's "extravagant claims" were statements of fact—that "the black stones broken into bits and used as fuel" were nothing more miraculous than coal; that "the nuts which I have seen and which are as large as a man's head" were cocoanuts; that "the country in which there is night for six months of the year" was northern Siberia; and that "the strange peoples, black, white and yellow, with their equally strange customs" were, and still are, to be found in the countries that he visited on his extensive journeys.

But let us look more closely at some of the "amazements and miracles" as described in the *Travels of Marco Polo*.

VI

"To the southwest of Armenia is the district of Mosul . . . near the confines of which there is a fountain of oil which discharges so great a quantity as to furnish loading for many camels . . ."

The skeptical generation of Marco Polo regarded this "fountain of oil" as a fantasy. It was not until 1940 that the reality of the Mosul oil fields came dramatically to the attention of a war-ridden world.

* * *

"The inhabitants of India have acquired the knowledge of magical and diabolical arts, by means of which they are enabled to produce darkness, obscuring the light of day to such a degree that persons are invisible to each other, unless within a very small distance . . ."

Modern travelers, while discounting the magic, have observed this phenomenon in certain parts of upper India. They call it the Dry Fog—an obscurity caused by the saturation of the air with the windblown dust.

* * *

"And then we arrived at the Desert of Lop . . . It is asserted . . . that this desert is the abode of many evil spirits which lure travelers to their destruction. If, during the day-time, any person remains behind the caravan, he suddenly hears himself called by name . . . Led away by the call from the direct road, he wanders away into the desert to his death . . . In the night-time the lost traveler is persuaded that he hears the march of a large cavalcade . . . and concluding the sound to be that of the footsteps of his own party, he follows the ghostly noise till daylight when he finds himself in the midst of the wilderness abandoned and alone . . . Marvelous indeed and almost unbelievable are the stories related about these spirits of the desert . . . which are said at times to fill the air with the clashing of cymbals and the beating of drums . . ."

To this day the natives of that region believe in the Evil Spirits of the Desert. The "voices" that reach the ear of the lonely traveler are the hallucinations of the fever resulting from the heat and the thirst. As for the music of the cymbals and the drums, modern explorers have observed that these sounds are produced by the contraction and the cooling of the sand in the sand-dunes of the desert.

* * *

"The men of Kamul are addicted to pleasure . . . When strangers arrive at their city, it affords them the highest gratification. They order their wives and their daughters and their sisters to indulge their guests in every wish, whilst they themselves depart from their homes . . . They do this because they are considerate of strangers who, after the perils and fatigues of a long journey, stand in need of relaxation . . ."

Recent travelers have again and again observed this custom among certain tribes of Asia.

* * *

"His Majesty (of Turkestan) has eagles which are trained to catch wolves, and such is the size and the strength of these eagles that no wolves, however large, can escape from their talons . . ."

Travelers in Turkestan have reported that eagles are thus employed in this country even at the present time.

* * *

"The people of Kardandan have the following singular custom: As soon as a woman is delivered of a child . . . her husband immediately takes her place in the bed and looks after the infant for forty days . . . whilst the woman attends to the household duties, carries food to the husband in his bed, and nurses the infant at his side . . ."

To this day the selfsame custom prevails in certain sections of India, Borneo and Siam.

* * *

"There is a curious custom in the province of Karazan. Whenever a stranger of superior quality, whether physical or spiritual, happens to lodge in the house of one of the inhabitants of this province, he is murdered during the night—not for the sake of his money, but in order that the spirit of the murdered man may remain forever in this house, to guide and to bless it in all its concerns . . ."

*   *   *

"In the land of the Great Khan it is the custom, at the funeral processions of the princes, for the mourners to sacrifice all such persons as they meet on their way, saying to them: 'Enter into the next world, there to attend upon your deceased lord.' Upon the occasion when Mongou Khan was escorted to his burial place, the mourners are said to have slain twenty thousand men."

*   *   *

"In the country of Ziamba no young woman can be given in marriage until she has first been approved by the king . . . In 1285, when I (Marco Polo) visited this country, the king had three hundred and twenty-six children, male and female."

*   *   *

"On the island of Zanzibar there is an extraordinary type of bird, called a *roc,* which is so large that it can seize an elephant in its talons . . ."

While this is probably an exaggeration, nevertheless there is today in the British Museum an egg which measures more than two gallons in capacity. The egg comes apparently from one of these "Marco Polo" birds.

*   *   *

And now we come to one of the most interesting of the Marco Polo stories—a legendary miracle which, if not true, at least inspired implicit belief in the poet-merchant of Venice.

"In the year of our Lord 1255," writes Marco Polo, "there lived in Bagdad a wicked Calif who was bent upon exterminating all the Christians within that city . . . One day he summoned them and propounded to them the question as to whether they believed everything that they read in their Gospel. They replied that they did. 'Very well, then,' said the Calif, 'you shall prove to me the power of your belief.' And he quoted to them the following passage in the Gospel—*If ye have faith as a grain of mustard seed, ye shall say unto this mountain, Remove hence to yonder place, and it shall remove.* And then the Calif went on and said: 'I give you ten days, before the end of which you must either, through the power of your Lord Jesus, remove the mountain now before you, or else embrace the law of Mohammed. And failing these two alternatives, you must expect, every one of you, to be put to death.'

"The Christians, trembling for their lives, prayed to the Lord to grant them the aid of His mercy. And the Lord answered their prayer, and directed their Bishop, in a dream, to seek out a certain cobbler—whose name is not known—having only one eye, who through Divine Grace would be able to remove the mountain . . .

"Having sought out the cobbler, they found him a man of strict morals, pure in mind and faithful to his God, regularly attending the Mass and other divine services, fervent in charity and rigid in the observance of the fasts . . . It had once happened to him that a beautiful young woman who came to his shop to be fitted for a pair of shoes, accidentally exposed a part of her leg, the beauty of which excited within him a fleeting sinful thought. Remembering the words of the Gospel, where it is said, 'If thine eye offend thee, pluck it out and cast it from thee; for it is better to enter the Kingdom of God with one eye, than having two eyes, to be cast into Hell Fire,' he immediately, with a sharp knife, scooped out his right eye. Such was the fervor of his faith . . .

"And now the day appointed by the Calif arrived . . . and the pious cobbler, in the presence of the assembled multitude including the Calif himself, knelt before the mountain and, lifting up his eyes to heaven, humbly besought his Creator that He would take compassion upon His faithful Christians and confound the infidels. And having concluded his prayer, he cried in a loud voice: 'In the name of the Father, the Son, and the Holy Ghost, I command thee, O mountain, to remove thyself!'

"Whereupon, lo and behold, the mountain moved and the earth trembled to its foundations . . . The Calif was struck with terror and secretly embraced Christianity, always wearing a cross which after his death was found upon him concealed under his royal robe . . ."

VII

MARCO POLO, together with his father and his uncle, remained in China for twenty years. They had found a warm place in the heart of Kublai Khan. The Great Khan refused them but a single request—that he accept the Christian faith. Although he entertained the greatest esteem for this faith, nevertheless he insisted that it was but one of several ways of salvation. "There are four great Prophets who are revered and worshiped by the different classes of mankind. The Christians honor Jesus Christ as their divinity; the Saracens, Mohammed; the Jews, Moses; and the Idolaters, Sogomombarkan. I honor and respect all four of them, and call to my aid whichsoever of them is in truth Supreme."

And now the Great Khan was growing old, and the Polos feared that after his death they might not find such great tolerance and respect in the kingdom of Cathay. And so they asked the Khan's permission to return to their native land. At first he was loath to let them go, for he had grown too deeply attached to them. But finally he gave them his reluctant consent. The Khan of Persia, grandson of the brother of Kublai Khan, had lost his wife; and Kublai requested the Polos to travel to the land of the Mongolians and to bring back from there a new bride for his sorrow-stricken kinsman. "But be sure to return to me," implored the Great Khan, "when your mission is fulfilled."

Thus he spoke, though he knew in his heart that he was looking for the last time upon his Venetian friends.

And the Polos left the palace of the Khan and never came back.

[*31*]

VIII

WHEN Marco Polo was released from the military prison of Genoa, he married a Venetian woman and became the father of three daughters. And then his adventurous life trailed off into the anticlimax of old age.

Seventy years old now. Marco Polo is on his deathbed. One final adventure—perhaps greater than all the rest? His friends beseech him, for the salvation of his soul, to retract some of the "falsehoods" which he has related in his book. But to the end he insists upon the truthfulness of his story. "What I have told you is not half of what I have seen."

COLUMBUS

Important Dates in Life of Columbus

1451—Born at Genoa.

1470-72—Engaged in trade at Genoa.

1476—Went to England.

1478—Married Felipa Perestrello.

1479—Corresponded with Toscanelli about the possible roundness of the earth.

1482—Tried to interest King John II of Portugal in voyage of discovery.

1492—April 17, signed agreement with Ferdinand and Isabella for voyage of discovery.

August 3, set sail into the Unknown.

October 12, discovered the New World.

1493—March 15, returned to Spain.

September 24, started on second voyage across the Atlantic.

1496—June 11, returned again to Spain.

1498—May 30, started once more for New World.

1499—Sent as prisoner in chains by Bobadilla back to Spain.

1502—Restored to royal favor, started on fourth and last great voyage.

1504—Returned to Spain.

1506—May 20, died.

Christopher Columbus

1451–1506

YOUNG CHRISTOPHER—he had been named after the patron saint of travelers—was serving wine to the customers in his father's tavern. A motley crowd of sailors and adventurers. French traders in silks and satins; Irish rovers with daggers in their eyes and laughter on their lips; Muscovite merchants, their unkempt beards agitated in lively conversation; Spanish cavaliers with long lean bodies and long lean swords; Moorish seamen, ebony statues of volcanic lava; Palestinian jobbers with hooked noses and shrewd kindly eyes; Greek courtesans, disturbing creatures with soft voices, soft skins, and hair the flame of the sunrise. The babel of sounds and sights and passions that were Genoa in the Year of Our Lord, 1470.

And the arguments that they had, and the stories that they told! About the Green Island of Barbary, whose oysters contained a fluid that cured lepers. About the cliffs of basalt in Madeira, a strange land that produced reeds of sugar. And beyond these, and past the Pillars of Hercules—said these outlandish adventurers—lay the island of Atlantis, wider than Europe and Africa combined—a kingdom of fabulous cities and fabulous riches and the most ravishing women in the world. And beyond Atlantis lay still other islands that contained still greater wonders.

And there were tales about a region beyond all these—the Enchanted Isles. "Nobody within our generation"—it was a Spanish sailor who was telling the story—"has ever seen these Islands, for a spell has been cast upon them. Long years ago, when the Moors were laying waste to Europe, a Spanish bishop sailed to these islands for refuge. And there he lived for a time; and when he departed, he cast an enchantment upon the islands, so that never again shall they be visible to mortal eye until all kingdoms of Europe have been embraced within the Catholic fold."

And how, if no one had ever seen these islands, could anyone know of their existence? Simply enough, answered the sailor. "I myself, and many others, have seen flocks of land-birds flying over the sea from the Enchanted Isles. And I have seen fragments of sweet-scented forests floating against our ship. And this, let me tell you, is no fairy tale. Why, King Charles of France has had his reading room at the Louvre paneled with this fragrant wood of the Enchanted Isles."

And more strange stories about the lands that lay even beyond the Enchanted Isles. The Land of Cypango, for instance. "In this land, they say, gold is so plentiful that the people use the grains for scouring their cooking pots . . ."

Young Christopher listened to these stories and thought about them as he lay in bed after the customers had left the tavern. And at such moments a deep yearning filled his soul. How grand it would be if some day he could sail beyond the Pillars of Hercules and go off adventuring after the secrets of those Enchanted Lands!

II

TWENTY YEARS OLD, and Christopher was now a partner in his father's business. Every few months he boarded a sloop and went coasting down to the vineyards along the shore in quest of shipments of wine. He loved the song of the surf and the singing of the wind and the salt sea tang of the air. It was no great tragedy to him, therefore, when his father went bankrupt and left his children—there were four of them besides Christopher—to shift for themselves.

Christopher left Genoa—and drifted away into several years of obscurity. It was the fault of Columbus himself that so little is known of those years. For later on, when he wrote the story of his early life, he was more anxious to be impressive than to be factual. Columbus was not only a sailor but a poet; and his poetical dreams often steered him into the uncharted seas of the imagination. Thus he informs us, probably without foundation, that for a time he served as commander of a pirate crew. In the course of this career, he wrote to King Ferdinand, "the good king Reinel . . . sent me to Tunisia, to capture the galley *La Fernandina.*" But—Columbus went on to relate—"on arriving at the harbor of San Pedro, in Sardinia, I learned that the galley was being protected by two ships and a carraca, which so alarmed the crew that they resolved to proceed no farther, but to return to Marseilles . . . Upon which"—and here Columbus describes a trick which he was to employ years later, on his first voyage to America—"I pretended to give in to their wish and to turn about for home—*first, however, having changed the points of the compass,* so that, while all believed that they were sailing for Marseilles, they were really sailing for Tunisia."

Shortly after his career as a pirate—he tells us—he took part in a "bloody naval engagement" out of which he barely escaped with his life. His vessel, hit by "a ball of fire," had burst into flames. "But, being a good swimmer, and finding myself two leagues from the land, I seized an oar, and by its aid succeeded in reaching the coast."

His next venture—he tells us, still spinning a good part of the story out of his imagination—was a voyage to Iceland. This island was then called *Ultima Thule,* the final shore on the edge of the world. "Yet I, in the year 1477, sailed one hundred leagues beyond the island of Thule."

[*37*]

All these stories, whether truthful or fanciful, combine to give us a vivid picture of the dreamer-pioneer ever on the alert, forever poised to reach out from the security of the known into the dangers of the unknown.

III

TWENTY-EIGHT YEARS OLD, and for a spell the adventurousness of Columbus seemed threatened to be submerged under the domesticity of marriage. His restless footsteps had taken him to Lisbon. Here, while kneeling one day at the Convent of Santos, the tall, suntanned and yellow-haired young rover with the dream in his eyes and the dimple in his chin, noticed a young woman who was kneeling at his side. A dark-eyed, dark-haired and dark-skinned little creature with a voluptuous smile. Even in repose she seemed a vision of graceful animation. Their eyes met.

After the services, mutual interrogations about each other from their various friends. This young man? Oh, he's a sailor from Genoa with strange ideas in his head. And this young woman? The daughter of a courtier—half Italian, half Portuguese. Donna Filepa Perestrello. A very pretty name.

They were introduced to each other. Her father too, before he had become a courtier, had sailed the seas with a strange quest in his heart. He had sought, like so many others, to fathom the mystery of the ocean which tumbled, as most people believed, over the edge of the world. But Perestrello, Filepa told Columbus, believed otherwise. He had collected quite a large library of books and manuscripts and maps that dealt with the possibility of unknown lands beyond the lands that were known. And with a new and startling theory. The world, in accordance with this theory, was not flat, but round.

Columbus thought a great deal about this matter. If the world really was round, then by sailing to the west you would come to the east. To the kingdoms described in the *Travels of Marco Polo*. To the jewels and the gold of the Great Khan of Cathay . . .

An impossible dream? To the foster-child of St. Christopher, the spirit of derring-do, nothing was impossible.

But for the present he was wrapped up in another dream. Donna Filepa. They were married, and the young Ligurian closed his eyes and sipped the fragrance of his love and rested from his adventures.

And in his spare moments he read the books in his father-in-law's library. And thought.

And before long his thoughts began once more to travel far away from home—all the way around the world. A rival had arisen to tear him away from the arms of Filepa. The lure of the unknown.

And—let it be admitted—the thirst for gold. Columbus was consumed by two passions: the love of adventure, and the yearning for wealth. And, in addition to these, by a third passion—an eagerness, like Marco Polo, to make Christian converts.

These three passions would be fulfilled, Columbus believed, by a single stroke. If only he could get a few ships to sail across the sea—it was a very narrow sea, Columbus thought—he would reach new lands and bring back new wealth and open the way for new souls into the Kingdom of Heaven.

At this time Columbus met an odd sort of fellow—a Galician pilot who had lost an eye in a shipwreck. This man had sailed on a Portuguese vessel with a cargo of merchandise for Flanders. The ship had been driven from its course. Day after day it had scudded before the tempest—westward, ever westward. Finally they had come to a land "far beyond the knowledge of any man."

The return voyage of the ship was even more terrible than the voyage out. "Without provisions, without water, without strength, one by one my comrades died. At last the ship went down, and I alone am left alive to tell the tale."

As Columbus kept questioning the sailor, he became more and more convinced that this "new and unknown land" was the eastern coast of Cathay—the land of spices and gold. And he was more eager than ever to seek out this land for himself.

But before he translated his eagerness into a final determination, he wrote for advice to Pagolo Toscanelli, the leading geographer of the day. And Maestro Pagolo sent in reply a warm letter of encouragement and Godspeed. "I learn of your great and magnificent desire to discover the way to the land of spices . . . I send you a marine chart which I have made and which will satisfy your needs . . . Although I know that this chart could best be made, like the world, in the form of a sphere, I have nevertheless decided, for greater clearness and ease, to draw it up in the way used to make marine charts . . .

"Upon the chart I have pointed out the best way *westward* . . . to reach the *eastward* regions that are richest in spices and precious stones . . .

"And be not surprised that I say these regions lie to the *westward,* although commonly they are called *oriental.* For to those who go by sea, these lands will lie always to the West; while he who goes by land will have them always to the East . . .

"This land to which you will come is populous and rich . . . the whole under the rule of one sovereign, called the Great Khan, which means the King of Kings . . .

"It is very fitting that we Latins should search out this land . . . of gold and silver and precious stones and aromatic plants and learned men . . . men who show a disposition to come to terms with the Christians . . .

"My best wishes to you, my dear friend."

A very encouraging letter from a very learned man. And now the time was past for further learning and further letters. The moment for action had arrived.

Columbus was ready for the Great Adventure.

IV

But nobody else was ready. To the rest of the world his project was still an impossible dream. He went with it to King John of Portugal, who turned him flatly down. He went to King Ferdinand and Queen Isabella of Spain. "Give me a few ships and a handful of men, and I will bring back to you innumerable coffers of gold." The queen hesitated, but the king put an end to her hesitation with a definite *no*.

In the meantime Donna Filepa had died. After a due period of mourning, Columbus went on with his quest for men, money and ships. He journeyed to England, to France, and then back again to Spain. Everywhere the selfsame answer—*No!*

"I will bring you gold enough to launch a new crusade against the Saracens."

"No!"

An endless series of wanderings from court to court. Eloquent pleas. Despair.

A brief passionate romance with Beatriz de Arana, "a woman without friend or fortune." They met at Cordova, whirlpool of passion and sunlight and sand. He left her with an infant in her arms, and went on.

He made and sold maps for a living, but his earnings were not enough for the nourishment of his body and his dreams. "At this period," writes a contemporary historian, "deprived of all human support, betrayed by his friends, besieged by poverty, Columbus had fallen into such a state that he was forced to go to a Franciscan monastery near the city of Marchena, as a humble suppliant begging food to sustain his very life."

But he had made friends—a Portuguese shipbuilder, a Jewish financier, a Spanish courtesan who had the ear of the king. And these friends spoke up boldly in his behalf. And when these had shown the way, a number of his other supporters plucked up the courage to speak. And on a midwinter day, as Columbus was dejectedly dragging his footsteps two leagues out of Granada, an alguazil on the gallop overtook him. "The King and the Queen have commanded you to come to them at once!"

Three months later (April 17, 1492) the contracts were signed for the beginning of the Adventure. Columbus was to retain all the glory of whatever conversions he might make, and one-tenth of the profits from whatever business he might transact—"leaving the other nine parts to the profit of Your Majesties."

There is an Oriental proverb: "The devil laughs at the credulity of the subject and the cruelty of the king." His majesties, as Columbus was to learn later on, were to defraud him both of his profit and of his glory. The entire investment of the Spanish crown in the discovery of America was $6000. The profits on this investment within a century, in gold alone, amounted to $1,750,000. And all the reward that Columbus was to get was a prisoner's chains.

But on the day that his ships floated out toward the unknown land (August 3, 1492), his heart was afloat somewhere among the stars.

V

FROM the Journal of Columbus on the first "voyage of his dreams":

Monday, August 6—"The helm of the *Pinta* broke . . . Suspect two mariners, Gomez Rascon and Cristobal Quintero, of conspiracy to turn back . . ."

Thursday, August 9—"The *Pinta* developed a leak. Stopped at Teneriffe for repairs . . ."

Sunday, September 9—"Went nineteen leagues and resolved to reckon less than he had gone"—Columbus, in his Journal, always referred to himself in the third person—"so that if the voyage be a long one, his people would not be frightened and discouraged . . ."

Monday, September 10—"Went sixty leagues . . . but computed only forty-eight leagues . . ."

Saturday, September 15—"At the beginning of this night . . . saw a marvelous branch of fire fall from the heavens into the sea . . . Mariners greatly disturbed thereat . . ."

Sunday, September 16—"Saw many tufts of very green grass . . . Land apparently not far away . . ."

Monday, September 17—"Sea water less salty than before

. . . Mariners all expectant and joyful . . . Fastest vessels hurried onward . . . Everybody eager to be the first to land . . ."

Sunday, September 23—"Still sailing on the westward course . . . No land in sight . . . Mariners disturbed, saying that . . . the wind would never blow for the return to Spain . . . Always the wind blew westward . . . Mariners muttered they would soon be blown over the rim of the world . . ."

Tuesday, September 25—"Land sighted from the stern of the ship . . . Proved to be only a mirage . . . Sailed on . . ."

Wednesday, October 3—Rebellion among the mariners . . . Calmed them down . . . Sailed on . . ."

Saturday, October 6—"No land . . . Sailed on . . ."

Thursday, October 11—"Signs of land again . . . petrels . . . a green branch . . . a little twig of dog-roses . . . At these signs everybody breathed and rejoiced . . ."

Another mirage perhaps? Another disappointment, another mutiny? But look at the entry in the Journal made several hours later:

"A sailor by the name of Roderigo de Traina reported that he definitely sighted land . . . At ten o'clock that night the Admiral (Columbus), standing in the forecastle, saw a light, but it was so concealed that he could not declare it to be land . . . Two or three others remarked that they, too, saw this light, and it was like a small wax candle, which rose and fell . . . The Admiral was now certain that they were near land . . . The sailors sang the *Salve* . . . At two hours after midnight the land stood clearly out of the sea . . ."

And thus, simply, Columbus announced the greatest discovery of the ages.

VI

COLUMBUS landed on an island which, in his opinion, was on the outskirts of Cypango (Japan). In reality it was one of the West Indies, just south of Florida. He had been right in his conjecture about the roundness of the earth, but he had underestimated its size. He thought that the Orient lay just about where America is situated. To his dying day he felt certain that he had reached Asia instead of a new continent.

And in the certainty of his belief, he set about searching for the riches that had been reported to exist so plentifully in Asia. "These islands which I have reached," he wrote to the king and the queen, "contain an infinite number of precious stones and gold incalculable . . . Their Highnesses can see that I will give them as much gold as they may need . . ."

And also, he reminded his sovereigns, he would enrich the Church with "an incalculable wealth" of converted souls. "For the which, all Christendom ought to feel delight and make great feasts and give solemn thanks to the Holy Trinity."

Columbus was to be disappointed in both of these hopes. It was not until thirty years later that the Spanish conquistadors discovered—and plundered—the gold of Montezuma. As for the conversion of the Indians, they would have nothing of the new faith. For they soon learned to distrust the visitors from over the sea. At first they had looked upon them as strange white gods who brought them beautiful gifts—pitchers and caps and sashes and slippers, and little glass beads that you strung around your neck and that held in them the colors of the rainbow. But before long they noticed that these newcomers were not white gods but white devils. They had come to these shores not to befriend them but to cheat them. ("Our men," wrote Columbus, "are defrauding the natives of their most valuable possessions in exchange for bits of broken pitchers.") And these white devils were kidnaping their strongest and their handsomest people and sending them off to hard labor across the sea. ("His Highnesses," wrote Columbus, "shall have as many Indian slaves as they shall order to be shipped.")

The Indians resented this treatment they received from the "white devils," who carried a crucifix in the one hand and a whip in the other. And when Columbus, after a short visit to Spain, returned to the West Indies, he found not a living trace of the garrison he had left behind him.

He paid, in all, four visits to America; and on each of these occasions he searched diligently for the gold and the jewels which he believed to be scattered throughout the islands. But his searching was all in vain.

King Ferdinand, in the meantime, had become impatient. He had expected gold from Columbus, and he received nothing but words. He determined to show this "wild and worthless dreamer" an example of his royal temper. First of all he deprived Columbus of his promised share in the profits that might accrue from his discovery. "A King's promises," Machiavelli had written, "are made only to be broken." And then Ferdinand sent one of his courtiers, Bobadilla, to the West Indies in order to spy upon the movements of Columbus. "I dare say this Genoese adventurer has found plenty of gold, but is keeping it all for himself."

Bobadilla, after a careful investigation, found Columbus innocent of the charge of dishonesty. But he found him guilty of another charge—stupidity. "This man has been stupid enough to discover a poor instead of a rich country." He therefore arrested Columbus and sent him back a chained prisoner to King Ferdinand.

This was quite in keeping with Spanish justice in the latter part of the fifteenth century. "I have done for my King," wrote Columbus, "more than any other prince has ever had from a subject . . . Now I am in such condition that even the vilest may affront me."

Yet even in his despair, he ends upon a note of hope. "God willing, the day will come when none can hear of my suffering without regret . . . and without some admiration for what I have done."

VII

THE hoped-for day did not come within the lifetime of Columbus. He died in obscure poverty.

The irony of the gods, with their lopsided and incomprehensible scales of justice. The strange and fragmentary gifts that they bestow upon the stepchildren of the earth. Talent without power, power without talent; beauty without goodness, goodness without beauty; success without merit, merit without success. Columbus discovered a continent; an impostor gave it his name. In 1503 an Italian adventurer, Amerigo Vespucci, published an account of a "new world" which he claimed to have discovered in 1497. The whole story was a fabrication. But a young German professor, who was publishing a geography at the time, named the new continent *America,* after the dishonest author of the fictitious discovery.

BENVENUTO CELLINI

Important Dates in Life of Benvenuto Cellini

1500—Born in Florence.
1515—Apprenticed to a gold-
    smith.
1519—Went to Rome.
1527—Took part in defense of
    Rome.
1537—Arrested on (apparently
    false) charge of embezzle-
    ment.

1540-45—Worked for King
    Francis I in Paris.
1545—Returned to Florence.
1558—Received the tonsure of
    the first ecclesiastical or-
    ders.
1560—Renounced orders and
    married.
1560-70—Wrote Autobiography.
1571—Died.

Benvenuto Cellini

1500–1571

THE NAME *Benvenuto* means *Welcome*. For twenty years his
parents had prayed for a manchild; but thus far, heaven had
answered their prayers with one daughter. Finally, on All Saints'
Day in 1500, the midwife came out of the delivery room with a
new child for Giovanni Cellini. "I bring you a fine gift," she said,
"a blessing such as you do not expect." Giovanni looked at the
infant, raised his eyes to Heaven, and exclaimed: "I thank Thee,
my Lord, for this welcome surprise!" And right then and there
he decided to name the child *Benvenuto*.

II

BENVENUTO had been slow in coming, but he was very fast in getting ahead. "The child is a hurricane of capability and conten-
tiousness." His father wanted him to be a flute-player, but the boy
insisted on becoming a goldsmith. "I hate the tinkle of music, but
I love the glitter of precious stones." At fifteen he apprenticed
himself, against the wish of his father, to a jeweler by the name of
Antonio di Sandro; and before long, he tells us unblushingly, "I
overtook even the ablest of the young goldsmiths of Florence."

His apprenticeship at Florence, however, was short-lived. At sixteen he got into a scrap—it was always the other fellow, he assures us, who started the fighting—and was banished from Florence. Within a few months he was recalled to his native city, only to leave it again as the result of a quarrel he had with his father. He went to Pisa, secured a job with a goldsmith "who adored me for my honesty and my talent," and left his "adoring" master for further adventures in Florence. Another quarrel with his father—"he still persisted in making a musician out of me"— and again he ran away from Florence. This time, a roughneck young genius of nineteen, he went to seek new fights and new fortunes in Rome.

For two years he fashioned his trinkets, reveled in his duels and his ducats and his glory, and finally attacked singlehanded an "entire tribeful" of his detractors. "Like a maddened bull I came among them, I threw four or five of them to the ground, and I fell on top of them, plying my dagger now on this one, now on that." For this escapade he was put under the ban, and for a while the firebrand of his temper burned low.

But the flames of his passion began to burn high. He collected and cast away his mistresses as recklessly as he collected and cast away his money. On one occasion, when the mother of his favorite courtesan took her away from Cellini and left for parts unknown, the distracted young lover traveled all over Italy to find her again. And when, to his delight, he did find her, he abruptly abandoned her because the mother had set too high a price upon her.

And yet, although he had no compunction about *throwing* away his mistresses, woe unto those who dared to *take* them away! One day he surprised his colleague, a goldsmith by the name of Pagolo Miccieri, in the arms of his mistress, Caterina. "When I beheld this stealing of my love," writes Cellini, "I felt a fever leap upon me." His first impulse was to kill Miccieri. But then he hit upon a far more subtle revenge. He compelled his rival to *marry* Caterina, and then he in turn stole her love from her husband.

Yet his dallyings and his duels were but of secondary importance to Cellini. Always foremost in his mind was the development of his genius. It was his ambition to perfect himself in "every phase of jewel-sculpture," from the carving of a tiny medallion to the modeling of a colossal statue. "In all these different branches I set myself to learn with very great attention." He realized that he had undertaken an almost superhuman task, but he believed that he was endowed with an almost superhuman talent. "No man before me has excelled in all these branches, because no man before me has received from Heaven a temperament of such diversified richness."

He believed so profoundly in his own genius that he inspired everybody else to believe in it. Bishops, cardinals, emperors and popes were ready to pay homage to him. And he, so proud was he of his achievements, was ready to pay homage to none. On one occasion, Pope Clement VII commissioned Cellini to model for him a chalice representing the Nativity of Christ. For this work, His Holiness undertook to pay him in regular installments. But when the installments were slow in reaching him, Cellini was equally slow in completing the work. Finally Pope Clement decided to call him to task. "I command you to attend to my chalice!"

"And I," replied Cellini, "request you to attend to my gold."

Unable to do anything himself with this young "upstart of a goldsmith," Pope Clement ordered his legate, Cardinal Salviati, to apply the necessary spur. "This beast of a Cardinal"—writes Cellini in his *Autobiography*—"sent for me at the end of eight days, telling me to bring along the chalice; to whom I went without it. When I arrived, the Cardinal said to me insolently: 'Where is that hodgepodge of yours? Have you finished it?'

"To which I replied with equal insolence: 'I shall not finish my hodgepodge until you give me the onions with which to season it.'

"At these words"—continues Cellini—"the Cardinal flew into a rage, and cried: 'I will send you to the galleys, and then you will have the grace to finish the job!'

" 'My Lord,' I rejoined, 'you cannot send me to the galleys unless I commit a crime. Until then, I am a free man and I refuse to bow to an uncivil tongue . . . A pleasant good day to you, sir!' "

And Cellini went home and sulked "like Achilles in his tent" until both the Cardinal and the Pope yielded to his demands. "They couldn't help it," concludes Cellini in his usual tone of arrogant naïveté. "For they knew that I was the greatest man that ever was born in my profession."

III

ONE DAY, as he was walking through the streets of Rome, Cellini met a group of "ruffians who disliked my work." When they arrived at about "the length of two Ave Marias" from Cellini, they stopped and "laughed with derision" in his direction. This act of disrespect so infuriated Cellini that he drew his dagger and rushed upon them. "As I aimed to strike their leader (Pompeo) in the face, the fear that he experienced made him turn his countenance away"—note how Cellini always puts the blame upon his adversary—"so that I caught him exactly under the ear." The man died of the blow, "a thing I had never intended— why *did* he turn his face away?"

Cellini was lucky enough to escape the consequences of this crime. The new Pope—Clement VII was now dead—granted him a pardon on the ground that the murder was an act of self-defense. "And it was a fortunate thing that they saved me. For I proceeded to astonish the world with the marvels of my creative genius." More adventures, more loves, more crimes. His super-abundant energy was forever boiling over into new quarrels, and his exuberant imagination was forever exaggerating small insults into great injuries. Once, as he was traveling toward Florence, he stopped at an inn where the landlord insisted upon being paid "before I went to sleep" instead of receiving his pay, "as was customary, in the morning." Fuming with rage, Cellini paid the inn-keeper "according to his evil method" and went to bed. "I had a very fine bed, entirely new, and very clean. For all this, I couldn't fall asleep, meditating all that night how I must act to avenge myself. Once it came into my thoughts to set fire to the house; at another moment, to cut the throats of four fine horses that he had in his stable . . ." Finally, in the morning, he hit upon the following revenge: "I took out of my pocket a small knife that cut like a razor, and with that knife I whittled four of his new beds into splinters." By the time the inn-keeper was up, Cellini was already too far away to be overtaken.

His fiery temper and his consuming energy resulted again and again in a physical breakdown. But out of every illness—once he was taken for dead and prepared for burial—he came out with greater vitality than before. "The reason why I always recovered was that I followed my own prescriptions rather than those of the doctor." Whatever Cellini did was—he was convinced—for Cellini's best.

And Cellini—he was equally convinced—was the greatest of artists and the noblest of men. "In art," he quotes from a sonnet written about himself, "he is superior to all men; in character, equal to all the angels." Whenever he undertook a job, he not only came up to everybody's expectations—he tells us—but he greatly surpassed them. In every new undertaking he tried not only to outdo his rivals, but to outdo himself. "Benvenuto," declares Cellini with the complacency of Little Jack Horner, "is the glory of the world."

Yet, on one occasion, his glory received the tarnish of a prison sentence. He was charged with having stolen a number of precious stones from the Pope's tiara. He defended himself vigorously against this charge and—he declares—completely established his innocence. "Yet so powerful were my enemies that I remained in prison as though I were guilty."

His active body was confined, but not his active brain. He set to work devising a plan of escape; and, having devised it, he at once put it into execution. He secured from one of the jailers a pair of pincers, wrested away the nails which held together the iron bands of his cell-door, slipped out at night through the loosened door, and then let himself down from the tower by a rope made out of a sheet which he had cut into strips. "In my descent from the tower, I had scraped the skin off the palms of my hands, which were bleeding . . ."

This, however, was not the end of his troubles. When he tried to rise, he found that his leg had been broken in the escape. "Yet this did not dismay me . . . Binding the leg together with a strip of the cloth which I had used for my rope, I crawled towards the city gate"—only to find it closed . . . "Nor did even this dismay me . . . Seeing a certain stone exactly beneath the gate, I laid hold of it and tore it loose . . . And by this means I entered the city of Rome."

Whereupon a pack of dogs "threw themselves upon me"—it is hard to tell where reality leaves off and Cellini's imagination begins—"and bit me severely." He fought the dogs off with his dagger, and dragged himself laboriously to the house of a friend.

But he was discovered and taken back to prison—this time, as he thought, for life.

His sufferings in prison were almost unendurable. "I was carried into a dark chamber . . . where there was much water, full of tarantulas and many noxious worms . . . I remained continuously on a pallet of coarse hemp without being able to move, since I had a broken leg . . . For one hour and a half of the day I had a little reflection of light, which entered that miserable cavern by a very tiny aperture; and, during that short space of time only could I read, and the rest of the day and of the night I remained always in the dark." His nails grew so long that he "couldn't touch himself without wounding himself," and his teeth "died in their sockets," so that their roots lacerated his gums. Again and again he tried to do away with himself; "but

Columbus

Benvenuto Cellini

some heavenly power always held me back." The world, he felt, still needed his genius, which somehow, some time, would be able to reassert itself. With a little charcoal that he had found imbedded in the earthen floor, he drew upon the wall of his cell a picture of Jesus surrounded by His angels. To this picture he prayed daily for his final deliverance.

And deliverance finally came. One day, just as he had concluded his prayer, his guardian angel lifted him up "after the manner of a whirlwind" and—he tells us—carried him to Heaven. Here he spoke "face to face with the Father, the Son, and the Holy Virgin." And they promised him to soften the hearts of his jailers so that they would set him free. "And that very day I was set free."

As a proof of the divine grace that had enveloped him in Heaven, Cellini pointed out to his friends—"and every one of them can see it"—a halo that hovered around his head. "This halo may be observed above my shadow in the morning from sunrise until two hours after sunrise . . . It may be observed also in the evening at sunset . . ."

Cellini had now arrived at the very apex of self-adoration.

IV

To CELEBRATE his deliverance from prison, Cellini got into another quarrel and committed another murder—a rather strange business for a man with a halo. And then, to escape further trouble, he went to Paris and entered the service of King Francis I. At the king's request, he undertook a group of three silver statues—"a work of genius such as even the ancients had never seen."

The king was delighted with Cellini's art. But Cellini was not at all pleased with the king's avarice. "When we talked about my salary, the prince tried to beat me down as if I were a load of wood." However, they finally compromised upon a payment of 750 gold ducats a year—"the same allowance that King Francis had given to Leonardo da Vinci. This sum, though far from sufficient, was at least respectable."

There now began a period of comparative quiet for "the greatest man that ever was born"—we are quoting Cellini's own words about himself. Under the cooler rays of the Parisian sun he was able—as a general rule—to restrain his temper and to channel his superabundant energy into creative work. Among the many things that he made for King Francis was a salt-cellar of ivory and gold. Cellini gives us a vivid description of its exquisite design. "This salt-cellar was oval in shape . . . and fashioned into the (figured) likeness of the Sea and Earth, both seated. And they intertwined their legs, just as . . . the Sea runs into the Earth and the Earth juts into the Sea . . . And in the right hand of the Sea I had fixed a trident, and in his left hand I had placed a boat . . . which was to receive the salt. There were beneath this said figure his four animals of the Sea, each of them represented with the head of a horse and the tail of a fish . . . The water was enameled in the various colors of the waves . . . For the Earth I had fashioned a very beauteous woman—with the Horn of Plenty in one hand, and in the other a small Ionian temple which was to receive the pepper. Beneath this female figure I had placed the handsomest animals that the Earth produces. And the rocks of the Earth I depicted partly in enamel and partly in gold . . . I had then placed this work upon a pedestal of black ebony carved into the four figures of the Night, the Day, the Twilight, and the Dawn . . . Interspersed among these were the figures of the four winds—the East, the North, the South and the West . . . a work to arouse the astonishment and the admiration of all men everywhere . . ."

Eloquent as he was in extolling the virtues of his own work, he was equally eloquent in disparaging the defects of his rivals' works. Asked to explain why he disliked the Hercules of Bandinello, he said: "Because it is bad, from top to toe . . . If you were to shave the hair off the skull, there wouldn't be left enough of a head to house his brain . . . As regards the face, there's no

telling whether it represents the features of a man or of an ox . . .
The shoulders resemble the two pommels of an ass's saddle . . .
His breasts and the rest of his muscles are not copied from those
of a man, but are drawn from an old sack full of melons . . .
And now look at the legs; they seem to have no connection with
that ugly body. You can't tell upon which of his legs he is resting
his weight . . . The calves have neither muscles nor sinews nor
blood . . . And his feet are so utterly devoid of life that one of
them seems to be buried in the earth and the other shriveled in a
flame . . ."

His caustic tongue finally resulted in a quarrel between Cellini
and the king. Disappointed at the royal neglect of an artist
"greater even than Michelangelo," Cellini returned to the hot sun
and the fiery adventures of his native Florence. Added to his
"natural" vices, he was now accused of an "unnatural" vice and
was compelled to flee from the city until the storm blew over. And
then came a pardon from the duke, and Cellini returned to his
aberrations under serene skies again. Serene, but for one dark
cloud that tempted him—to quote his picturesque expression—
"to throw myself into despair." Among his illegitimate children
there was a two-year-old son whom he loved better than his own
life. One day he went to visit this child whom he had placed with
a wet-nurse. "When I reached him, I found him in good health,
and I so unhappy kissed him." But when Cellini rose to depart,
the child clung to him with his little hands, and "with a passion
of tears and screams" begged his father not to go. "It seemed as
if he had a presentiment of some great tragedy." And sure
enough, three days after his return to Florence, Cellini heard that
the wet-nurse had accidentally smothered his little son. "And this
news," writes Cellini, "gave me so great a sorrow as I have never
felt a greater."

V

THE FIRES and the desires of his youth had now almost completely subsided. When his enemies insulted him, he no longer

rushed upon them with his sword. Instead, he transfixed them with his pen. But his lampoons were no less keen than his sword-thrusts.

And equally keen was the ever-shining instrument of his genius. Like Michelangelo, he had that rare faculty of improving with age. "My last works"—and he spoke the simple truth—"were the best." When he unveiled his statue of *Perseus,* hundreds of sonnets in praise of the work were nailed to the posts of his door. "For, since it was the vacation at the University of Pisa, all those most excellently learned scholars vied with one another upon that subject."

This unveiling of the *Perseus* was the culmination of Cellini's triumph. He was now universally recognized as one of the greatest artists of all time.

And now, having tasted all the exciting pleasures of life, he settled down to the more quieting contentments of old age. He bought a farm, entered the primary grade of the Holy Orders, and—at the age of sixty—married for the first time. He ushered into the world—with or without benefit of clergy—five daughters and three sons, the last of whom was born when Cellini was sixty-nine years old.

The following year the young-old artist laid down the burden of a too impetuous life. And the world was so much the emptier for the passing of one who had proved himself "a master of the greatest as well as of the smallest things."

SIR WALTER RALEIGH

Important Dates in Life of Sir Walter Raleigh

1552—Born.

1568—Entered Oxford (but never graduated).

1569—Volunteered to serve with French Huguenots.

1580—Served as captain in British infantry.

1581—Became favorite at British court.

1583—Received, from Queen Elizabeth, grant of Durham House.

1584—Knighted.

1584-87—Sent expeditions to Virginia.

1587—Appointed Captain of the Royal Guard.

1592—Lost Queen Elizabeth's favor.

1595—Explored South America.

1597—Regained Queen's favor.

1600—Appointed governor of Jersey.

1603—Sent by King James to Tower.

1616—Released. Made second voyage to South America.

1618—October 29, executed.

Sir Walter Raleigh

1552–1618

"He hath been a star at which the world hath gazed. But stars . . . must fall when they trouble the sphere wherein they abide." A guiding star he appeared to those who dared to follow—too brilliant for the early dawn that was the age in which his course was set. Eyes that had long looked on darkness were dazzled and afraid. And in their fear, they needs must destroy that which they could not comprehend.

Of Walter Raleigh's childhood, there is little known. Born (1552) of seafaring people in the West Country, he seemed from the start to have been compounded of tempest and fire. Early his eyes were drawn toward the sails that slipped silently beyond the horizon, embarked upon the exciting adventure of the unexplored.

An insatiable curiosity for the unknown impelled him to seek in every field where there was knowledge to be gleaned. Yet no dull bookworm he. His quick mind soon absorbed a subject and turned to fresher fields.

At sixteen he entered Oxford where he was "worthily esteemed a proficient in oratory and philosophy." But his attendance was far from being worthy of esteem.

Like a small boat on a large sea, his early years—now in full view upon a wave's crest, now lost to sight in the trough. Enlisting in the French and Irish wars, he displayed for the first time the quality that was to mark his entire career. In the presence of danger he was without thought of self but full of concern for those under him. See him standing "with a pistol in the one hand and his iron-shod quarter-staff in the other," fending off a small army, whilst his escort passes safely over a river.

Ruthless in the protection of his comrades, he was all-too-lenient in the defense of his own interests. Again and again it was to prove his undoing, this too great generosity toward an enemy. A man too big for his age, he was unable to conceive of souls so small that they wouldn't treat him as he treated them.

Such is the rather hazy picture of Raleigh in his youth. That this picture is not more concrete is due partly to Raleigh's own fault. "Whosoever in writing a modern history shall follow truth too near the heels," he observed, "it may haply strike out his teeth."

Yet this much we know from his subsequent life. Fate has prepared him for a stellar role. At twenty-nine, formed as to character and endowed with personal charm, he is led to where the stage is set. He is sent to court bearing dispatches. There, attracting the Queen's notice, he becomes the central figure in a drama that has thrilled and horrified the ages.

II

RALEIGH "requested the Queen's ear; he got it in a trice." Destiny had brought together these two for many purposes. Elizabeth loved a soldier. She was a woman peculiarly sensible to masculine attractions. Wearied by the heavy-handed fawning of her courtiers, she found in Raleigh an intellect equal to her own, a counsel she could respect.

Raleigh, "darling of the English Cleopatra," is a figure to fire the imagination. Adequate to all situations, he rises gallantly to the romantic gestures demanded of him. As when—for example

—"spreading his cloak in a plashy place, whereupon the Queen treads gently over," he receives the Royal smile with bended head. And is rewarded by many a cloak in return.

Knowing the Queen's love of public devotion, gaily he fulfills his role. With a diamond he inscribes his admiration on a windowpane where all may see:

"Fain would I rise, yet fear to fall."

And waiting he receives the Queen's reply, transferred through the selfsame medium:

"If thy heart fails thee, climb not at all."

He had passed the first test; Elizabeth was satisfied. And now began an association that was to change the course of history. For Raleigh was the first Englishman to dream of Empire—the first colonizer in a nation that was to colonize one-third of the world. The Queen was "much taken with his elocution," and night and day she listened to his plans. Elizabeth possessed an intellect that could follow his fancy far beyond the boundaries of her little island. Understandable, then, that she wished him always by her side. Having appointed him to a post in Ireland, she changed her mind and ordered him to stay at court, lest in his travels he "get knockt on the head."

Steadily he rises in the Queen's esteem. Grant follows grant, until Raleigh is a man of wealth. But prosperity is the father of envy. With the growth of his prestige, there is an equal growth of his unpopularity. He is too impatient to court the opinion of the rabble—"the dogs that bark at those they know not." At every turn his swift searching stride causes him to tread on sensitive toes. And when they retaliate, there is venom in their kick.

Yet thus far they are unable to do him harm. The arc of his fortune is on the upward swing. Elizabeth is generous with her favorite. He is Lord Warden of the Tanneries. He is knighted. He is Captain of the Queen's Guard. Though generally "the best hated man in the world," in his own province he is adored. There he has established a miners' council. Slipping away from the satins and the perfumes of the court, he meets his own people. There, upon a high tower, mist enshrouded, he confers with the miners —speaking that soft West Country burr that Elizabeth finds so enchanting.

III

RALEIGH scorned the rabble in the mass, yet loved the individual common man. Throughout his life he tried to bring decency and justice into a world whose only justice was might and whose only decency was victory.

None better than Raleigh knew the wanton cruelty inflicted upon the Irish, those stubborn people who loved their land better than their life. It was he who first propounded self-rule for them. Reminding Elizabeth of their courage, he suggested that she gain the confidence of their chieftains who in turn would gain the confidence of their people. Thus they might establish a protectorate, and end the wholesale slaughter of a nation in religion's name.

Elizabeth saw the wisdom of his reasoning, and in all his plans concurred. But the Irish leaders were not ready for this civilizing influence. At such distance, royal commands could be disobeyed, and words made to appear other than what they meant. There was only one Raleigh, and he could not be everywhere.

Not when his presence is demanded at court, and his heart is centered upon his first love—the American colonies. Time and again he stands at the water's edge and gazes with a sad exaltation upon the men "going down to the sea in ships." His spirit sails to Virginia, while his person remains at the command of the Queen. Elizabeth has promised to defray all his expenses if only he will stay near her and let others go to Virginia in his place.

More grants, more lands. On his Irish estates Raleigh has cultivated the lowly potato, has popularized the smoking of the "vile-weed"—tobacco. These, with the trees and the shrubs from the colony which he has transplanted onto English soil are the only tangible proofs of his dream. The first Virginia colony had prospered for a while and then ended in the desertion of all the settlers. Of the second colony, all the members had been massacred. He sends out a third colony. Virginia has become a sieve into which he pours his fortune. An endless stream of more men, more ships, more supplies. Leashed like a restless mastiff at the court, he must watch the bungling of those permitted to go, must fret at those who antagonize the natives in defiance of his repeated counsel to friendliness and peace.

Eventually he turns the whole project over to the Virginia Company. For now there are other matters that occupy the attention of Raleigh, of all England. The long dreaded Spanish Armada is on the way. Galvanized into action, Raleigh throws himself into the planning of fortifications and of coastal defenses. But when the actual fighting commences, Raleigh is left without a command. The Queen's favorite must not risk his neck. Chafing at the inactivity, he must remain at court—chained to a petticoat.

And then, release at last. Elizabeth sends him to order an attack. Gallantly the little fleet, outmanned twenty to one, sets forth. The elements have espoused the English cause. A strong tempest on the day of the battle. With wind and wave fighting on their side, they drive off the Spanish Armada. Raleigh cries for pursuit and complete annihilation. But England is satisfied. She accepts her victory with modest gratitude. "God blew with his winds, and the enemy was scattered."

IV

RALEIGH is in danger of being superseded. Another man has caught the Queen's roving eye. Young Essex. A strange rivalry has arisen between these two men. The nineteen-year-old Essex is jealous of the Queen's high regard for the mature Raleigh. He tries to poison the Queen's ear against him. And Raleigh, as Captain of the Queen's Guard, is compelled to listen to the aspersions cast upon him by this saucy little schoolboy. Elizabeth enjoys the rivalry. Yet for all of Essex's youthful charms, Raleigh is the man whose wisdom she esteems. Staunchly she defends him. Essex complains against her partiality. "She came to speak of that knave Raleigh, and it seemed she could not well endure anything to be spoken against him."

Essex is losing ground. His attempts to dislodge his rival have served only to strengthen Raleigh's position. The mysterious winding of the thread of Destiny. What might have seemed a misfortune, proved actually to be Raleigh's good luck. England had decided on reprisals against Spain. Raleigh received permission to join the crusade while Essex was ordered to remain behind in silken dalliance. But Essex was young and impetuous. Defying the Queen, he joined the fleet. And the strange rivalry continued on the high seas. With a stubborn perversity, Essex overruled every one of Raleigh's plans, and the man of judgment must needs yield to Essex's greater rank.

Strangely enough—again that mysterious winding of Destiny's thread—Raleigh had conceived a genuine fondness for the headstrong youth. In dispatches to the Queen, he made excuses for his rival's mistakes even while Essex was peevishly endeavoring to undermine him. Score another point for Raleigh. From Elizabeth he receives a gold chain—token of her trust in him, the snub direct to Essex.

But Raleigh's position is far from secure. At home the jackals are making holiday. Interpreting his absence as disfavor on the part of the Queen, they greedily set about usurping his properties and rights. In Ireland, too, the natives confiscate his lands— those bogs which he has reclaimed through his system of drainage and converted into rich soil for their advantage.

And then, another twist of Destiny's thread, and Raleigh's fortune is again on the rise. Essex has committed the unforgivable sin. He has taken himself a bride. Banishing Essex, Elizabeth reinstates Raleigh and showers gifts upon him. She presents him with Sherborne—a manor house of breath-taking beauty but of an accursed history. It is whispered that all who come into possession of Sherborne are destined to die on the scaffold.

In the meantime, Raleigh's wealth has melted away. Gone in reckless gifts to his friends. "When will you cease to be a pauper?" the Queen asks him.

"When your Majesty ceases to be a benefactor," Raleigh replies.

For the moment he basks in the sun of the Queen's favor. But this moment is of brief duration. There are whispered rumors, they grow louder, they reach the Queen. Raleigh has seduced Elizabeth Throckmorton. He "hath been too inward with one of her Majesty's maids. The explorer hath discovered not a new continent, but a new incontinent." The Queen's wrath is dreadful to behold. Raleigh tries to escape, but he is overtaken and with his paramour sent to the Tower. Eventually, a secret marriage comes to light. Lady Raleigh is banished to Sherborne, there to begin her married life alone. But Raleigh remains a prisoner. His hot blood has spurned Elizabeth Tudor for Elizabeth Throckmorton. Let him cool it off amidst the damp stones of the Tower.

V

NOMINALLY a prisoner, Raleigh is—within limitations—at liberty under guard. Yet his complete freedom is a hope that Elizabeth stubbornly is determined to postpone. And then once again Destiny takes a hand. A number of heavily freighted Portuguese vessels, driven by the English, have run aground. The countryside in fevered activity is looting and carrying away the treasure. The English sailors, shocked at Raleigh's imprisonment, demand his presence to restore order. Under guard, he is sent to their aid. His mission having been accomplished, Raleigh is denied his share of the prize. His freedom, the Queen contends, is more than ample payment for his service. With this he must be content, and with "banishment from the Royal Presence."

Contentment for the first time. As Raleigh the courtier disappears, Raleigh the man emerges. His rich personality has blossomed into full flower. With his devoted wife—"Dear Bess"—he improves Sherborne, experimenting with the healing qualities of many herbs. Marriage has sounded a deep chord in his nature. He has become a man of rich emotions and large thoughts. Poet himself, he is the friend of poets. He is preoccupied with the mystery of death, and with the transient futility of all earthly progress. "The long day of mankind draweth fast toward an evening, and the world's time and tragedy are nearly at an end."

He has begun to question the narrow sectarian system of his age. Deeply religious, he tries to find a universal truth, a common basis for all religion. The Puritans are making heard their small voice, crying in the wilderness of intolerance. Raleigh enlists in defense of their right to worship as they will. But he himself is in disgrace and powerless to lend them substantial aid.

Restless again. No extended interludes of pastoral contentment for Raleigh. That dreaming look has once more overspread his countenance. Those brooding eyes are now focused upon Guiana. It is believed that the deposed Incas have formed a new civilization of fabulous wealth. "Through the veins of Guiana flows a stream of gold."

Elizabeth grants him a patent to "discover and subdue heathen lands." In 1595 he sets sail for Guiana, whose chieftains joyously acclaim their liberator from across the sea. With new hope they join forces against the Spanish whose cruelties have depopulated their towns and confiscated their treasures. Raleigh returns to England, with a promise to send ships and supplies to Guiana. A great vision has fired his mind—the vision of a new world "where men shall live in fruitful amity." Justice and peace shall reign in this new world under the protection of the old.

In England once again, he can find no audience for his brave dream. The Queen is "old and full of sleep." The court and council have no time for this "impractical dreamer with his grandiose schemes." The Elizabethan Age is fast drawing to a close.

Dark shadows hover in the offing—darkest of all, the Scotch James, who seems the likeliest successor to the English throne. Already the opportunists are courting that weak and depraved spirit. False lips are pouring poison into that willing ear. "Raleigh is the man that you must fear and hate." Raleigh, sturdy oak with head cloud-wreathed in thoughts of bright tomorrows, is all unaware of the sly foxes gnawing at his roots.

VI

THERE ARE sad days ahead for England. Raleigh views with misgiving a dismal future in which James, with Robert Cecil and his ilk, will guide the destinies of their country. Elizabeth is feeble; the reins rest loosely in her palsied hands. But Raleigh still labors faithfully in her behalf. At last he is permitted to track the Spaniard to his lair.

With a small fleet, he surprises the unsuspecting enemy. His courage, like a giant magnet, draws the entire contingent behind him to a superhuman effort. The city of Cadiz is overwhelmed and sacked. The Spanish domination is at an end. England is now supreme upon the waves.

But the Queen is not as jubilant as once she might have been. Sick and confined to the Palace, she is tired of her public affairs and saddened by the puerile blusterings of Essex.

Raleigh, too, is sad at the sight of a courageous life wasted. He attempts to reason with him. But a dread disease is consuming Essex, is gnawing at his brain. His wild rantings culminate in an insurrection against Elizabeth. Captured, he remains vindictive to the end, striving to implicate Raleigh in a treason plot. With great reluctance the Queen signs the young insurgent's death warrant. The execution makes heartsick both Elizabeth and Raleigh. With very real affection they had watched this wayward child, hoping that eventually he might come into the fold. And their hope was dead.

Raleigh's health is failing. One by one his contemporaries are

[69]

disappearing from the scene. The gallant days of adventure in Merrie England are over. Ponderous, petty men are setting the stage for the advent of King James.

The Queen is dead. Long live the King! Elizabeth has joined her Maker (March, 1603) and James has ascended the throne. Raleigh remains alone. Last of the Elizabethans, first of the Moderns, he hovers suspended between two worlds. And England lies submerged in the darkness into which her lecherous king has plunged her. The arts and the sciences—the glory of Elizabeth's reign—are discouraged. Superstition and witchcraft have spread over the land. There is no seat for Raleigh at this "banquet of backwardness." Slowly James and his little men weave the net in which they intend to stifle Sir Walter's life.

One by one his grants, lands, privileges, titles are stripped from him. Only Sherborne remains; and on this, too, James has fixed his greedy gaze. Now they pull the drawstring, and the net closes. Raleigh is arrested, charged with treason. He is granted a "trial," the injustice of which has rarely been equaled. Not a single witness could be found to testify against Raleigh. The only evidence as to his guilt was a deposition wrung from a coward whom they dared not summon into court. From a Tower cell, this pusillanimous Cobham every morning penned notes implicating Raleigh, and every afternoon wrote letters vindicating him. Finally, after several days of this legalistic farce, the judges found Raleigh guilty—at the King's command. With head held high, he received the sentence: "To be hanged by the neck, cut down living, and his heart removed, before the populace."

VII

RALEIGH'S FINAL SPEECH before the judges. A plea not for mercy, not for justice, but that he may die an honorable death instead of being barbarously mangled in accordance with their verdict. The judges, aghast at what they have been compelled to do, give their consent—some, with tear-dimmed eyes.

A stunned silence descends upon the court as Raleigh is led away. Cecil, as he accompanies him to the Tower, weeps. "Raleigh," he reports, "conducted himself with admirable erection, yet in such sort as a condemned man should."

All England was shocked at the farcical trial. So transparent had been the sham, so obvious Raleigh's innocence, that nobody had anticipated the outcome. The very judges who had tried him were appalled at their own deed. "We are sending an innocent man to his death."

As the Tower door clangs shut, he leaves behind an affectionate people. Raleigh pampered was despised. But Raleigh condemned is the idol of England. Everybody clamors for his release. Even Queen Anne has added her voice to the general outcry. But the cards are stacked against him. James is determined to get him out of the way. His mind has been too completely poisoned by the enemies of Raleigh. The condemned man awaits his end with calm resignation. His thoughts are for others. On the eve of execution he writes to his Dear Bess. "I beseech you for the love you bare me living, that you do not hide yourself many days . . . Your mourning cannot avail me that am but dust."

The day is come. Sadistic James has prepared an extra treat for the man he hates. The scaffold is set up beneath Raleigh's window, and he is the last to be executed. He is to watch the others die, in order that his agony may be "thus duly prolonged."

And now we see enacted a comedy so fraught with vicious cunning that only a warped mentality could have conceived it. Each of the condemned men is led onto the scaffold, then granted a reprieve. The crowd mutters. The last man has been led away. But what of Raleigh? He has witnessed the release of his fellow prisoners, but what is to be his own fate? As long as he dares, James withholds the climax—savoring to the full his grim jest. But the crowd grows restive, the mutterings become louder. Now, at last, James announces the finale. Raleigh's sentence is commuted to life imprisonment. A glorious joke! Living death for the man who loves life so well.

VIII

A POIGNANT DRAMA—the story of Raleigh's imprisonment in the Tower. His cell had become a place of pilgrimage. A new savior of his people. While the magic-makers were concocting poisonous love philters and charms, Raleigh had learned to brew herbs into healing medicines. To him came the sickly Queen Anne, now his staunch friend. He cured her of her illness with his Oil of Balsam. Ceaselessly she extolled its virtues, and ceaselessly she sued for Raleigh's pardon.

A strange man, Raleigh—officially dead, who yet refused to die. Innumerable legends sprang up about him. The world's great journeyed to his side. The warden, jealous of his prisoner, attempted through restrictions to curb his growing popularity. "Sir Walter hath converted a little hen-house in the garden into a still, where he doth spend his time all the day in his distillations . . . If a brick wall were built, it would be more safe and convenient." The wall was built, and Raleigh even more closely confined.

And now Raleigh is very ill. The prison dampness and the river mists are taking their toll. His left side is paralyzed, speech is difficult. It is necessary to remove him from the riverside. Once again he has his little hen-house.

But not his peace. With petty persecutions the warden continues to plague him. Raleigh endeavors to rise above these vexations. He is happy in a new friend. Prince Henry, a youngster with a prodigious intellect, has found his way into the Tower. With Raleigh he discusses the affairs of state. And for his guidance Raleigh writes *A History of the Modern World*. The young Prince has exacted from James the promise that at Christmas Raleigh will be released. But shortly before Christmas Prince Henry dies. The rumor of poison flies from tongue to tongue. And Raleigh remains in the Tower . . .

Always he protests his innocence, proclaims his loyalty to the crown. At last James attends to his pleas. The prison doors swing open (1616) and Raleigh steps forth. But not into freedom. No pardon accompanies the release. King James has other plans for Raleigh.

All unsuspecting, Raleigh accepts the terms proposed. He is to head an expedition to Guiana, there to locate and to work the gold mine discovered on the previous voyage. For this venture he is made Admiral. All expenses are to be met from his own purse, but the crown is to receive the lion's share of the profits. A royal bargain, this. James, cringing beneath the threats of the Spanish ambassador, has promised Raleigh's head to Spain.

In Guiana, Raleigh knows a few short weeks of happiness. He roams over the countryside collecting herbs for medicinal purposes. But one day a small company of his men sails up the Orinoco, seeking the mine. Met with fire from a Spanish town, they return the fire. These unfortunate shots reach round the world. Spain proclaims that England has violated her peace pact, and that Raleigh is the culprit. Word reaches Guiana that James has denounced him as a traitor, has sworn that he must hang. Down tumbles Raleigh's house of gilded cards, as the truth flashes upon his stunned mind. He is the victim of a plot. Actually, he had sailed from England with a noose already draped about his neck.

IX

RALEIGH, left to rot in prison, had stirred the world. And now, tossed to the Spaniards, once more he refused to stay put. He rushed back to England, determined to clear his name.

King James is in a fury. Can't a monarch rid himself of this troublesome visionary, whose courage verges on the foolhardy? Yes, there still remains the execution block. Again the Tower receives its guest. And James demands the death sentence on any charge that can be trumped up.

The rotten timber of James's reign is crumbling. Trembling behind his barricade of evil deeds, he wields now but little power.

Valiantly Raleigh defends himself, refuting all charges brought against him. The judges are unable to convict him.

But James must have his life. That old trick again. The unproved and forgotten treason charge is dusted off and hung once more upon Raleigh. Again he hears his death sentence pronounced. Again he prepares himself for the end.

X

AWARE of Raleigh's widespread popularity and of his own despised position, James hastens the execution.

To the Tower come friends to offer consolation. They find an exalted Raleigh, who proceeds to console *them*. Already he has cast off his earthly bonds. He walks in realms that transcend the flesh and all things temporal. "The world's but a larger prison out of which some are daily selected for execution," he writes.

Lord Mayor's Day. A vast crowd is gathered around the scaffold. They pity and admire as Raleigh is led forth. Too weak to walk alone, he is supported on each side. Tall and erect, with white head raised high, he has a jest or a word of encouragement for every one of them. Draining the proffered cup of sack, he observes, " 'Tis a good drink if a man might but tarry by it." His warm smile moves even his enemies to tears.

From the scaffold he begs indulgence. Should he tremble, let it not be mistaken for cowardice. " 'Tis but that the hour of his ague is upon him."

Many feared that Raleigh might sway the crowd against the King. But even at this hour, he is without malice. "What have I to do with kings, who am about to go before the King of Kings!"

The executioner breaks down, and weeps. Kneeling beside him, Raleigh places his palms upon the man's shoulders and exhorts him to do his appointed task well. "When I hold forth my hands," he tells him, "strike." Raleigh rests his head upon the block and holds out his hands. Still the axe is stayed. "Strike, man, strike!" he cries. Two swift strokes, and all is over. An awed

hush descends upon the spectators. They draw away from one another. A man's voice cries, "There was never such another head
to be cut off!"

"Aye," cries an answering voice, "and will there ever be such
another hand to help a poor soul?"

SHAKESPEARE

Important Dates in Life of Shakespeare

1564—Born at Stratford-on-Avon.

1582—Married Ann Hathaway.

1584—Compelled to leave Stratford for poaching.

1592—Attained success as actor and playwright.

1593—Published Venus and Adonis.

1594–1610—Acted and wrote plays, at the rate of two a year.

1597—Bought a house at Stratford.

1602—Bought a large estate at Stratford.

1609—Published collection of his sonnets.

1610—Retired to Stratford.

1616—March 25, wrote his will. April 23, died.

William Shakespeare

1564–1616

O F ALL the mysteries in the world, the genius of Shakespeare is the most difficult to explain. His parents were rather less than ordinary. His father, a glover and wool-stapler, was not able even to sign his name. Shakespeare came of an obscure line, blazed across the skies, and then left an equally obscure line after him. Of his three daughters, two were of average intelligence and the third was downright stupid.

Much ink has been spilled in the battle of scholars who have tried to prove that the plays of Shakespeare were written by a man with another name. What a useless thing to waste our time in such empty pedantries! The work that goes under the name of Shakespeare seems as infinitely beyond the ability of a professor as it is above the capacity of a butcher. Whatever may have been the training or the social standing of the author, it is amazing that anyone bearing a mere human name should have produced a rose of such divine sweetness.

Shakespeare was a freak of nature—a demigod born out of the race of men. No critic as yet, not even Carlyle or Emerson or Brandes or Kittredge or Taine, has been able to probe to the depths of Shakespeare's mind. And the chances are that no critic

ever will. To understand Shakespeare is to understand the com-
plex mystery of creation. For his plays are a reproduction, in
miniature, of the whole stupendous drama of life.

Shakespeare was a man gifted with the thoughts and the language of a god. Yet, externally, his life was anything but godlike.
The career of this greatest of poets was quite unpoetical. At fourteen he was apprenticed to a butcher. At seventeen he was looked
upon as one of the most reckless tipplers and wildest roisterers in
the town of Stratford. At eighteen he seduced—or perhaps was
seduced by—Ann Hathaway, a woman of twenty-six. He married
her in the nick of time, as she was about to become a mother.
Shortly after his marriage to her, he fled from Stratford in order
to avoid arrest for deer-stealing. Coming up to London, he drifted
into the theatrical channels and started out as a low comedian—
one of "His Majesty's poor players." For the next seventeen years
he devoted himself to the writing of sublime dramas and to the
acting of motley parts in them. He was an indifferent actor; and
as for his plays, he never thought enough of them to get them
published during his lifetime.

He made money in his profession, lent out some of it on interest, invested the profits in real estate, knew how to drive a hard
bargain, had his debtors imprisoned when they were delinquent
in their payments, visited his family once a year, and finally
bought an estate in Stratford and settled down to a life of com-
monplace respectability as a gentleman farmer.

His conduct during his stage career, however, was anything but
respectable. On one occasion he drank himself into such a stupor
that he was found the next morning under a tree by the roadside.
He had his share of unsuccessful love affairs. "When my love
swears that she is made of truth," he complains (Sonnet 138),
"I do believe her, though I know she lies." Apparently he was
not much of a ladies' man. The gentlewomen of London preferred the young lords, with their yellow curls and courtly manners, to the somewhat uncouth country bumpkin who wrote
poetry and played the clown. Yet within his own little circle of

actors and playwrights he was able now and then to outwit his rivals. An anecdote, written in 1602 on the authority of Tooley, relates how "his comrade Burbadge, who played Richard III, having a rendezvous with the wife of a citizen, Shakespeare went before, was well received, and was pleasantly occupied when Burbadge arrived, to whom he sent the message that William the Conqueror came before Richard III."

His family life seems to have been rather stormy. Whatever his success with other people's wives, he enjoyed very little success with his own. To Ann Hathaway, he was anything but William the Conqueror. She nagged him to the very end of his life, and he retaliated by leaving her in his will his "second-best" bed— nothing more.

This, in brief, is the story of Shakespeare's life. But it gives us not the slightest insight into the story of Shakespeare's mind. As a man he was, like most of us, just a little higher than Caliban— one of the earthiest of his creations. But as a teacher of mankind, he seems to belong to another planet, born as if by accident into this puny-minded race of ours.

The foremost intellects in the world have tried to grapple with the intellect of Shakespeare and to reduce his ideas to a logical sequence. But in vain. The critics have made him out to be, in turn, a patriot and a pacifist, a Catholic and an infidel, a ser- monizer and a cynic, a humanitarian and a misanthrope, a democratic utopian and a royalist snob. He was none of these; or rather—amazing paradox!—all of these in one. His genius tran- scended the ideas and the beliefs of any one man, or of any group of men. He entered with an equal degree of sympathy and affec- tion into the mind of every character that he created. Caliban was as intimate a part of Shakespeare as Prospero. The mind of Shakespeare was co-extensive with the mind of the human race.

We shall make no effort to analyze Shakespeare or to delve extensively into the "antres vast and magical groves" of his un- fathomable genius. It would be useless to try it. For greater minds have made the attempt and failed. The art of literary criticism has not as yet invented the yardstick that can gauge the dimensions of Shakespeare's intellect. All we shall try to do here is to explore a little way into one of the many corners of Shakespeare's mind—to dip up, as it were, a mere thimbleful of wisdom out of the inexhaustible ocean of his genius.

With this object in view, let us glance at three of his plays which represent him in three of his distinct attitudes toward life —first as a satirist, then as a man of the world, and finally as a philosopher. These three plays are—*Timon of Athens, Hamlet,* and *The Tempest.*

II

IN *Timon of Athens* Shakespeare cries out against the injustice of the world with the bitterness of an Isaiah. In his other plays he simply mirrors life, but he rarely moralizes about it. When, occasionally, he does stop in his dramatic action to offer a hasty comment on life, he dismisses it, like some superior visitor from another planet, as an insubstantial and worthless dream—"a tale told by an idiot, full of sound and fury, signifying nothing." But in *Timon of Athens* his contempt flares up into indignation. Life here is a tale told, not by an idiot, but by a crafty devil. And far from signifying nothing, it signifies treachery, meanness, hatred, hypocrisy and fraud. Timon was a wealthy citizen of Athens who generously gave all his money away to his friends. When they were troubled by their creditors, he paid their debts. When they were married, he gave them a dowry and set them up in their new life. When he invited them to a banquet, he sent them home with presents of money and of precious stones. His steward, Flavius, warned him time and again that his generosity would bring about his ruin. But Timon, overestimating both the extent of his resources and the gratitude of his friends, paid no attention to Flavius. He kept spending all his money on other people until he had nothing left for himself.

When his own creditors began to bother him, he felt certain

that his friends, to whom he had given away everything, would come to his rescue. But one by one they refused to help him, each of them offering a different excuse for his refusal.

Whereupon Timon invited them once more to a banquet—and this time he served them nothing but dishes of warm water. Then, before the "affable wolves"—miscalled in the past his friends— were able to recover from their surprise, he dashed the water in their faces and ended by throwing the dishes at them and driving them out of the house.

And thus, having learned the bitter lesson that unselfishness is dangerous in a selfish world, Timon left the city of Athens and went to live in a cave in the woods. Here he found "the unkindest beast more kinder than mankind." While digging in front of his cave for roots to eat, he discovered hidden gold—the "yellow slave and tyrant" of the human race. But its glitter had lost its power. It aroused now within him nothing but contempt. He threw it back into the earth and kept only a few pieces to be used as stones against unwelcome strangers.

When the Athenians learn of this discovery, they come one by one to his cave. Poets, painters, warriors, prostitutes, statesmen, beggarmen, thieves—all of them are eager once more to become the friends of Timon. To each of them in turn he gives a handful of gold, and then like a scornful god he sends them scurrying back to hoard it or spend it in the pigsty of their city. "Go," he cries to several of the thieves as he hands them the gold. "Rob one another. There's more gold. Cut throats. All that you meet are thieves. To Athens go, break open shops; nothing can you steal but thieves do lose it."

All the world, to Timon, is a den of thieves. That is, all the world with the exception of one man. When Timon's old steward, Flavius, arrives to commiserate with his master in the hour of bitterness, Timon feels persuaded that there is, after all, some decency left in the world. "I do proclaim one honest man—mistake me not—but one; no more, I pray—and he's a steward." But he warns Flavius against his own goodness. "Methinks thou art more honest now than wise; for, by oppressing and betraying me, thou mightst have sooner got another service. For many so arrive at second masters upon their first lord's neck."

Shakespeare has been accused of despising the so-called lower classes. His critics tell us that he never showed any sympathy for them, that he always spoke of them with an aristocratic sneer, and that he looked upon them as mere "sticks and stones and worse than senseless things." Such critics do not understand the universality of Shakespeare's genius. The only lovable character in the entire human race, as represented in *Timon of Athens,* is a Roman slave. There are more sympathies in the mind of Shakespeare than are dreamt of in the philosophy of his critics.

Shakespeare was perhaps the only man in the world who could see life from every angle. He could be, on occasion, as revolutionary as Shelley, as bitter as Heine, as pessimistic as Euripides, as cynical as Byron, as disillusioned as Swinburne, as philosophical as Goethe, and as hopefully resigned as Tennyson. He was a poet who consecutively looked upon life through spectacles of different colors. In *Timon of Athens* he sees life through the dark glass of despair. Nothing in the world seems worthwhile. The erstwhile friend of Timon, Alcibiades, has tried to help his native city of Athens in a crisis. His city repays him with exile for his trouble. He raises an army and marches against the city in retaliation for his unjust banishment. The senators, alarmed over the approaching danger, visit Timon in his cavern and implore him to return to Athens in the hour of their need. But Timon pays no attention to their entreaties. He invokes upon them all the noxious pestilences he can think of. And then, as if on second thought, he informs them that there is something he *will* do for them to save them from death at the hands of Alcibiades:

> I have a tree, which grows here in my close,
> That mine own use invites me to cut down,
> And shortly must I fell it; tell my friends,
> Tell Athens, in the sequence of degree

From high to low throughout, that whoso please
To stop affliction, let him take his haste,
Come hither ere my tree have felt the axe,
And hang himself.

And then, having sent the final shaft of venomous cynicism
after his retreating countrymen, Timon digs his grave on the
"verge of the salt flood" and puts an end to the evil nightmare
of his life. Better to feast the grateful worms underneath, than the
two-legged beasts who grovel thanklessly above.

Timon is not the only cynic in the play. The churlish philosopher, Apemantus, is also contemptuous of the stupidity of mankind. But there is a vast difference between the mournful bitterness of Timon and the sarcastic vulgarity of Apemantus. Timon
kills himself because he cannot endure the spectacle of man's
inhumanity to man. Apemantus, on the other hand, derives the
keenest joy out of the selfsame spectacle. Timon would like to
destroy the world and to build in its place a world of true friends.
But Apemantus would rather find fault with the world than im-
prove it. When one of the noblemen of Athens asks him what
time it is, he replies, "Time to be honest." Yet if he ever found
himself in an honest world, he would set about immediately to
corrupt it, in order that he might be able once more to snarl about
its dishonesty. The ingratitude of friends is to Timon no less than
a mortal blow. To Apemantus, it is merely an occasion for laughter. It required the most subtle shading of character to draw both
Timon and Apemantus in the same play. Yet each without the
other would be incomplete. The two men together are the complete answer of Shakespeare, the satirist, to the injustice of the
world.

III

In *Hamlet,* we get the answer of Shakespeare, the man of the
world, to the selfsame problem. Confronted with the baseness of
humanity, Timon kills himself and Apemantus is merely amused.

But Hamlet, less sensitive than Timon but more noble than Apemantus, tries to meet injustice with punishment and murder with revenge. He believes in the Old Testament doctrine of an eye for an eye, a tooth for a tooth, a life for a life. His reaction toward evil is the reaction of the average man. He does not run away from it like Timon, or mock at it like Apemantus. Instead, he broods over it and philosophizes about the meaning of it all; and finally, when his courage and his frenzy have been nursed to the highest pitch, he strikes—not against the evil deed but against the evil doer. And in so striking, he destroys himself as well as the object of his wrath.

Revenge, to Hamlet, was a noble mission. Nothing else, not even his love for Ophelia, must stand in the way. The world of *Hamlet,* in spite of its beautiful maxims and philosophical meditations, is a world of barbarians in which the highest ethical principle is the spirit of vengeance. Strip it of its poetry, and *Hamlet* is an ugly play. A young prince of fairly average intelligence loses his reason through his belief in spirits. Thinking that his father's ghost has urged him to avenge his murder, he goes crazy, reviles his mother, spurns and drives to suicide the girl he is about to marry, kills her father and her brother, and then brings about his mother's death and his own—all because he has promised a ghost that he will punish the king for having committed a murder. It is a rather high and stupid price to pay for a single act of vengeance. This play would indeed seem to be, as Voltaire called it, "the work of a drunken savage." The whole drama of our human existence, for that matter, often appears like the work of a drunken savage. But that is because we regard life, as some of the critics regard Shakespeare, from too narrow a point of view. *Hamlet* represents but a single aspect of Shakespeare's genius, just as vengeance represents but a single aspect of human life. Shakespeare, the magician who could imitate Nature so perfectly, knew better than to let Hamlet stand for his entire philosophy. He had other, and higher, ideas in his dramatic bag of tricks. Nature could produce a Confucius as well as an Orestes, and

Sir Walter Raleigh

Shakespeare

Shakespeare was able to create a Prospero as well as a Hamlet. In their final analysis, both Nature and Shakespeare have something finer to show to the world than the spirit of mere revenge. Just what this "something finer" is, we shall see in *The Tempest*.

IV

In *Timon of Athens*, Shakespeare repays injustice with bitterness; in *Hamlet*, with revenge; in *The Tempest*, with forgiveness. Like Timon and Hamlet, Prospero has been tried by suffering. But his sadness makes him all the more compassionate even toward those who have brought the suffering upon him. He does not storm against the world, he does not even laugh at its foolishness, but he smiles with the indulgence of a man who looks upon the follies of children. In *The Tempest*, Shakespeare has risen above the spirit of satire. He has entered into the world of true philosophy. In many of his other dramas he makes merry, like a heartless god, over the pettiness of humanity. He loves to drag the king down from the throne and to point out to him how with all his pomp he will some day be eaten by a worm, which in turn will be swallowed by a fish, which then in *its* turn will go into the guts of a beggar. But in *The Tempest*, even when he scolds, he scolds in a gentle voice. The tone of bitter scorn which he often employed in his earlier dramas has been transformed, in this play, into a tender note of pity.

And now—the story of *The Tempest*.

Prospero, the exiled Duke of Milan, lives with his daughter, Miranda, upon an enchanted island. Twelve years before his brother Antonio, with the aid of Alonso, King of Naples, had treacherously driven him out of Milan and set him afloat, with his three-year-old daughter, in a leaky ship upon the open sea. Having fortunately drifted to this enchanted island, Prospero has spent his time in the education of his daughter and in the study of magic. He has enlisted in his service the faithful spirit, Ariel, and the treacherous savage, Caliban.

One day a ship passes by the island. There is a wedding party on board, returning from Tunis to Italy. Among others in this wedding party are King Alonso and Antonio, who have brought about the banishment of Prospero; and with them are the King's brother, Sebastian, and the King's son, Ferdinand.

Prospero, by means of his magic art, unleashes a tempest over the ocean and drives the vessel upon the enchanted island. He orders Ariel to rescue all the passengers, but to scatter them, in various groups, over the seashore. Ferdinand, thus separated from his father and believing him lost, wanders as it seems to him aimlessly over the island. In reality, however, he is being guided by Prospero's magic to the old enchanter's cell. Here the prince and Miranda, seeing each other for the first time, transact a mutual exchange of hearts even before they have had the opportunity to exchange a single word.

Meanwhile, in one part of the island, Sebastian and Antonio are plotting the murder of the King; and in another part, Caliban and a couple of drunken sailors from the shipwrecked crew are plotting to murder Prospero. Unaware of the fact that this island is enchanted, the newcomers are already trying to establish upon it the immoralities and the stupidities of the world from which they have come. But Prospero, all-knowing and all-powerful, frustrates their savage plans.

At first he is inclined to punish the King and his company for the injuries that they have inflicted upon him. But Ariel, with his more than human wisdom, converts him to a saner point of view. "The King, his brother, and yours," Ariel points out to him, "are all distracted, and . . . brimful of sorrow and dismay . . . Your (magic) charm so strongly works 'em, that if you now beheld them, your affections would become tender."

Prospero: Dost thou think so, spirit?
Ariel: Mine would, sir, were I human.
Prospero: Hast thou, which art but air, a touch, a feeling
Of their afflictions? and shall not myself,
One of their kind, that relish all as sharply,

> Passion as they, be kindlier moved than thou art?
> Though with their high wrongs I am struck to the quick,
> Yet, with my nobler reason, 'gainst my fury
> Do I take part . . . Go, release them, Ariel . . .

Compare the words that Timon spoke to the senators with these words that Prospero speaks to Ariel, and you have the difference between the reaction of the man and that of the superman toward the injustice of the world.

For Prospero is a superman—the most sublime type of human character that either Shakespeare or Nature has been able to create. He is the Confucius of the Shakespearean world. He forgives—not so much because of his superior sympathy, but because of his superior wisdom. His mind works upon a plane which is far removed from the quarrels and the hatreds, the ambitions and the passions, the betrayals and the jealousies, and the oppressions and the retributions of the world into which he has been sent down to live. He is not a "stern censurer" of life, but an amused, though somewhat sorrowful, onlooker. When Miranda for the first time sees human beings other than her father on the enchanted island, she rapturously exclaims, "O wonder . . . How beauteous mankind is! O brave new world, that has such people in't!" But Prospero, smiling at her enthusiasm, replies, " 'Tis new to thee." He knows from experience that every human creature is "a devil, a born devil," on whom his teachings are "all, all lost, quite lost." He believes no man, and yet he loves all mankind.

Prospero is not only the best of Shakespeare's creations, but he is Shakespeare himself at his best. Like Prospero, Shakespeare too is an enchanter whose magic art has peopled the earth with elves and puppets and sprites and men, who has "bedimm'd the noon-tide sun, call'd forth the mutinous winds, and 'twixt the green sea and the azured vault set roaring war." Graves at his command "have waked their sleepers, oped, and let 'em forth" by his so potent art.

V

AND NOW, having reached the height of creation by creating *The Tempest,* Shakespeare, like Prospero, abjured his magic, broke his staff, and, folding up the bag of his enchantments, retired from the stage. He was through with teaching and amusing and scolding this dull-witted race of ours. From now on, he preferred to be an interested spectator.

He died in obscurity. The world knew nothing about the genius of Shakespeare. But then, Shakespeare cared nothing about the plaudits of the world.

SAMUEL JOHNSON

Important Dates in Life of Samuel Johnson

1709—September 18, born at Lichfield.

1731—Left Oxford without a degree.

1735—Married Elizabeth Porter.

1736—Went to London.

1738—Published satire, London.

1743—Published biography of Richard Savage.

1747—Began Dictionary.

1750-52—Published paper, The Rambler.

1755—Completed Dictionary.

1762—Received pension from George III.

1763—Met Boswell.

1765—Published edition of Shakespeare. Met the Thrales.

1775—Published Journey to the Hebrides.

1779-81—Wrote Lives of the Poets.

1784—December 13, died.

Samuel Johnson

1709–1784

Meet Samuel Johnson—a big, brutal bear of a man, an implacable controversialist who laid his opponents low with a bludgeon, a morose, blubbering and blustering combination of the invalid and the prize-fighter, a glutton who started his daily round of voracity with eight peaches before breakfast, a pedant of pomposity who always put on his wig before he sat down to write, a bundle of superstitions who insisted upon touching every lamp post that he passed on the street, a roughneck who took delight in answering "every fool according to his folly" and who regarded everybody but himself as a fool. A young man once came to him for advice as to whether he should marry. "Sir," said Johnson, "I would advise no man to marry who is not likely to propagate understanding." His one purpose in life, said his critics, was to slay his opponent in a conversational duel . . . "This man is the most disagreeable snob in England."

Meet Samuel Johnson—a man who, to quote Oliver Goldsmith, "had nothing of the bear but his skin," an opponent who was always the first to seek a reconciliation, a fighter who knew how to smile in defeat, a cheerful accepter of pain—once, when the doctors were operating on him (it was in the days before ether), he urged them to cut deeper and finally took the knife into his own hands to show them how—a philosopher with strange ideas but with a "central sanity" in his mind, a lifelong invalid who bathed at Brighton in October and who, when he got drenched to the skin in the rain, refused to change his clothes because a friend was expecting him for dinner, a believer in social inequality who befriended the poor and insulted the rich— "you are certainly not better than the poor; give thanks to God that you are happier"—a lover of independence and hater of slavery—"how is it," he said referring to the Americans, "that we hear the loudest yelps for liberty among the drivers of Negroes?" —an eccentric whose greatest eccentricity was a kind heart in an unkind world. He had a habit of picking up all the stray animals and all the stray people from the gutters of London and of bringing them to live with him in his household. Let us for a moment visit him in this gloomy tenement of his on the north side of Fleet Street. As we mount the stairs, our ears are deafened by the barking of dogs and the meowing of cats and the screeching of parrots. We get to the top floor and enter the crowded rooms. Four old women and an old quack doctor are quarreling about the evils of destiny, whilst a Negro evangelist is trying to pacify them with quotations from the Scripture. We pass through this bedlam into the inner chamber, and here we find the "master" propped up in bed and entertaining a group of distinguished ladies and gentlemen with his favorite amusement—conversation about life . . . "This man is the most human creature in England."

Such was the paradox that was Samuel Johnson—"rough, wise, severe, gentle, limited, lovable" pattern of the English character in the eighteenth century.

II

A FLOWER out of the mud. Johnson's paternal ancestry was so obscure that he once said, "I can hardly tell who was my grandfather." His mother's antecedents were equally obscure—simple, unlettered and unremembered yeomen of Warwickshire.

Johnson's earliest memories, however, were concerned with literature. His father, a bookseller of Lichfield, allowed his awkward little son, "with a head too big for his years," to browse freely among the pastures of the printed page. Samuel learned to philosophize long before he learned to play.

He was a sickly child. Once his mother took him to London to be "touched" by Queen Anne for the scrofula. The Queen's touch had no effect on his disease, but it had a tremendous effect on his lifelong adoration for royalty.

And for learning. "I must be an educated man. I have had the privilege to meet the Queen!"

His mentality, even as a child, was amazing. The spinster who first taught him to read gave him a present of gingerbread and told him he was the smartest scholar she had ever had. At Lichfield School, though he played none of the games, he was the acknowledged leader of the boys because "he knew something about everything." At Stourbridge, the school which he entered at fifteen, he astounded his teachers by reciting a Latin poem which he had read only once. "Don't you ever forget what you read?" asked his instructor, Baretti. "Who can forget, sir?" replied Johnson.

After his graduation from Stourbridge he spent two years in his father's bookshop, reading—"not voyages and travels, but all literature, sir." When he came up to Oxford, the Master of the college said he was "the best qualified" student that had ever matriculated there.

The best qualified, but not the most disciplined. He spent a great part of his time "lounging at the college gates with a circle of young students, whom he was entertaining with his wit and keeping from their studies."

Speaking later of his college life, Johnson confessed that he neglected his studies, especially in the classics. "The result is that I have remained an ignoramus in Greek and in Latin." The word "ignoramus" must be taken with a rather generous pinch of salt when we remember that Johnson's remedy for sleeplessness was to turn Greek epigrams into Latin verse.

Johnson was a poor scholar in but a single sense—the material. Indeed, his poverty prevented him from finishing his course at Oxford and from getting his degree. Frequently he was unable to attend his lectures because he didn't have any shoes. His two financial props—his father's book business and a promised loan from a Shropshire friend—both failed him; and he was obliged (December, 1729) to leave Oxford and to return to Lichfield.

Two months later his father died, leaving him an inheritance of twenty pounds and a handful of unsalable books.

With this capital he set out to conquer the world—and failed. He tried ushering in a school at Market Bosworth, clerking in a bookstore at Birmingham, translating a Jesuit treatise on Abyssinia, and raising subscriptions for the poems of Politian—a man very few had heard of, and nobody cared to read. Johnson's talents were definitely not of the financial type.

Nor of the practical type in any sense whatsoever. Unable to support himself, he took on the additional burden of a wife—a woman twice his age who even in her youthful days had been "nothing to look at."

And—miracle of miracles!—he loved her with a romantic and passionate devotion. While his friends snickered at his "blindness," he spoke to them rapturously of his "beautiful Tetty." A somewhat domineering Tetty, who led him by the leash—and he liked it. "Sir, she had read the old romances, and had got into her head the fantastical notion that a woman of spirit should use her lover like a dog." But what could he do? Whenever he upbraided her, she burst into tears. "And how can you see a woman you love in tears?"

His love for his wife continued long beyond the grave. Eighteen years after her death he noted in his diary that he had "less pleasure in any good that happens to me, because she is not here to share it." And thirty years after her death, when his own end was approaching, he wrote, "Perhaps Tetty knows that I pray for her. Perhaps Tetty is now praying for me. God help us both."

Love is timeless. The climate of May is not unlike the climate of October; and the difference in the color of the foliage is but an added zest to the lover of beauty. "Sir," said Johnson to his friend, Beauclerk, "ours was a love marriage on both sides."

A love marriage, and a marriage which brought new ambitions with the new responsibilities. Johnson began to write books that were closer to the interests of his day. He composed a tragedy, *Irene;* a satiric poem, *London,* after the manner of Juvenal; a series of articles for the *Gentleman's Magazine;* and a number of speeches for the members of Parliament. Once, when a friend at a dinner praised a famous oration of Chatham's, Johnson startled the company with the quiet remark, "That speech I wrote in a garret on Exeter Street."

The most important work that he wrote at this period, however, was his biography of Richard Savage. This mysterious friend of Johnson's, who "suffered from much misfortune and many vices," possessed an insatiable thirst for brandy and beauty. He and Johnson found little in common save their mutual delight in intellectual conversation. They spent many a night together walking the streets and talking about the world and Richard Savage. Johnson was fascinated by his friend's story—most likely fictitious. Savage claimed that he was the illegitimate son of Lady Macclesfield by Lord Rivers. His mother, he said, had repudiated him from childhood, leaving him to the untender mercies of a poor and ignorant woman. His father, unable to determine either the identity or the number of his offspring, had left his entire fortune "to about twenty paltry whores." And then, to add injury to insult, Lady Macclesfield had tried her utmost to have her son hanged on a trumped-up charge of murder.

These, and many other lurid details, form the story of "the life of a blackguard written by the pen of an angel." And so interesting was this story that Sir Joshua Reynolds, having taken it up casually with his elbow leaning upon a mantelpiece, finished the entire book while standing in the same position and "found his arm quite benumbed when he got to the end."

Johnson was now acquiring the friendship of important people —the painter Reynolds, the historian Gibbon, the orator Edmund Burke, the poet Goldsmith, the statesman Charles Fox, the actor Garrick. It was through the help of Garrick that he secured the production of *Irene*—a financial success and artistic failure. Johnson himself was aware of the shortcomings of *Irene*. The story is told that a certain Mr. Pot called it "the finest tragedy of modern times"—to which extravagant compliment Johnson retorted, "If Pot says so, Pot lies."

Johnson realized that the stage was not his medium. All his characters talked like Johnson—and when everybody's so brilliant, nobody shines. The "master" decided to exercise his conversational genius in the clubroom, at the tavern, on the sidewalk—wherever the sunlight of his wisdom would not only outsparkle his companions, but inspire them to richer feelings and better thoughts.

And fortunately for Johnson, and for the world, he met (in 1763) James Boswell, a man who became inseparable from the "master," and who absorbed his genius as the charcoal absorbs the sun. The brilliance of Boswell has been eclipsed under the glow of Johnson's personality. But Boswell's *Life of Johnson* is perhaps the greatest biography ever penned by the hand of man. In the fire of the charcoal we get a good reproduction of the flaming sun.

Boswell worshiped Johnson; and Johnson, to quote his own expression, held Boswell "in my heart of hearts." He realized Boswell's weakness; he acknowledged that his biographer was "vain, a babbler, a wine-bibber, a man of frequently irregular and ill-governed life." But he pardoned his friend's follies, looking upon them as the common follies of mankind. "All the decent people at Lichfield get drunk every night." He knew that under a faulty covering lay a faultless heart. Though heir to the life and the fortune of a Scottish laird, young Boswell—he was Johnson's junior by twenty-one years—had generously thrown himself into the struggle for Corsican independence, had mingled with the disinherited stepchildren of the world, had finally placed himself at the feet, not of a minister or a king, but of a man of lowly origin and vulgar habits whose only claim to distinction was a wise and noble soul.

They were as two brothers—the man of boorish nobility and the man of noble birth. They ate, talked, traveled together— Johnson observing and recording every aspect of life, and Boswell observing and recording every aspect of Johnson. And it is largely through Boswell's eyes that we see Johnson today.

For Johnson's literary work is hardly known today. His *Dictionary* is more prejudiced than accurate—he defines *patriotism,* for example, as *the last refuge of a scoundrel.* His *Rasselas*—a fantasy which he wrote in a week to pay for his mother's funeral—has about as much lift to it as an eagle with feathers of lead. His annotated edition of Shakespeare overwhelms the fire of poetry under an avalanche of Johnsonian erudition. His essays in *The Rambler*—a semi-weekly newspaper which he published for three years—are uncharted excursions into boredom. And even the lightest of his work, the *Lives of the Poets,* violates the one vital formula for biographical writing—"the art of biography is that of giving life to the dead." Johnson's *Lives,* on the contrary, are full of learning and empty of life. He presents the poets as a row of symmetrical mummies instead of living men.

Johnson's writing is dead. But his conversation, as recorded by Boswell, will remain forever alive. The range of his eloquence covered every subject under the sun. Like Socrates, he confessed that he knew nothing; but most people, he insisted, knew even less—for they didn't know that they knew nothing. Above all things he hated hypocrisy, insincerity and pretense. "Clear your mind of cant . . . Never lay claim to goods or to thoughts that you do not possess." No matter what the subject of his conversation, he always reduced everything to the "bottom of sense." If his writings are for the pedants, his conversations are for the man in the street. "After all," a London cabman recently remarked to an American visitor, "I agree with Doctor Johnson who says, a man may travel all over the world and see nothing better than his dinner." When people met him for the first time after having read his work, they were amazed. They had expected to see an author, and they found a man. A man who loved to stick pins into the bubbles of idle gossip. An acquaintance once remarked that every fashionable Frenchman, as soon as he married, took an opera girl into his keeping. And this, concluded the acquaintance, is a universal custom. "Pray, sir," said Johnson, "how many opera girls are there in France?"

"About fourscore."

"Well, then," observed Johnson, "in that case there can be only fourscore fashionable Frenchmen who resort to this practice."

His tongue was caustic, but never mean. Above all, he liked to approach the problems of life—and of death—with an honest gaiety. One day a Quaker was denouncing the vanity of the current fashions in dress. "My friend," said Johnson, "let us not be found, when our Master calls us, ripping the lace off our waistcoats, but the spirit of contention from our souls and tongues." On another occasion, referring to the same subject, he declared that "a man who cannot get to Heaven in a green coat will not find his way thither in a grey one."

His honest and good-natured tolerance extended to everything save his two pet aversions—the Whigs and the Scotch. "The first Whig," he said, "was the Devil." And his closest descendants are the Scotchmen. Once a friend remarked that "poor old England is lost." Whereupon Johnson retorted: "Sir, it is not so much to be lamented that poor old England is lost, as that the Scotch have found it." Together with Boswell he paid a visit to Scotland, and came back unimpressed. "The noblest prospect which a Scotchman ever sees is the highway that leads him to London."

Johnson loved his London above everything else. He loved it, not for its commercial preëminence, but for its intellectual pleasures which, to him, were the only justification for human existence. "He who is tired of London is tired of life."

III

JOHNSON never grew tired of life. And he found twenty-four hours too few for a day of zestful living. He hated to go to bed; and when he did, he was always ready to "tumble out" for an extra round of the taverns. One night his friend Beauclerk thought he would "go and knock up" old Sam Johnson. In answer to his pounding, Johnson came to the door, poker in hand and nightcap on his head. "Who is it, a burglar?"

"No, it's only Topham Beauclerk."

"What time is it?"

"Three A.M."

"Time for a good frisk, you dog."

A few minutes later the two cronies, hand in hand, went to meet the dawn at a Covent Garden tavern, and then topped it off with a boatride to Billingsgate.

Always ready for a frisk. Always full of laughter. "Echoes of that huge laughter," writes Max Beerbohm, "have come ringing down the ages."

It was with this ringing laughter that he greeted his friends, confounded his enemies, parried his misfortunes, and waited for his death. A big, shapeless, hulking, mischievous child-philosopher to the very end. Once, at sixty, he rolled down a hill because "I haven't had a roll for a long time."

It was with this ringing laughter that he enlivened the household of the Thrales—a wealthy brewer and his wife—with whom he made a "second home" for sixteen years. And it was with this cosmic laughter at the incongruity of life that he once picked up a woman lying in the gutter, "so much exhausted"—we are quoting Boswell—"that she could not walk. He took her upon his back and carried her to his house, where he discovered that she was one of those wretched females who had fallen into the lowest state of vice, poverty, and disease. Instead of harshly upbraiding her, he had her taken care of with all tenderness for a long time at considerable expense till she was restored to health."

Laughter is akin to pity—and to piety. Like Voltaire, Johnson laughed at life in order to keep himself from crying. And in his laughter he found hope. Life is a matter of great sadness. Without hope—that is, without faith in an ultimate righting of wrongs—human existence is a succession of losses. To this evil there is but a single remedy—religious hope. "He that grows old without religious hope, as he declines into imbecility and feels pains and sorrows crowding upon him, falls into a gulf of bottomless miseries . . . where he finds only new gradations of anguish and precipices of horror."

From this "gulf of bottomless miseries" Johnson found an escape in a laughing acceptance of the ultimate rightness of things. With Browning he might have said, "God's in His heaven" and consequently "all's right with the world." He composed, for his guidance, a number of prayers; and he felt always, whether in his serious or in his serene moments, that he was "under the eye of Omnipotence." One night at dinner someone mentioned the nineteenth psalm, whereupon Johnson recited it while his face "was almost as if it had been the face of an angel."

"The law of the Lord is perfect, restoring the soul; the testimony of the Lord is certain, making wise the simple; the precepts of the Lord are righteous, rejoicing the heart." In this faith he approached his end. "I may be conquered, but I will not capitulate." In 1783 he suffered a paralytic stroke from which he recovered sufficiently to take a trip to Kent and Wiltshire. The following year he suffered a relapse, recovered, and "began life anew" with the formation of a dining club among those of his friends who were still alive. "Let us die feasting."

But his friends knew that the black camel was kneeling at the door. And on December 14, 1784, the *Gentleman's Magazine* recorded the passing, "without a pang," of "the great and good Samuel Johnson, the pride of English literature and of human nature."

GOETHE

Important Dates in Life of Goethe

1749—*Born at Frankfort-on-Main.*

1765—*Entered Leipzig University.*

1770—*Began legal studies at Strassburg.*

1773—*Wrote first important drama,* Götz von Berlichingen.

1774—*Wrote* The Sorrows of Werther.

1775—*Settled down at Weimar.*

1777—*Began* Wilhelm Meister.

1786—*Went to Italy.*

1789—*Had son by Christiane Vulpius.*

1791—*Appointed director of ducal theater.*

1794—*Started friendship with Schiller.*

1800—*Completed* Wilhelm Meister.

Completed first part of Faust.

1805—*Schiller died.*

1832—*Completed second part of* Faust.

Died.

Johann Wolfgang Von Goethe

1749–1832

THE YOUNG MEN and the young women of the eighteenth century were Modernists. Like the young men and women of today, they were dissatisfied with the world in which they found themselves and tried to create in its place a world that would be nearer to their heart's desire. In France and in America the rebellion took a political turn. In other countries, however, and especially in Germany, the revolt against tradition was purely intellectual. The soldiers of the German revolution discarded the antiquated ideas of their nation, but they left the antiquated government alone. Theirs was a revolution of the pen, and not of the sword. They liberated the minds of their countrymen, but they were not much concerned about their bodies. They believed in free thought, but not in free action. They were the conservative radicals of the eighteenth century.

The leader of these intellectual revolutionists was Johann Wolfgang von Goethe. At the age of six he rebelled against God. At seven he expressed his doubts about the justice of men. At eight he composed a Latin essay in which he compared the wisdom of the Pagans with that of the Christians. At eleven he wrote a cosmopolitan novel in seven languages. At twelve he fought a duel. At fourteen he fell violently in love for the first time. At seventy-four he fell violently in love for the last time. And at eighty-two he completed his greatest poem, the second part of *Faust.*

II

GOETHE was born in 1749. His great-grandfather had been a blacksmith and his grandfather was a tailor. But the tailor made a man out of his son, Johann Caspar, who became the Imperial Councilor of Frankfurt and promptly forgot about his humble origin.

Goethe, the son of Johann Caspar, never mentioned the black-smith and the tailor among his ancestors.

Like the great French philosopher, Voltaire, he was born half-dead. But unlike Voltaire, he enjoyed good health for the greater part of his life. In all his eighty-three years he suffered only three serious illnesses. He was one of those few fortunate mortals endowed with a perfect mind in a perfect body.

He was educated at home. His father, somewhat of a classical scholar and a strict disciplinarian, put him through a course of study which trained the intellect rather than the imagination. His mother, on the other hand, a simple, hearty, joyous and well-read *Jungfrau*—she was only eighteen at the time of Goethe's birth—stimulated his poetic faculty by telling him stories of her own making and by encouraging him to help her in the weaving of the plots and in the creation of the characters. "To my father," he said, "I owe my serious outlook on life; to my little mother, my love for telling tales."

His father wanted him to study law and to become a college professor. But Goethe was interested neither in law nor in teaching. To please his father, he entered the University of Leipzig (1765); but to please himself, he became a student of life rather than of books.

Plentifully supplied with money, for his father was well-to-do, he proceeded to break through the conventional shell of his home environment and to experiment recklessly with the ways of the world. For his teachers he had not the slightest respect. "I fancied I knew as much about God and the world as the professors themselves." He felt that he could learn much more about life if he neglected the classroom and went into the haunts of the people. "In society, concerts, theater, feastings, promenades, the time flies. Ha, it goes gloriously! But also expensively. The devil knows how my purse feels it!"

One of his fellow-students, writing about the unrestrained conduct of Goethe at this time, remarked that it would be easier to "influence the trees and the rocks than to bring Goethe to his senses."

But he came to his senses of his own accord. Throughout his life he experimented with wine and women, and then he transmuted his experience into song. Having learned all he needed to know about the society of Leipzig, he left it for the solitude of the country, where he took long rambles, reading his Shakespeare and his Homer and dreaming his poetical dreams.

For he lived in order to sing. He had begun his literary career as a mere child. And now, at the age of seventeen, he dashed off his first important drama, dealing—of all the subjects in the world—with the rascalities and the adulteries of married people! *Die Mitschuldigen* (*The Fellow Sinners*) is written with a sophistication that is astonishing in a youngster of seventeen. Like most of the adolescent dramas, it is a story with a moral; but the moral has within it the concentrated wisdom of all the sad old men who have sinned and suffered for their sins. "Inasmuch as the majority of us are guilty," concludes the indulgent young philosopher of Leipzig, "the wisest thing for all of us to do is to forgive and forget."

III

THE dissipation of his Leipzig days—and nights—came near to putting an end to his life. In the summer of 1768 he was seized with a violent hemorrhage, and for a time it was doubtful whether he would recover. When at last he was able to leave his bed, he returned home—to an adoring mother and a disappointed father. Herr Johann Caspar Goethe had tried to make a lawyer out of his son, and the boy had turned out to be nothing but a poet!

The Councilor made another attempt to put Wolfgang on what he considered to be the right road. This time he sent him to Strassburg, to complete his studies "without any further nonsense" and to get his doctor's degree in Jurisprudence.

But here too, as in Leipzig, Goethe neglected his law and resumed his study of life. He dabbled in art, he learned to play the cello, he took up medicine, he philosophized, he flirted, and he became the leader of the Strassburg intelligentsia. His health was completely restored now. He walked through the streets of the city like a Greek God. On one occasion, when he entered a restaurant, the diners laid down their knives and their forks to stare at the magnificent young stranger.

He was, to use his own expression, "intoxicated with youth," and all those who came into contact with him were infected with something of his own spirit.

An excellent swordsman and rider, and a singer of magical phrases such as Germany had never heard before, he turned the heads of all the Strassburg Fräuleins. And his own head was almost always in a whirl.

But if he loved easily, he easily forgot. Whether jilting or jilted, he translated his experience into a poem and then turned to his next adventure.

In his eagerness to study life from every possible angle, he fell in with all sorts of people—inn-keepers, inn-keepers' daughters, evangelists, dancing masters, merchants, manufacturers, workers, rabbis and priests. And, like Spinoza, he found something lovable and divine in everyone that he met.

He was especially fond of the stage. A passionate admirer of Shakespeare, he tried to transfuse some of the rich blood of the Elizabethan drama into the anemic productions of the German theater. With the exuberant optimism of youth, he set out to revolutionize not only the *art* but the very *thought* of his nation. He examined the history of Germany for dramatic material that would give full scope to his lawless genius. He found it in the life of Götz von Berlichingen, the Robin Hood of Germany. This man's exploits against the bishops and the barons in behalf of the peasants inflamed Goethe's imagination into producing one of the wildest, yet one of the most magnificent, of German dramas. It became for a time the Bible of the younger generation, and Goethe was worshiped as the prophet of the new religion of unrestraint.

Yet, much to his father's gratification, he was able to spare enough time from his "lawless activities" to obtain a degree as doctor of law. His father sent him, for further training, to the Supreme Court of Wetzlar. But Goethe noticed on his arrival that there were twenty thousand cases awaiting the Imperial Judges' decision, and that it would take them no less than three hundred and thirty-three years to get through with all these cases. This settled his own case. He lost all respect for the law and definitely turned to literature as his life's work.

During his short stay at Wetzlar he fell, as usual, desperately in love. This time the situation was complicated by the fact that Lottchen, the young lady of his choice, was already engaged. For a time he thought of committing suicide. He kept a dagger under his pillow, and every night he tried to muster up sufficient courage to plunge it into his heart. Finally, however, he decided to write a novel about his unfortunate love affair, and to kill the hero in the novel instead of killing himself. The result was *The Sorrows of Werther,* a book of romantic nonsense and sublime beauty. It is the autobiography of a misfit—a sensitive artist who does not feel at home among his fellows and who finds companionship only in the solitude of the fields. It is an elegy on the sadness of life, a hymn to the joyousness of death.

The Sorrows of Werther produced a tremendous effect upon the German public. All the young men imitated Werther's blue coat and yellow waistcoat, and the girls adopted Lottchen's white dress with the pink bows. In Germany the book was sold like a newspaper on the street corners; and even in China, Werther and Lottchen were modeled in porcelain. In some places the more sentimental admirers of the book went so far as to organize "Werther societies for the suppression of life." An epidemic of suicides swept over Europe as a tribute to the genius of Goethe.

But Goethe himself had no desire to put an end to his life now. Leaving his love and his book and his admirers behind, he pressed on to new fields and new adventures.

IV

ALTHOUGH he flouted the conventions, Goethe had a deep-seated reverence for authority. "I cannot blame you," he writes to one of his friends, "for living in the world and making acquaintances amongst men of power and influence. Intercourse with the great is always advantageous to him who knows properly how to use it." And so, when Prince Karl August asked him to come to his court at Weimar, Goethe accepted the invitation with alacrity.

He reached Weimar (in 1775) at the age of twenty-six. He stayed there for the rest of his life. Taking up his residence in a "garden-house" near the palace, he divided his time between poetry and politics. He became not only the devoted priest of Apollo, but the equally devoted servant of Karl August. He was the German Confucius who tried to teach his prince how to rule; and in so doing, he gave up his own independence. Confining his rebellious spirit to his books, he became in his private life one of the most submissive of courtiers. On one occasion, when he was walking with Beethoven, the prince's retinue happened to pass by. The composer, who respected nothing but his art, threw out his chest and walked defiantly through the pompous crowd. Goethe, however, who worshiped royalty even more than his art, stepped aside, took off his hat, and bowed in deepest reverence. For he was a true son of Germany. He was proud of his

distinction as the poet-laureate of the world; but he was even
more proud of his dignity as the private secretary of one of the
least important of German princes.

Saxe-Weimar, the little province over which Karl August
ruled, boasted an army of only 600 men. But it was an army of
little tin gods adored by the military idolatry of the Germans.
Every German prince, even though his domain consisted of only
a few acres, was constrained to support an army for the worship
of his subjects. One of Karl August's fellow princes, for example,
boasted a "superb military force" of seven officers and two men
in the ranks!

Such was the childish pretentiousness of official Germany in
the eighteenth century. And Goethe, in spite of his great genius,
was not altogether free from it. Yet life at the court of Weimar
was gay, and his duties sat lightly upon his shoulders. He made
hunting and skating popular, and he turned flirting into one of
the most fashionable amusements of the day. "We are somewhat
mad here," he writes in one of his letters, "and play the devil's
own game." If he sacrificed his independence to Karl August,
he got from him in return "what the great seldom bestow—affection, leisure, confidence, garden and house." He loved his art,
but he was equally fond of his comfort. He was not a prophet
who was willing to die for Truth, but a poet who was anxious to
live for Beauty.

V

FOR FIFTY YEARS he made Weimar the literary center of the
world. He gathered about him a group of brilliant men and
women who, under his leadership, discussed philosophy, devoted
themselves to poetry, and played at love. He organized and became the director of a Little Theater, and he wrote for it some
of the greatest dramas of the century. As long as his youth lasted,
the tone of his writing remained wild, and at times flippant. In
Stella, for example, he allowed the hero to live with his wife
and his mistress at the same time—to the mutual satisfaction of

all three. This "plea in favor of bigamy" aroused violent opposition on the part of the public. And so, with his tongue in his cheek, Goethe rewrote the end of the play. He got his hero, who was unable to quit either his wife or his mistress, to solve the difficulty by blowing out his brains.

Gradually, however, we find this note of exuberant irregularity less and less dominant in Goethe's works. Finally it disappeared altogether. The intoxication of his youth had subsided. From now on, he was no longer a rebel who wanted to destroy the world, but a philosopher who tried to understand it.

His lifelong quest was now for more light—more beauty. He sought for beauty even in ugliness, and for dignity in the midst of humility. Like Walt Whitman, he was passionately fond of human beings, however lowly their station. If he bowed to princes, he did not shun the society of paupers. Throughout his life he was on the most intimate terms with "the butchers and the bakers and the candlestick makers" of the world. "How strong my love has returned upon me for these lower classes!" he wrote after visiting a group of miners. "These so-called lower classes are, in God's eyes, assuredly the highest!"

His expressions of sympathy for the underdog were not mere rhetoric. Out of the meager salary of $1000 a year which he received as the Councilor of Karl August, he supported two strangers who had appealed to him for aid. Though spared from suffering for the greater part of his life, he could yet sympathize with the sufferings of others. For he possessed the imaginative faculty to see beyond the horizon of his own existence.

His was perhaps the most versatile mind of the eighteenth century. He was not only a poet and a painter and a musician, but a scientist of no mean achievement. As a poet, he recognized the absolute unity under the apparent diversity of things. And as a scientist, he tried to demonstrate this unity. He made a thorough study of botany and anatomy and the theory of colors. He wrote a book on the metamorphoses (the structural changes) of plants in which he showed that flowers are nothing but glorified leaves—leaves turned into poems, so to speak. He examined the human skull and he discovered in it a bone—the intermaxillary—which established the relationship between man and the lower animals.

Like Terence, he was interested in everything pertaining to the human race—in everything, except war. For Goethe was essentially a man of peace. There was nothing in him of the Prussian lust for conquest. When Karl August was fighting against the French, he invited Goethe to come to his camp and to watch the maneuvers of his troops. Goethe accepted the invitation; but instead of interesting himself in the battles, he made a study of the stones and the flowers in the neighborhood of the camp. He had a deep and passionate love for his country, but he refused to be a chauvinist. Charged with being a slacker because he would not write inflammatory war songs, he replied: "I have never uttered anything which I have not experienced . . . I have composed love songs only when I have loved. How, then, can I write songs of hatred without having hated?"

VI

THE middle period of his life was blessed with three of the greatest of human blessings: a loving wife, a son, and a devoted friend. In 1788, at the age of 39, he met Christiane Vulpius. At first they indulged in a free relationship; but after several years of this freedom they yielded to the "greater freedom of marriage." In 1789 his son was born; and in 1794 he became intimately acquainted with Schiller. Goethe was 45 at the time, and Schiller was 35.

The friendship between Goethe and Schiller was a more radiant poem than any which either Goethe or Schiller ever wrote. It was a friendship between a demigod and a dying man (for Schiller had already lost one of his lungs). Goethe was a Pagan, with a reverence for beauty. Schiller was a Christian, with a passion for justice. Both had started out as rebels, but both had surrendered at last. Goethe had been tamed by his good fortune, and Schiller by his poverty. But the two poets still believed in the rebelliousness of Art. Poetry, to them, was the sacred medium which would transform men into supermen. And so they worked together, these two apostles of salvation through the religion of the Word, and each of them supplemented and encouraged the genius of the other. When Schiller died, after their all-too-brief comradeship of eleven years, Goethe shut himself up into his room and wept like a child. "The half of my existence," he wrote to an acquaintance, "is gone from me . . . My diary is a blank at this period. The white pages intimate the blank in my life."

Goethe lived to an old age, but he had to pay the price of loneliness in return for the gift of a long life. One by one he lost all those whom he loved—his dearest friends, his sister, his wife, and finally his only son. But he went bravely ahead, turning his sorrows as well as his joys into immortal song. "I have never uttered anything which I have not experienced." He wrote sixty books of his spiritual and his mental experiences—lyrics, elegies, satires, epics, dramas, essays and novels—fantastic fables about elves and ghosts and goblins, and philosophical stories about myths and mortals and devils and gods. Finally he gathered all his genius into one masterpiece and created *Faust*. It took him thirty years to write the first half, and twenty-five years longer to complete the second half.

VII

THE purpose of Goethe in writing this drama was to understand Humanity—to measure its powers and to define its duties. The keynote of the drama is struck in the Prologue. God and the Devil make a wager about the soul of Man. The Devil has no respect for mortals. He is the everlasting Skeptic, the spirit of denial. He believes that *not to be* is better than *to be*. He sees no sense in "destiny's ceaseless play" which creates men only to destroy them. He would prefer the "eternal emptiness" out of which the universe started upon its "needless journey" through time and space. His business, therefore, is to thwart the creation of God and to deny the goodness of men. "Even the old Doctor Faust, the most learned and the most upright of mortals," maintains the Devil, "can easily fall a prey to my wiles if only I should take the trouble to tempt him."

But God knows better. It is true, he admits, that the vision of Man is imperfect, so that he struggles forever through a haze of semi-darkness. "He strives and sins throughout his life." And yet, through his very sinning, "he struggles instinctively toward the light."

And so it is agreed that the Devil is to tempt Faust and to see whether he can destroy the immortal part of his soul. In accordance with the wager, the Devil is to be declared the winner if Faust ever finds the passing moment (of mortal existence) so beautiful that he is loath to move on from that moment to the next.

In the first half of the story, which is familiar to most readers, Goethe relates how the Devil restores the youth of Faust and tempts him with many of the selfish joys of life—beauty, wealth, sensuality, recklessness, and the pleasures without the responsibilities of love. Guided by the Devil, Faust seduces Marguerite and then abandons her to her sins and her sorrows. Throughout this first part of the story, Faust is possessed by "a passion for error." But in all his erring ways he finds not a moment of happiness, not a single incident to which he is able to say, "Verweile doch, du bist so schön." (Linger awhile, thou art so beautiful.)

After the death of Marguerite, the Devil tries to win him with temptations of a different sort. Faust, who is the symbol of Universal Man, is eager to try every experience of life, "to bare his breast to every pang, to know all human joy and sorrow," to live and work with men, "and to share with them the shipwreck of mankind."

Accordingly the Devil enables Faust to become (like Goethe)

a councilor at the royal court. Here, by his able service, Faust wins gratitude and honors—but no happiness. Dissatisfied with his present life, he conjures up for himself the life of the past. He brings out of antiquity the spirit of Helen of Troy, restores her to life, and tries to become wedded to her (just as Goethe tried to become wedded to the classical thought of the Greek poets). But when Faust embraces Helen, she vanishes, leaving only her cloak behind. It is useless even for a Faust, or a Goethe, to try to understand the glory that was Greece. In spite of all their endeavors, the beautiful soul of antiquity escapes them, and they are left with nothing but the outward garment in their hands.

And thus Faust moves on from one experience to another, and finds satisfaction in none. "His very walk is a series of falls." Whatever he undertakes to do, whether of good or of evil, ends in failure, or in an empty triumph which is even worse than failure. He wins an important battle for his emperor, and he finds that his victory in war means death and devastation for both sides. The Devil offers him cities, kingdoms, castles, beautiful women, glorious achievements, and eternal fame. But Faust is sick of it all. The arc of his life has begun to turn downward. The pleasures of youth and the achievements of middle age have brought him nothing but disillusion. Care has taken possession of his house, and the fires and desires of his youth have all turned to ashes. He is stricken with blindness, and he is ready at last to give up his lifelong quest for happiness.

But—strangely enough—at the very moment that he renounces happiness, he finds it. He starts upon a vast project to reclaim the swamps near the sea and to make them fit for human habitation. Here he plans to build homes, upon free soil, for millions of people who will best enjoy their freedom by conquering it anew with their labor every day. This thought fills him with a great joy. This is the self-forgetful goal toward which he has subconsciously struggled all his life. This at last is the golden moment to which he can say, "Linger awhile, thou art so beautiful!"

GOETHE

And now that he has arrived at the supreme moment of his life, his life comes to an end. Apparently the Devil has won the bet. He claims the soul of Faust as the price of his victory. But the angels descend amidst a shower of roses and carry his soul to heaven. Faust has erred grievously, to be sure, but through all his erring he has struggled instinctively toward the light.

The first to greet him in heaven is Marguerite. She has sinned and died through the sins of Faust. But all this is forgiven and forgotten. It is her mission now to show him the way. *Das ewig Weibliche zieht uns hinan.* Woman is the eternal savior of Man.

VIII

AND NOW, having completed the supreme work of his life, Goethe —like Faust—was ready to sleep. His numerous admirers were preparing a royal celebration in honor of his eighty-second birthday. In order to escape from the festivities, he went to the mountains of Ilmenau. There, in a hut where he and Karl August had often stayed together, he saw the lines which he had penciled on the wall a number of years ago.

"Over all the hilltops, there is quiet peace; in the treetops, thou canst scarce perceive the slightest breath; the little birds in the forest have stilled their voices. Be patient now—soon thou too wilt be at rest."

Brushing away the tears from his eyes, he re-echoed the last words—"Soon thou too wilt be at rest."

He returned home. For a little while longer he sang those magical songs in which—as Heine observes—"the word embraces you while the thought imprints a kiss." At last, on the 16th of March in 1832, he was unable to get up from his bed. Six days later, amidst the hushed whispers of his household, he closed his eyes—and the song of his life trailed off into eternal silence.

His last audible words were—*"More light!"*

Samuel Johnson

Goethe

SIMON BOLIVAR

Important Dates in Life of Simon Bolivar

1783—Born in Caracas.
1801—Married Maria Teresa Toro.
1803—Wife died.
1805—Traveled in Europe.
1806—Returned to Caracas, "a rebel dedicated to freedom."
1811—Declared Venezuelan independence from Spain.
1813—Started war for liberation of Venezuela.
1815—Defeated, exiled to Jamaica.
1817—Returned to Venezuela.

1819—Crossed Andes with "Army of Liberation." Defeated the Spanish army at Boyaca (August 7). Became president of liberated Venezuela (December 17).
1820–26—Fought for liberation of other South American countries.
1828—Escaped attempt to assassinate him.
1830—Died at San Pedro.

Simon Bolivar

1783–1830

I T WAS a dangerous thing to rebel against the Spanish rule in South America. In 1781, when Tupac-Amaru attempted to liberate Peru, the Spanish governor tore out his tongue and then compelled him to look on while his wife and his son were being pulled apart by four horses driven in different directions. At the end of the spectacle, he himself was accorded the same treatment.

The story of this atrocity was still fresh upon everybody's lips when Bolivar was born (July 24, 1783). His father wanted to call him Santiago. But the priest who baptized the infant gave him the name of Simon. "I have a presentiment that this child will some day become the Simon Maccabeus (the old Judean liberator) of the New World."

Dedicated from his infancy to rebellion, this child of a noble family in Venezuela grew up into a reckless, restless and audacious youngster. Having lost his father at the age of three, he was put into the care of the distinguished Caracas jurist, Miguel José Sanz. His escapades were at once the admiration and the terror of Don José. "My child," he once remarked, "you are a regular *polvorin* (horn of gunpowder)." Whereupon the child retorted, "Then you had better keep away from me—I'm liable to explode."

Slight, wiry, effervescent, he captivated everybody with his impudent dark eyes and his ingratiating bright smile. He lived like a prince in an enchanted tale. At the death of his mother—he was nine years old at the time—he came into a considerable estate. Mines of valuable mineral deposits, spacious *haciendas,* vast acres of sugar cane, mills, ranches, distilleries, fruit orchards and thousands upon thousands of animals and slaves—all these were his to share with his brother and his two sisters.

But Simon cared next to nothing for his wealth. He was interested only in his adventures. Gathering around him a group of mischievous youngsters, he became a "constant pain and irritation" to the conventional old magistrates and merchants of Caracas. He accepted as his tutor in all his escapades a vagabond philosopher by the name of Rodriguez—a half-cracked utopian who walked around with a copy of Rousseau's *Émile* in his pocket and with all sorts of social and political panaceas in his head. "In this crazy world of ours," he remarked to Bolivar, "there are two outstanding facts—the sacredness of the human body and the stupidity of the human mind." And to demonstrate the "sacredness" of his own body to the "stupid" minds of his contemporaries, he occasionally appeared in public *au naturel.* He was among the first of the nudists.

But the crazy doctrines of Rodriguez had their serious as well as their frivolous side. This "Socrates of South America" taught Bolivar the importance of a healthy body for the spiritual tussle in the arena of life. He took his young pupil on long and dangerous hikes through the forests and over the mountains of Venezuela. Together they traveled on muleback to the Bolivar ranches where Simon learned from the *vaqueros* (cowboys) the art of taming wild horses, of wielding the lasso and the lance, and of galloping full tilt to the side of a bull, seizing his tail with one hand and hurling him to the ground with a sudden snap of the wrist.

Rodriguez looked on with admiration as his young protégé became the most iron-muscled expert among the *vaqueros.* "You will need this iron constitution in the great battles that await you." Venezuela, South America, the entire world needed to be reshaped. The priest had named him Simon because he was destined to be a liberator. Eagerly he absorbed his tutor's ideas about a new age of freedom. There were great events stirring in South America—rebellions, suppressions, executions, new rebellions. Bolivar and his tutor were among those who witnessed the decapitation of the revolutionist, José Chirinos, in the public square of Caracas. In one of the numerous uprisings Rodriguez himself was involved. Thanks to the influence of Bolivar's family, he managed to escape the death penalty. But he was compelled to leave the country.

Bolivar missed his tutor. But he found consolation in the arms of his beautiful cousins, the Aristiguietas—a couple of warm-blooded young ladies with receptive ears and prodigal hearts. "When I die," he observed to a friend, "I hope to go to Purgatory; for there I shall be able to continue my flirtations with the Aristiguietas."

His flirtations, however, formed but an episode in his restless life. He enlisted in the militia, and the impetuous lover proved himself an equally impetuous soldier. At the end of two years of maneuvering over the *llanos,* he was commissioned *alferez* (sub-lieutenant).

And then he directed his adventures toward the Old World. On January 19, 1799, he set sail for Madrid where his uncle, Esteban Palacio, enjoyed a favored position in the palace of the king and—it was whispered—in the boudoir of the queen.

Bolivar came to Madrid highly recommended as a loyal subject of King Carlos and Queen Maria Luisa. Yet within a few months an order was issued for his arrest. He was suspected of having joined a conspiracy, together with his uncle Esteban, against the royal couple. He fled to Paris where he paid homage to Napoleon, the "savior of the French Republic," and made love to another member of the far-flung and fascinating Aristiguieta family. In the midst of his flirtation he learned that the king's charges against him had been dropped. Whereupon he promptly left his French girl, returned to Madrid, and married a Spanish girl. Bolivar was only nineteen at the time.

The young couple set sail for Caracas. Here they enjoyed a honeymoon of uninterrupted fiestas given by their friends in their honor. And after their honeymoon they settled down to a life of idyllic happiness in one of Bolivar's *haciendas* at San Mateo.

Their idyl continued for eight months and then ended abruptly when his wife died of a sudden malignant fever. "This tragedy," he observed, "marked the end of my playtime, and the beginning of my work."

II

To FORGET his grief, he returned to Madrid. Here he fell in with a group of South American intellectuals who, like himself, were dreaming dreams of freedom. They organized themselves into a secret society and accepted Bolivar as one of their leaders. Though of medium height, he produced the impression of commanding stature because of his well-proportioned muscles and his supple slenderness. His deep-set, dark and thoughtful eyes, his high, broad forehead, his long, thin, aristocratic face and his fiery voice demanded—and received—the respect of his fellows.

And aroused once more the suspicion of the Spanish court. A royal edict ordered him out of Madrid.

Again, as before, he went to Paris where he became the life of the fashionable *salons*. With his ingratiating smile he won the affection of practically all the French men and women of any importance—Talleyrand, General Duroc, Marshal Oudinot, Napoleon's young stepson Beauharnais, the great French actor François Talma, Madame Recamier and Madame de Staël. He became especially intimate with Alexander von Humboldt, the great German naturalist who was then visiting Paris. Humboldt had just returned from his scientific expedition to South America. "Do you think," Bolivar asked him one day, "that South America is ready for independence?"

"Yes," replied Humboldt, "I think it is. All that your country needs is a great leader."

Bolivar's heart leaped up when he heard these words. "A great leader." Perhaps he himself might prove to be the man. His old tutor, Rodriguez, had finally drifted to Paris with his *Émile* and his utopian dreams. "Of course you are to be the man!" But, first of all, Bolivar must complete his education. Rodriguez supplied him with those books that had served as a bugle call to freedom —Plato, Voltaire, Rousseau, Montesquieu, Helvetius, Hobbes, Hume, Spinoza. And then, after the strengthening of Bolivar's mind, must come a further toughening of his body. "An end to your luxurious living!" A modest house. A hard mattress. A strict diet. A rigorous course in fencing until Bolivar became equally adept with either hand. And finally, Bolivar and Rodriguez started off on a walking tour over southern Europe. Down the valley of the Saône, across the Alps, and into the plains of Italy. Milan, Venice, Verona, Padua, Ferrara. At Naples, Bolivar was the guest of Humboldt's brother. At Alessandria, he saw Napoleon reviewing his army on the battlefield of Marengo. The "savior of the French Republic" was on his way to crown himself king of Italy. "What a mighty fall is this!" exclaimed Bolivar. Napoleon had degenerated from a demigod into a dictator.

Rome, and a visit to the Vatican. Here, to the amazement of the onlookers, Bolivar refused to kneel and to kiss the Pontiff's slipper. "I respect His Holiness, but I bow to no man."

One day the two pilgrims climbed the hill of Monte Sacro. The city below them was golden-red under the light of the setting sun. Rodriguez was delivering a stirring dissertation on the glory that was Rome. For a long time Bolivar was silent. And then, "his eyes moist, his breast palpitating, his face flushed with a feverish animation," he spoke:

"Rodriguez, I swear by the God of my forefathers that my hands shall never rest until they have delivered my country from the shackles of Spain!"

III

BOLIVAR returned to his country by way of the United States where he saw the spirit of independence in its practical application. When he arrived at his native city of Caracas, he found it in an uproar. A liberator had appeared in Venezuela—a strange fighter-prophet by the name of Miranda. This "soldier of misfortune," like Bolivar a native of Venezuela, had fought in the American Revolution and in the French Revolution. He had distinguished himself under Napoleon and had attained the rank of general. And now he was back in South America in an effort to inspire a rebellion against the Spanish king. In the summer of 1811 he gathered together a number of Venezuelan patriots at Caracas, and on July 5 he issued a South American Declaration of Independence.

His next step was to establish this independence by force of arms. He took to the field and examined the troops. His heart sank. A rabble of undisciplined and barefoot peasants who could neither shoot nor drill. But he didn't give up. They were brave men, and with hard work they might be transformed into good soldiers.

Incessant drill under exacting taskmasters, the foremost of whom was Colonel Simon Bolivar. Irregular meals, irregular pay and nondescript rags in place of uniforms. But finally they were whipped into a fighting army. With this army of amateur soldiers Miranda twice defeated the troops of the Spanish king.

And then, treachery. A Venezuelan sentinel had delivered to the enemy the stronghold of Puerto Cabello. Miranda was giving a victory dinner to a hundred officers when he received the news of the betrayal. "Gentlemen," he said, "Venezuela is wounded to the heart."

The Spaniards were victorious. Miranda was captured and imprisoned at Cadiz where he died of a broken heart. The Venezuelan rebellion was at an end.

One of the leaders of the rebellion, however, had managed to make his escape from the Spaniards. Under cover of the night Bolivar had boarded a ship that sailed safely away from the fortress of Puerto Cabello. He returned to Caracas where, concealing himself in the hut of a friendly Indian, he laid the plans for another and more successful revolution.

IV

MIRANDA had failed because he couldn't perform the impossible. Bolivar succeeded because he could. His property had been confiscated, his army had melted away and twenty thousand Venezuelans had been swallowed up in an earthquake. "Nature herself is fighting against us!" wailed the survivors. "Very well," shouted Bolivar into the clamor. "Then we shall compel Nature, too, to give in to us!"

And he did compel Nature to give in to his indomitable will. Captured and exiled to the Island of Curaçao, he escaped and set sail westward and southward to New Granada—a country across the Andes from Venezuela. Here, in a land which he had never seen and in which his name had never been heard, he issued a manifesto of liberation and a call to arms. And the people, captivated by the magnetism of his personality, listened and obeyed. An army sprang up as if by magic. "Let us free Granada—and then, on to Venezuela!" With a company of two hundred men loaded upon ten rafts he poled up the Magdalena River to Teneriffe, a stronghold occupied by a sizable Spanish force. He reached the stronghold in the dead of the night. Out of the darkness came the sentinel's call, *"Quién vive?"*

Bolivar fell upon the sentinel and cut his throat. Then, concealing his handful of soldiers behind the rocks and the trees, he ordered them to make a terrific clatter so as to convey an exaggerated impression of their numbers. The Spaniards thought that an entire army had descended upon them. Bolivar called upon their commander to give himself up. "If you refuse, I shall blow the fortress to smithereens with my cannons!" The commander fled precipitately with his entire force, and Bolivar entered the town without the loss of a single man.

The townspeople looked with amazement at the soldier who had "routed an army by the mere sound of his voice." But where were his cannon? they wanted to know. "My cannon?" laughed Bolivar. "I didn't have any." And then, as he surveyed the arsenal that he had just captured, "But I see that we shall have plenty of arms for our future campaigns."

His next objective after Teneriffe was the fortress of Mompox, further up the river. Here, too, he was able to enter without a fight, for the Spaniards had fled at the word of his approach.

Higher and higher toward the source of the river he advanced, up amongst the cliffs of the Andes; and wherever his army encamped, hundreds of recruits rallied to his standard. The Spanish army "melted like the sands" before his onslaught. Within six days he fought six battles and won them all.

And then, an eastward and upward ascent into the peaks of the Andes toward his native Venezuela. "It is a feat beyond human endurance," his lieutenants warned him. "Then our endurance," he retorted, "must be *more* than human."

He started the crossing of the Andes in the middle of the winter. His soldiers, brought up in the tropical valleys of New Granada, were unaccustomed to the snowdrifts and the sleetstorms of the upper ranges. But into the teeth of the tempest they marched, scrambled up the faces of slippery rocks, held on precariously with their knees and their fingers, crawled in single file across ledges so narrow that two mules could not pass each other, and groped their way through the blinding mists that swirled around the mountaintops. Again and again, after an exhausting climb, they found it necessary to retrace their steps in order to avoid gorges too deep to cross. Hardly a day passed without the loss of men and animals who missed their footing and crashed down over the precipices as the mountains reëchoed their cries amidst the howling of the wind. "We shall never get across," moaned the living. But a fiery spirit drove them on. Bolivar seemed to be everywhere—smiling, tireless, undismayed, impervious to the cold, unconcerned about his life. "We have a mission to fulfill, and nothing shall stop us!"

And nothing *did* stop them. With five hundred crusaders he charged down from the Andes into Venezuela. The Spanish royalists looked upon them with superstitious amazement. "These soldiers are veritable devils!" To which Bolivar retorted—"Not devils, but avenging spirits!" He addressed his men as they reached the boundaries of his native land: "Soldiers, your arms have brought freedom to the gates of Venezuela . . . As the darkness scatters before the light of the dawn, the Spaniards will disappear at the mere sound of your guns . . . Brave soldiers, it is to your hands that America looks for salvation . . . You have conquered the Andes. It is now your proud task to conquer the Spanish king!"

V

THROUGH scenes of indescribable enthusiasm he marched across Venezuela toward his native city of Caracas. In every town and village he found eager volunteers for his army—not only South Americans but native Spaniards as well. For the resentment against the Spanish misrule was intense. One of Bolivar's Spanish volunteers, Major Vicente Elías, was so fanatical in his hatred of his countrymen that he vowed destruction to every last one of them. "When I have killed all the Spaniards I will do away with my own family and then with myself, so that none of that race will be left alive."

Major Elias had brought along with him an entire company of volunteers. Bolivar was now the commander of a considerable force, an army of inspired men determined to see but a single end to their crusade—victory. Reckless of their lives and regardless of the odds, they kept charging again and again at the enemy until they put them to flight. In one of their stubborn battles they renewed the charge twenty times, with Bolivar always galloping at their head. He seemed to lead a charmed life. "God is preserving him for America's sake." His followers had become imbued with a religious conviction of their invincibility. "America is destined to be free!"

On August 6, 1813, they entered Caracas in triumph. The city lay in the hollow of the mountains like a huge bowl filled with flowers. Bolivar, in full dress uniform, marched at the head of the column amidst the garlands and the banners and the happy throngs that lined the streets. Shouts of acclamation on every side. The soldiers, ragged, barefoot, covered with wounds but with faces aglow, displayed the flags they had captured from the enemy.

They marched into the public square. Here, upon a raised platform, the notables of the city bestowed upon Bolivar the title by which he was henceforth to be known to his countrymen—*Libertador*—the Liberator of Venezuela.

VI

Bolivar had conquered his enemies. But he was unable to conquer his friends. Many of them had become envious of his success. They accused him of dictatorial ambitions. Several of his former lieutenants had set themselves up as dictators on their own account. They refused to acknowledge the authority of their Commander-in-Chief. Venezuela had become entangled in a confusion of civil wars. Street broils, mutinies, desertions. Bolivar tried to keep his people united by every psychological weapon at his command—flattery, persuasion, encouragement, reprehension, rewards, promises, threats, appeals to their self-interest, their patriotism, their common sense. Sometimes, when the occasion demanded, he resorted to *physical* weapons in order to rid his country of its malcontents. One day he ordered the execution of five hundred men. "If I am forced to retaliate by terrible means, which are repugnant to me, it is solely to deliver my country from its enemies."

Bolivar was not a cruel man. But he was obliged to fight fire with fire. His enemies, both Spanish and American, were the type that would stop at nothing. One of them, Morales, was always followed by a gigantic slave known as "the Executioner," a monster whose chief amusement was to clear his master's path of its "human vermin." Another of Bolivar's enemies, Zuazola, had adorned his hat with the ear of a slain rebel. Still another, Antonanzas, was in the habit of presenting his friends with boxes full of hands and feet and noses—the trophies of his battles. Such was the character of some of the men against whom Bolivar was obliged to fight.

But he fought against them and overthrew them, one by one. Time and again he came near to losing his life, either in open combat or as the result of treachery. One night he left his house to meet an Englishman sympathetic to the Venezuelan cause. During his absence an intimate friend came to visit him. Finding the house empty, the visitor lay down in Bolivar's hammock to await his return. When Bolivar came home, he saw his friend lying in a pool of blood, stabbed to the heart. Some enemy had mistaken this man for the Liberator.

This was but one of many seemingly miraculous escapes. The assassins never knew where or when to find him. "It's hard to shoot the shadow of an eagle on the wing," remarked his admiring friends.

And the "eagle on the wing" covered an amazing range of territory in his crusade to disemburden his country of its tyrants and its traitors. North, east, south, west—across unfordable rivers, insurmountable mountains and impenetrable forests he struck at the enemy with the swiftness of lightning. And with the tantalizing *irregularity* of lightning. His blows invariably descended upon the places where they were least expected. Everywhere he was hailed as a savior. The Liberator of Venezuela, New Granada, Colombia, Ecuador, Bolivia, Chile, Peru. "The Spanish domination in South America is now nothing but a memory."

VII

By SEPTEMBER 4, 1826, Bolivar had completed his work of liberation. "Whatever remains of his life after that date," writes his great biographer, Rodo, "is tragedy." His campaigns had broken down his health. He suffered from recurrent attacks of fever. He saw the disintegration of the countries he had tried to unite. He tried to convene a Pan-American Congress in Panama, but failed in his attempt. "I am like the crazy Greek who stood on a rocky headland and tried to direct the vessels that sailed around it." The cross currents of personal envy and national intrigue were everywhere threatening to whirl his beloved countries into anarchy. He started on a personal tour of these countries. "Let there be no more regionalism—no more Venezuela, no more Ecuador or Bolivia or Chile or Peru. Let us all be united into a single family of Americans." Everywhere the people cheered these words and promised to heed them—and promptly forgot them the moment Bolivar was out of sight.

Rivalries, conspiracies, assassinations. In Bolivia there were three presidents, two of whom were killed, within a single week. Revolts in Ecuador, New Granada, Venezuela. Bolivar, too ill to take an active part in the suppression of the revolts, implored his countrymen to come to their senses. They voted him a pension of 30,000 pesos—to keep him quiet—and went on with their fighting. He refused the pension although he was now penniless, having sacrificed his entire fortune to the cause.

He was left virtually alone. Nearly all his friends had either died or deserted. Only a handful had remained loyal to him— his lieutenant Sucre, his old tutor Rodriguez, his Irish aide-de-camp O'Leary, his mistress Mansuela. He had met Mansuela in Quito, when he rode triumphantly into the city after his victorious Battle of Pichincha. She tossed him a flower from a balcony and a few days later she tossed him her heart. The wife of an English doctor in Quito, she left her husband to follow Bolivar in his adventures. And she remained with him in his sorrow. Time and again her husband had begged her to return. But she always refused. "I am more honored by being the mistress of General Bolivar than the wife of any other living man."

Bolivar was her god, and she stood by him even after his crucifixion.

But Bolivar wanted to be alone in his sorrow. He had determined to exile himself from the painful scene of his military victories and his political defeats. Where would he go? It didn't matter. Anywhere away from the hatreds, the jealousies and the squabbles of his countrymen. He had brought freedom to a people who did not know how to use it. The Americans had won their war, and they had lost their peace. So much toil, so little gain! "Those of us who have served the Revolution have ploughed the sea."

Quietly he boarded a frigate and sailed away to his lonely death. The ship was bound for Jamaica; but when Bolivar's illness took a turn for the worse, the captain decided to sail for Santa Marta on the Colombian coast. They carried him to the shore on a litter—a shivering bundle of bones that had been the Liberator of South America.

He lingered on for a few days. "My last wish, as I die, is to see my countrymen united."

Twelve years after his death his wish came partially true. On a December day in 1842, a united fleet of all the nations he had liberated escorted his body home to his native city. Now at last they knew him for the great man that he was.

DISRAELI

Important Dates in Life of Disraeli

1804—Born, December 21, in London.

1821—Apprenticed to firm of solicitors.

1825—Lost heavily in South American stock gamble. Started paper, The Representative.

1826—Published first novel, Vivian Grey.

1830—Left on trip to Orient.

1832—Ran for House of Commons as a radical. Defeated.

1837—Elected to House of Commons as a Conservative.

1839—Married Mrs. Wyndham Lewis.

1847—Acknowledged as leader of House of Commons.

1848—Bought estate of Hughenden.

1852—Appointed Chancellor of the Exchequer.

1861–65—Advocated British neutrality in American Civil War.

1868—Became Premier.

1869—Compelled to give up this office.

1872—His wife died.

1874—Again appointed Premier.

1876—Elected to peerage as Earl of Beaconsfield. Gave Victoria new title, Empress of India.

1878—Took prominent part in Treaty of Berlin.

1881—Died.

Benjamin Disraeli

1804–1881

What lies behind the inscrutable mask of the man they call the Sphinx? What tempests have so wracked the emaciated frame that, in audience before the Queen, tired lids droop over the once piercing eyes, and slightly he sways? So that the Queen, champion of conventions, violates the most rigid of them all, and bids him be seated in her presence. Deeply moved, he shakes his smiling sad face in denial and remains standing before his sovereign—her loyal servant to the last.

"Life is too short to be little," he wrote. Man of mystery, poet and statesman, builder of empires and weaver of dreams, he crowded a dozen lives into a single lifetime. "Poetry," he said, "is but the safety-valve of my emotions. I wish to put my writings into action."

Born in England (1804), he loves passionately all that is English. Combining the hot blood of Spain and of Italy, together with the poetry and the indomitable spirit of the Orient, he is at times almost consumed by the fires that rage within him. Yet he keeps himself in check under an overpowering will—a single unswerving desire to serve and to dominate the pale Nordics of his adoration.

A sheltered childhood, a haphazard schooling, a pair of gentle, affectionate, but utterly impractical parents. Hardly the ingredients for the making of a great man.

And then there was an additional handicap. Thrust young into an alien world, he was left to cope with a bewildering problem—his racial origin. No visible signs marked him apart, and yet he was an outsider, a Jew. Father Isaac, himself a follower of Voltaire, gave ground before the stronger grandfather, engaging a rabbi for extra-curricular studies and thus adding fuel to the fires of humiliation.

When grandfather Benjamin joined his Maker, Isaac yielded to family pressure and consented to his son's conversion to Christianity. Discarded the Hebrew lessons; and in their place, baptism and catechisms. Ben heaved a great sigh of relief.

At thirteen, he entered Dr. Cogan's school—at last, an English gentleman!

But now came a new surprise. Prayers and priests do not make an Englishman. The tall youth, olive-skinned, with jet curls and meticulous attire and alien manners, became the laughingstock of the other boys. He met their jeers with head upraised. "Some day I will be master over them."

And before long, he got his first opportunity for mastering his schoolmates. Directing and acting in plays of his own composition, he became the central figure of the social life in Dr. Cogan's school.

But play-acting was against the rules. The school's former leaders, disgruntled at the success of this "arrogant intruder," went to their master with tales of secret sessions. The Reverend Dr. Cogan denounced Disraeli in a scathing speech. "No doubt it is a foreign and seditious mind that has conceived such plans."

The glittering castle toppled, and Ben became the target of insulting jibes. "We've been led long enough by a foreigner!" cried a boy much bigger than Disraeli. To the amazement of the assembled scholars, Ben beat him with his fists. But this empty triumph held a bitter taste.

Mark this lesson well, Benjamin, for you will meet it all your life. "The foreigner, the usurper, the Jew."

School days thus ingloriously terminated at Dr. Cogan's suggestion, Ben came home.

II

To a bewildered boy, the remote parents provided small help. It was to his sister Sarah that he turned. Together they discussed this strange handicap that birth had set upon them. For long hours she listened to the outpouring of his ambitions. Ben had recognized himself for a child of Destiny, and Sarah shared his conviction.

Deciding that education was the first step along the path to greatness, he attacked his father's library. With more zest than method, he devoured every volume within reach and filled notebook after notebook with his comments and conclusions. To Isaac the sight of the tall youth, wandering "aimlessly" about the house and uttering pompous judgments about everything under the sun, was a source of great irritation. "Pray, my dear boy," he scolded, "keep your papers in order."

Anxious to give direction to his boy's aimlessness, father Isaac suggested that he enter a lawyer's office. Ben loftily dismissed the suggestion. "The Bar. Pooh! To be a great lawyer, I must give up my chances of becoming a great man."

"Beware," Isaac warned, "of endeavoring to become great too soon."

Isaac argued, Ben scoffed. "Think," Isaac said, "of the opportunity this would give you for studying men." Finally Ben capitulated.

He entered the office of the solicitor, Mr. Maples, and began to survey the human scene. To shine amongst worldly men, one must be more worldly than the rest. Two characters in particular captivated his imagination—Lord Byron, master of wit, as pattern for literary style; Beau Brummell, master of insolence, as model for manner and attire. Never one to act halfway, Disraeli affected a sartorial extravagance that would have startled Brummell himself.

A zestful, colorful, exciting life. Side by side with the stream of statesmen, bankers, bon vivants, flowed a stream of jingling coin —sweetest sound. His imagination flared up at the huge fortunes that were being made on a runaway market in South American mining stocks. Together with another young clerk, he gambled for a turn. As he watched the growth of his small stakes, a sense of self-sufficiency gripped him. Here was a world in which he might bring into play all his occult powers and analytical judgment.

His clerkship had begun to irk him. And so, at the suggestion of his father who recognized his restlessness, he took a trip to Germany. There, traveling down the Rhine beneath ivy-clad castles, he bade farewell to dull tomes and dusty desks. The wide world was too wonderful, and it was waiting.

His sortie into finance had brought him into contact with John Diston Powles, a controlling power in the market. Struck by the keenness of the young man's mind, Powles commissioned him to compile a pamphlet on South American mining. Disraeli's comparative ignorance of the subject disconcerted him not at all. In a few days the material was gathered, the pamphlet completed, and a publisher induced to print it. To Powles fell the doubtful pleasure of footing the bill.

During their conferences John Murray, the publisher, unwittingly delivered himself into Ben's hands. Fired by his brilliance, Murray confided his fondest dream—to start a daily paper. Ben grasped eagerly at the idea. Murray, a cautious man, attempted retraction, but found himself trapped in a landslide, the exuberant Ben leaping joyously into the lead.

Neither inexperience nor lack of capital could halt the young enthusiast. Ben arranged for everything. With Murray supplying half the funds, and Powles a quarter, only a fourth of the burden fell upon his own shoulders. A mere bagatelle to one whose operations on the stock market were proving his worth as a financier.

It was decided that Lockhart, son-in-law of Sir Walter Scott, was to be editor. To Scotland next, to make known to Lockhart his great good fortune. But a chill reception greeted him. Lockhart, having mistaken the signature for that of the elder Disraeli, looked askance at the intrusion of this youngster. An insult to his dignity! A situation to try a young man's mettle. Assuming a poise far beyond his years, and attributing his ideas to Murray, Ben waxed eloquent. Beneath his glib tongue the project became "the most considerable enterprise of the day." Still wary, Lockhart presented Disraeli to his illustrious father-in-law.

Here was reception more to his liking. Within baronial halls, Sir Walter received him graciously and at once espoused his cause. But with one proviso—a seat in Parliament for Lockhart. Just another bagatelle. Quickly and graciously Ben gave his promise—having not the slightest idea as to how he was going to fulfill it.

Onward plunges the avalanche. Even the doubting souls are carried along. Murray writes to Lockhart that never has he seen such promise in so young a man; that his discretion warrants any amount of confidence.

Back to London, with all in readiness, even to the waiting presses. And then the blow falls. Croker, powerful Secretary to the Admiralty, violently opposes the project. Prominent contributor to the *Quarterly*, another of Murray's publications, he demands to be told why all the scheming has taken place without his knowledge. And who is this young upstart of a Disraeli who dares such an undertaking without consulting him? Lashed by the vindictive tongue of Croker, Murray wilts. He places all the blame at Ben's door. "He alone is responsible for the divulging of the secret plans."

The avalanche has reached bottom; it crashes about Ben's feet. And almost simultaneously there comes another crash—in the stock market. Ben and his partner, young Evans, are wiped out. Their losses amount to 7,000 pounds.

Out of the double catastrophe Disraeli finds himself friendless and alone. His late collaborators have deserted him in a body. Yesterday's backslappers, today they turn relentless backs.

III

DISRAELI comes home. He finds comfort in his father's advice. Ridiculous at twenty-one to think that all's lost. Why, life is just beginning. Ben says nothing of the 7,000 pounds—nor of the debts he has accumulated in his effort to get rich.

Not long, however, can he dwell upon his debts. Benjamin, man of action, has met with reverses; but Benjamin, man of vision, stands ready to receive the torch.

Unknown to his family, he undertakes his first novel. Eager to justify himself to ears now closed, he fashions a hero in his own image. The story of Vivian Grey is the autobiography of Benjamin Disraeli. But it is more than that. Not content with the past, Disraeli projected his hero into the future, supplying him with all those qualities which analysis showed that he himself lacked. It was himself, of course, he meant when he wrote of Vivian Grey: "He had long come to the comfortable conclusion that it was impossible that his career could be anything but brilliant."

As in his writing, so now in his life, Disraeli found the exact type of character of whom he had need. Thus far, his fear of women had kept him apart from them. Yet his emotional spirit felt a great hunger for female companionship. Sarah had but partially satisfied this hunger. For the rest, he addressed his romantic yearnings to an imaginary creature, embodying within her all the gentle understanding, minus the physical demands, of incarnate womanhood. This creature of his imaginings materialized in the person of Mrs. Austen, neighbor of his parents, the first of many women whose platonic friendships were to play a leading part in his history.

Mrs. Austen was a great help to Disraeli. Sensing unusual depths of tenderness beneath the frivolous exterior, she courted his confidence. Overjoyed to lay aside the mountebank trappings,

Ben met honesty with candor. To her he revealed his hurts and fears, and finally the secret of his manuscript.

Mrs. Austen liked the story and found a publisher for it. The book was issued anonymously. A vigorous advertising campaign. London read, London laughed. Everybody recognized in this story not himself, but his neighbor, held up to ridicule. The book had a meteoric success; and the two chief conspirators, luxuriating under the shelter of Disraeli's anonymity, laughed like a couple of mischievous schoolchildren.

Another triumph, another fall. And once again it was that shadow that lurks in the pathway of the great—the little man—who struck at Disraeli. An indiscreet subordinate in the publishing house reveals the secret of the authorship. The acclamations of the public turn into threats. The impudence of this nobody who dares to sit in judgment over his betters! One critic wrote: "The class of the author was a little revealed by his frequent recurrence to topics about which the mere man of fashion knows nothing and cares less." And another referred to the "comic pretentiousness with which the author affects a distinction he does not possess." Murray, thinking he recognized himself in one of the unfavorable portraits, angrily severed all connections with the Disraeli family.

Ben's mind was in a turmoil. Could they be right, this furious rabble denouncing him as a fraud? Of a certainty, no! Only a great book could cause such furore. He would go on to become author of authors. Let the pack howl now; later they must come to heel.

Disraeli's health had given way under the stress of his emotions. The Austens, deeply concerned, persuaded him to accompany them to Venice. Gliding in gondolas over moonlit canals to the accompaniment of soft music, he recovered his spirits. But his body lagged behind. Home once more, he found work impossible because of torturing headaches.

Isaac, grown tired of London, had purchased a spacious home near Bradenham. Here, within lofty halls and sweeping grounds, Ben's love of grandeur found satisfaction. For months, discussing his predicament with Sarah, he roamed the woods and fields. But this retirement, tonic for a time to a bruised spirit, made him finally restive. Even across these far fields, London sang her siren song of glories yet to come, and he must follow.

IV

HE HAD STUDIED MEN, but with the eye of youth. To this field he must now bring his maturer judgment. Having made the acquaintance of Edward Bulwer-Lytton, he became a frequent visitor at this man's home. Here foregathered the poetically and politically prominent. Into this gay circle stepped Disraeli, in attire more exaggerated than ever, but in manner and speech much subdued. His faithful notebook yields up his present formula for acquiring social success. "Do not talk too much . . . Never argue . . . Talk to women as much as you can . . . Nothing is of so much importance . . . as to be well criticized by women."

Charmed by the lavish entertainment of the fashionable world, Disraeli wrote and sold *The Young Duke*. But what does Ben know of dukes, inquires Isaac, bewildered. Sarah shrugs. What *doesn't* Ben know!

Disraeli knows everything, and he criticizes everything. Introduced into the House of Parliament, he finds fault even with the great orators of the day. A new world has now opened before his searching eyes. The pen is mightier than the sword; but how much mightier the silver tongue of oratory! Bewitched, he wanders through the corridors. What an enviable life! To stand before the elect, swaying them like saplings before a tempest of words. The telling phrase, the biting wit—until, wild with enthusiasm, they rise to drown all sound in thunderous applause. Sending the name of Disraeli ringing down through the centuries . . .

Watch out, Ben! Almost you collided with that hansom cab. That deafening sound is but the roaring traffic of a busy London street. And who are these little people that hurry past, unconscious of the prophet they are jostling in their midst? Unknown to them, one Benjamin Disraeli; but time will remedy that. First there must be travel—has not Byron himself set the pattern? And the world must have time to forget your failures.

To Spain, cradle of his ancestors; thence through Greece and Turkey; finally to Palestine. William Meredith, engaged to Sarah, is to join the tour. To their combined entreaties, Isaac yields; and in June, 1830, the pilgrimage begins. With some sadness, he bids farewell to Bradenham. And with some trepidation, he envisages his reception among the ultra English of the Empire's colonies. But—"adventures are to the adventurous." Your own words, Ben.

A gay rainbow trailing across the continent, the astounding wardrobe he exhibits. Through Turkey, where all that is eastern in him responds to the rhythm of the Orient. Ambition for the nonce is lulled, submerged in sensuous sound and smell.

Through Syria, an infinitude of burning sands, where no green thing can thrive. The majesty of such timeless austerity sounds deep chords within him.

At last, having shared with nomad tribes their tents and travels, he stands upon *The Mount of Olives*. Here, viewing the city of Jerusalem and the Holy Sepulchre, he yields to a wave of religious ecstasy. A great peace enwraps him, fold upon comforting fold. For here, within these hallowed walls, lies the answer to the old bewildering question. We are all Christians, created in the image of our Christ.

Wandering through the dusty streets, he shaped the story that would carry this message to the world. *Alroy,* a young Jew who would free his race from worldwide prejudice.

On to Egypt, to join Meredith. Here tragedy cut short the journey. Meredith died of smallpox. Grieving over Sarah's grief, Ben lost all taste for travel and turned his face toward home.

Reaching Bradenham in October, somber amid falling leaves, he found Isaac half blind from constant reading and Sarah, broken by her bereavement, dedicating her life to him.

Travel has broadened Ben's vision, stilled much of his restlessness. Realizing that a literary career can never be enough, he turns undivided interest toward the political scene. Surveying the field for some foothold, he finds but a single means of entrance—through the drawing room. The Bulwers, the springboard from which to make the plunge.

V

FOLLOWING his pattern of speaking little and to the point, Disraeli acquires a reputation as a brilliant conversationalist with a store of colorful tales from the East. The formula for interesting the ladies bears fruit. Among the many women requesting to be presented to him are Mrs. Wyndham Lewis and Mrs. Caroline Norton.

Of Mrs. Lewis he wrote: ". . . a flirt, and a rattle . . ." Mrs. Norton he found, for the present, more satisfactory. Together with her mother and her sisters, she entertained him often in her home. Here, amongst the "noble and the fashionable," delighted by the audacity of these people of birth, he felt at home. And drawing up an imaginary footstool he placed himself at the feet of these gentlefolk—a self-styled page boy, ready to absorb and adore.

This gay social whirl, however, is but the means to an end. It is the men of action whose opinion he really courts. Slowly, and because their women are favorably impressed, they accept him. At last the long coveted goal is reached. Ben is invited to small political luncheons. At times grave doubts assail him. Seated next to Sir Robert Peel and to others whose birth has bestowed upon them all that he himself must struggle ceaselessly to attain, he wonders whether the end is worthy of the means. Is it really essential to enter Parliament? Can it be that gracious living has tamed his flaming spirit, he asks himself as homeward bound from some frivolous evening he contemplates a life complete in social dalliance. He feels that now it is only pride that drives him on. Or is this but a breathing spell, a lull before the storm?

It must be the latter. For a gathering storm bursts. In 1832 the reform bill is passed; all England is in upheaval. Responding to the trumpet call of opportunity, Ben rushes to Bradenham to enter the mêlée as independent candidate. Defeated at the elections, he is not discouraged. Leaping upon the carved figure of a lion, he has delivered an impromptu oration to an electrified audience. And having tasted of this heady potion, he needs must drink more deeply thereof.

Back to the drawing rooms of London, for more campaigning.

Ben has acquired a mistress. In her company he mingles with the sporting crowd, setting himself the task of becoming a fine horseman. This he accomplishes without pleasure but with satisfaction. The blond Anglo-Saxon giants, followers of the hounds, fascinate him. "The magnificent asses," he calls them. The epithet contains no rancor, but rather admiration and a little envy. In honor of his paramour, he writes and publishes a novel, *Henrietta Temple*.

But these side journeys are unimportant. The things that count are the contacts with great men—such as those made in the home of Lady Blessington. "I am dying for action, and rust like a Damascus saber in the sheath of a poltroon," he tells her. How he envies these men, with power to translate words into action! If only he could get their help.

And help did come to him in the person of Lord Melbourne, who was attracted by his originality. Melbourne's question as to what Ben wanted to be, had drawn a prompt reply, "I want to be Prime Minister." "No chance of that in our time," Melbourne had told him. "Go into politics . . . With patience I dare say you will do very well . . . But put all these foolish ideas out of your head."

Lord Melbourne, you know not whereof you speak. No idea of patience has ever entered that curly head. Chafing beneath enforced inaction, he cries in answer to a query as to what would constitute a desirable life—"A continued grand procession from manhood to the tomb."

VI

DISRAELI is still clinging to the idea of independent candidacy. But the public has no admiration for such apparent lack of fealty. A politician must have a party's backing. But which party? Although the chances for an unknown are better with the Whigs, Ben's sympathies lean with the Tories. And with the Tories, under the leadership of Robert Peel, he takes oath.

For yet awhile, fate turns an immobile cheek. But we are on the eve of swift events. Victoria, a girl of eighteen, ascends the throne. With Victoria's accession comes the dissolution of Parliament. Safe now within the party fold, Disraeli receives many offers of constituency. Mrs. Wyndham Lewis, whom he has learned to respect and admire, steps forward. Through her husband, she holds out to Disraeli a fellow constituency at Maidenstone. Having dropped into his lap this political plum she proceeds, with all the energy and good sense at her command, to campaign by his side. "When I meet you again," Disraeli promises his electors, "not a person will look upon me without some degree of satisfaction . . . and many of you perhaps with some degree of pride."

The voting over, Wyndham and Disraeli are in. Benjamin Disraeli, M.P. At Bradenham, awaiting the opening of Parliament, he contemplates his triumph—and his responsibility. Owing to the harassed history of his people, he loves England's solidity more than the English themselves love it. For to them their heritage is a matter of course. There, beneath the templed trees of his father's estate, he dedicates himself to the service of his country. To keep England noble, undivided and great.

In Parliament now. Seated behind Sir Robert, he listens to the speakers, dreaming of the day when he is to deliver his own first address. He is quite unaware of the sidelong glances that mistrust him. These stolid men resent the un-English-looking interloper thrust into their most British midst.

The great day dawns. Benjamin arises to make real his cherished dream. But the dream turns out to be a nightmare. His star seems destined never to ascend the heavens in a gentle curve. His opening words bring titters, which gradually expand into a crescendo of laughter. Cries of "Hear, hear" and "Question, please" interrupt every sentence. Valiantly he struggles against the rising tide of derision. At first squeaky of voice and slightly nervous, he finally grows calm and sure of himself. But the contest proves unequal. He faces his tormentors and sends a challenge ringing through the hall: "Though I sit down now, the time will come when you will hear me!"

To continued laughter, he resumes his seat with bowed head. Another dismal failure added to the growing list.

There is a glimmer of comfort, however—the supporting voice of his chief, Sir Robert Peel. To Disraeli's comment that his effort had been "a reverse," Sir Robert's retort is: "I say anything but reverse; you will make your way."

Lift that heavy head, Benjamin. Others of your loyal friends are with you. Listen to the famous Sheil, as he berates your detractors: "I tell you, if ever the spirit of oratory was in a man, it is in that man. Nothing can prevent him from becoming one of the first speakers of the House of Commons."

A fig for dull orderly beginnings! What seemed the sword-thrust of defeat was but the birth-pang of glory. The voice of genius had spoken. Soon it would have for an audience—the entire world.

VII

SLOWLY his star rises, and steadily. True, there are setbacks still; but no career is complete without its strengthening obstacles. Six months after Disraeli's entry into Parliament, death claimed his colleague, Lewis. Hastening to console the widow, he remained to admire. Attracted by her warmth and steadfastness, he grew to recognize her as the woman necessary to complete his life. In answer to his marriage proposal, Mary Anne Lewis asked a year in which to study his character.

Bringing to his courtship that ardor typical of his every venture, he wrote to her continuously and without restraint. "I wish to be with you, to live with you, never to be away from you." But once again he seemed headed for failure. Mary Anne's answers became less and less frequent until finally there was only silence.

In great alarm, Benjamin begged for an interview. Mary Anne received him coldly. Rosina Bulwer had convinced her that it was her small income, and not herself, that Disraeli was after. How else could it be, since she was forty-five, and he but a little over thirty? Dismissed and desolate, he penned a final letter. ". . . As far as worldly interests are concerned, your alliance could not benefit me . . . Farewell . . . The time will come when you will sigh for any heart that could be fond . . . and then you will recall to your memory the passionate heart that you forfeited, and the genius that you betrayed."

This proved too much for Mary Anne. She melted utterly. "For God's sake, come to me," she wrote, "I am ill and almost distracted. I am devoted to you."

At St. Peter's, in Hanover Square, they were married (August, 1839). To say that the marriage was perfect may draw smiles from the sophisticates, but so it was. Mary Anne's good nature and unquestioning devotion never wavered. On his part, Benjamin was the most devoted and appreciative of husbands. Her tactless honesty, which irritated many another, delighted him, and her constant chatter soothed him. Adoring till the very end, he turned always to her as the one rock in a weary land.

VIII

IN HER YOUTH, Victoria had disliked Disraeli's patron, the austere Sir Robert Peel. Now, married to Albert Saxe-Coburg, a man who thoroughly approved of Sir Robert, the mature Queen had grown to trust him. At last the scene arranges itself for the climax. Disraeli is ready to advance the long step toward his goal. His name is on the lists of those proposed for ministerial posts.

Simon Bolivar

Disraeli

But once again Destiny shakes her head. No, Benjamin, not yet. One by one the posts are filled, and no summons has come to Disraeli.

Perplexed, both Mary Anne and Benjamin address notes to Sir Robert—and receive cool answers. Sir Robert's actions, however, are not of his own choosing. It is the old distrust of the foreigner, and Peel is helpless against the pressure of opinion.

When the next Parliament met, Benjamin's position was most unenviable. A conservative without a post, with nothing to do but to cast his vote. Loyally he took his place, the object of surprised glances, and gracefully he did his part.

This inactivity, so irksome to a strong man, could not long endure. Seeing for the present no roads open, he said to Mary Anne: "This is the time to imitate Talleyrand who, when he could not see very clearly what ought to be done, took to his bed."

Instead of taking to his bed, however, he betook himself, together with his wife, to Paris for a winter of gaiety punctuated by frequent entertainments in the palace of the French king and queen.

That winter in Paris there came to him the representatives of a group of young men. Impatient with the old political forms, they wished to form an opposition party. Disraeli appealed to them as the logical leader.

He listens, and lays his plans. In England once again, they set in motion the wheels that will roll out the old, roll in the new. Eventually, the once indomitable Peel is overthrown. Disraeli is now riding upon the crest of a tidal wave!

IX

Success has given him renewed assurance. Soberer now his manner and attire; his speech, less fiery, more devastating. Yet still the public refuses to take him to its heart. Though he no longer struts before them as the flashy mountebank, they love this new Disraeli no better. They find in him now a little of the sinister, much of the mysterious. Albert and Victoria view with alarm his growing popularity among the younger generation. They resent, too, the blows he has dealt their devoted friend, Peel.

Faster now the march of events. Isaac is dead. Benjamin purchases Hughenden Manor, installing Mary Anne as its Lady. Benjamin is Chancellor of the Exchequer, the Queen having accepted him on Stanley's recommendation. "I was not born Chancellor of the Exchequer," he says. "I am one of the Parliamentary rabble."

And now, another turn of events. Disraeli is ousted as Chancellor, with Gladstone leading the attack.

Time passes now too rapidly for Disraeli. He is fifty-five. The once lithe figure is grown gaunt; the once aesthetic face, thin almost to emaciation. "Dizzy" is beginning to show the strain. Ugly, many think him. But to Mary Anne he is still the dreamy poet of their courting days. "He is very handsome," she declares. "I should like them to see him when he is asleep."

Old friends are disappearing, new friends take their place. His beloved Sarah is gone. Albert, too, is dead; and Victoria, powerful and determined monarch, has learned to trust him. She treats him with kindness, even. New friends, new honors. At Oxford he receives a doctor's degree. Never since Wellington has a public figure been accorded such an ovation.

Faster, faster. The Victorian Age is in full swing. The Industrial Era. Machines, inventions, speculations, adventures, plans— and Disraeli keeping abreast of them all.

But now the years are beginning to slow him. Sixty-one, and the body lags behind the spirit. Seated in the pew at Hughenden, he still dreams of being Prime Minister. Many now share that dream, for England has at last accepted the inevitable. She cannot love this man, but she respects and trusts him.

Factories and mills bring people together, and they talk. The day of articulation for the workingman is dawning. Rioting and demonstrations. The workers demand a voice in Parliament. Against Gladstone and terrific odds, Disraeli puts through a bill granting more general suffrage. The man is a wizard. What next? How taciturn he has grown! Almost never laughs. Only Mary Anne and his intimates know the warm simplicity that dwells within this man called the Sphinx.

Eighteen-sixty-eight, year of years. Lord Derby retires, the inevitable is at hand. Victoria summons Disraeli to Osborne. Without surprise he receives the message, for Victoria herself has told him she intends to make him her Prime Minister. But with what pounding pulse he reads the note! And who would give scorn to a few tears, wrung from eyes which for so long have gazed on triumph from afar and now view it in a lean and trembling palm.

"You must kiss hands," Victoria declares upon receiving him. And falling on his knees, he kisses the soft small hand in real devotion. For actually he loves this woman. Within him well great floods of emotion. With every fiber of his being, he vows to serve faithfully his little Queen. What a pair they make, this tall lean Eagle, and this small plump Pigeon!

To a reception in his honor flock the great. Mary Anne, on the arm of the Prince of Wales, presides graciously. If she leans a little heavily, now and then, there is a reason. For some time past she has been suffering from cancer; but not Mary Anne to burden her hero when now, more than ever, he needs his every faculty.

One other shadow hovers over the brilliant assembly. Sarah's absence. Turning aside a moment in his hour of triumph, Benjamin sends his thoughts to her whose faith in him not once had wavered.

X

NOT YET is Disraeli to bring to public life the full powers of his genius. At Hughenden, tortured by asthma and rheumatic pains, he receives news of his overwhelming defeat. Weighed down by infirmities, he contemplates retirement. But it is not in his nature to abandon a defeated party. Following precedent, the Queen offers a peerage. For himself he refuses, but for his wife he asks a title. Mary Anne becomes Viscountess of Beaconsfield, while her illustrious husband remains plain Dizzy.

This honor, come so late, sits on the shoulders of a strange pair. She eighty-one, and he sixty-eight, both very ill. Mostly they are bedridden. Short periods of health permitting, they take their place in society. A startling sight. Mary Anne, an overdressed mummy. Benjamin, with one remaining curl dyed black, an alien with the features of a hawk.

At last, unable to take nourishment—for the cancer was of the stomach—Mary Anne died. Disraeli's overwhelming grief drew sympathy even from his enemies. Gladstone himself wrote a warm and friendly letter.

With Mary Anne's going, life changed completely for the widower. The house passed to her heirs, and Disraeli removed himself to a hotel. "This," said everybody, "is the end of his career."

And then, contrary to all expectations, he came with new vigor back into the political arena. Seeking surcease from the hollow pain.

Victoria welcomed the return. For Gladstone she had little fondness; for his policies, still less. With satisfaction she viewed the events leading to his downfall. Watched happily Disraeli's deft manipulations and certain victory. Now at last (1874) they were re-united in power and in friendship—this amazing pair who could see so surely eye to eye, whose devotion to Empire superseded all else, who in honesty and in steadfastness met on common ground.

Bringing now to Victoria's service the ardor of an undivided purpose, Disraeli lays at her feet prize after prize. The Wizard waves his wand (1875): the Suez Canal is an accomplished fact. Greater glory to the Empire! Once more he works his magic (1876): Victoria becomes Empress of India. Greater grandeur to the Crown! In reciprocity, she wields her scepter—and behold, Disraeli is Lord Beaconsfield. He is leader of the House of Lords.

Seventy-four now. And though the will and the spirit soar on high, the years have taken their toll of the flesh. More frequently illness absents him from the House. Always the Queen sends flowers from her own gardens. Often he speaks to her of retirement, but she will have none of it. A sick eagle is still an eagle, and no pigeon can wing the dizzying heights alone.

There is much work to be done; he rallies. Turkey, Russia, the Balkans—a smoking volcano about to erupt. Russia threatens to seize all the Mediterranean ports. The Queen urges action, fuming at these men who procrastinate. Calmly Disraeli counsels patience. "We will have peace if we are firm," he promises.

Seated next to him at dinner, one of the Princesses exclaims, "I cannot imagine what you are waiting for." "Potatoes, at this moment, Madam," he answers quietly.

Inch by inch, Russia yields in the territorial card game, but not finally until the news breaks about the secret landing of Indian troops. All this victory without a single blow, or the loss of a single Englishman. He is still the master magician. But how tired he is! He longs for release, but he cannot face her Majesty's *scenes*.

XI

To BERLIN, for the signing of the treaty granting all his demands. How he must have chuckled on the way! In youth, adventures to the adventurous; in age, victory to the audacious. Audacity he needed, for here he found the cards cunningly stacked against him. Russia agreed to non-aggression in Turkey; but Turkey was not to defend her borders against occupied Bulgaria. A direct negation of the London treaty. Gortchakoff and Beaconsfield lock arms; the battle is on. To Gortchakoff's thundering, Beaconsfield replies quietly that England's terms constitute an ultimatum. The Russians send an emissary to their Emperor; the Congress is at a standstill. To the Queen he writes, "I have no fear of the result . . ."

The expiration date of the ultimatum. With calm deliberation the gambler plays his last card. He orders a special train to carry him and his entourage to Calais. The winning hand! Results are swift. Bismarck calls, offering compromise. "Compromise," retorts Disraeli, "was found at the moment of the London agreements, and it is impossible to go back on those." They stand facing each other—the stout blunt Teuton and the lean suave Jew. Bismarck hastens to the Emperor, having first asked Beaconsfield to dine. Of this interview Disraeli writes Victoria: ". . . he (Bismarck) was convinced that the ultimatum was not a sham, and before I went to bed, I had the satisfaction of knowing that St. Petersburg had surrendered."

Bismarck's high regard for Beaconsfield advances to admiration. "The Old Jew," he declares, "*that* is a Man!"

Never was the Wizard's popularity so great. All England adores its Dizzy, who has done it again . . .

Another short day of triumph—and then the clouds gather once more on the horizon. Trouble in India, uprisings in South Africa, threatened famine at home. And always Gladstone waging verbal warfare against "the heretic and his mad policies." Differences arise between Disraeli and the Faery Queen.

But the Wizard has not lost his magic touch. The Queen is pacified; elsewhere, too, quiet is restored. Only on the home front do the doves of peace decline to perch. The threat of famine grows more serious, as rains pour continuously from leaden skies. Slushing through the mud at Hughenden, he receives devastating news. A mission to Kabul has been slaughtered to a man.

And then the elections. The conservative party sinks in crushing defeat. To Gladstone, grown fanatic in his denunciation of "the instrument of the devil," this conclusion is but pre-ordained.

Defeat brings to Beaconsfield what he has desired above all else —relief. His mind has turned once more to letters and the arts. True, he will miss the stimulating conferences with the Queen. But the sands are running low, and the body cries for rest.

Deeply touching, the final scene between the two. The Queen bestows upon him a statuette of herself in bronze. For the last time he kisses the small plump hand, promising to write often.

Several letters he does write—and then the Eagle and the Pigeon settle down in their separate nests . . .

XII

HUGHENDEN receives its master, home at last. The few who visit him are startled by the almost lifeless figure. A mass of skin and bones, the one lacquered curl resting ridiculously on the parchment forehead. Only now and then one eyelid flutters upward, when some pointed phrase strikes home. The mind has not lost its keenness, nor the tongue its edge. Yet speech is possible only at intervals, when drugs have given him momentarily his failing breath. "Dreams . . . dreams," he murmurs, poking at a dying fire.

Along the stairway hang portraits of the many people he has loved so well. "The gallery of friendship," he calls it.

Several visits, against his physician's orders, to the House of Lords. He delivers a number of addresses to his former colleagues speaking with eloquence but with great difficulty.

Back home. A chill confines him to his bed. The Queen's own physician promises hope, but Disraeli knows better. "I should prefer to live, but I am not afraid to die." In the midst of his final agonies, he corrects proofs for a speech. "I will not go down to posterity talking bad grammar."

Two o'clock in the morning. Slowly the dying man rises and, throwing back his head, prepares to speak. The old familiar gesture. Then he falls back. April 19, 1881. Benjamin Disraeli has embarked upon his last adventure.

Unable to attend the funeral, the Queen afterwards trod afoot the pathway taken by the procession. She wanted to stand alone before the grave of a dear friend. In the church she caused to be erected a monument to his memory. The inscription ended in this revelatory passage: "Kings love him who speaketh right."

GARIBALDI

Important Dates in Life of Garibaldi

1807—Born, July 4, at Nice.

1834—Condemned to death as revolutionist.
Escaped to Marseilles.

1836—Arrived in South America.

1836-46—Liberated Rio Grande and Uruguay.

1848—Returned to Italy.

1848-49—Fought for the liberation of Rome.

1860—Liberated Sicily from the king of Naples.

1862—Fought again for liberation of Rome and a united Italy.

1870—Helped French Republic in war against Germany.

1875—Became member of parliament in Rome.

1882—Died June 2.

Giuseppe Garibaldi

1807–1882

T HERE HAVE BEEN many heroic soldiers of fortune. Garibaldi, one of the outstanding heroes of all time, was a soldier of *misfortune*. And through his own choice. He always sought out the most unprofitable causes to fight for. Always he took up arms for the oppressed and the dispossessed. Wherever there was a nation to be liberated, whether in the Old World or in the New, Garibaldi was to be found at the head of the liberating forces. And in return for his services he asked for no glory or reward. In 1842, when he had won a series of victories for Uruguay, he was living with his wife in a tumbledown hut with no door and with broken windows. One night the leader of a French squadron in South America, Admiral Lainé, came to congratulate him on his success. The hut was plunged in darkness.

"Does General Garibaldi live here?"

When Garibaldi heard his name called, he turned to his wife, "Anita, bring a light!"

"Sorry," said Anita, "there's no light to bring."

"Oh, I forgot," apologized Garibaldi. "Candles have not been included in our military rations."

"And so," wrote the Admiral, "I heard Garibaldi's golden voice, but I was unable to see Garibaldi's golden smile."

II

THAT GOLDEN SMILE of Garibaldi's was famous the world over. In appearance he was a combination of Mars and Apollo. There was strength in his body and beauty in his face. Tall, lithe, muscular, with a halo of gold-brown hair and a gold-brown beard, he was like a painting of Michelangelo's. A god in a red blouse and patched-up trousers.

It was a curious circumstance that impelled Garibaldi and his "legion of liberation" to adopt the red blouse for a uniform. Finding it necessary, because of the lack of funds, to clothe his soldiers as economically as possible, Garibaldi had made an offer for a consignment of red woolen shirts that a merchant in Montevideo was about to send to a slaughter house in Buenos Aires. "The red color," explained the merchant, "will help to absorb the blood in the shambles."

"And on the battlefield, too. Just the thing for us!"

And thus the red shirt became the symbol of Garibaldi's fight for freedom.

III

THE SON of a sea-captain, Garibaldi was born (at Nice) with two strong instincts in his blood: a love for wild wide spaces, and a passion for freedom. His favorite amusements as a child were roaming over the hills and swimming in the sea. "I seem," he once remarked to Alexandre Dumas, "to have been born amphibious."

And fearless. Strolling one day along a riverbank, he chanced upon a group of women washing flax. One of the women lost her footing and fell into the water. Treacherous water, full of cross currents and whirlpools. Garibaldi leaped in after her and pulled her ashore.

It would have been an act of unusual courage for a full-grown man. Garibaldi at the time was only eight years old.

At fifteen he left school—"the freedom of the open appealed to me more than the confinement of the classroom"—and sailed off by himself to Genoa in search of adventure. This was a great blow to his father, who had intended Giuseppe for the priesthood. "The peace of the cloister for my son; I have had enough hurricanes for the two of us." But he realized now that his son was not made for peace. He bowed to the inevitable and hired "Peppino" as cabin boy on his own ship.

Peppino—nickname for Giuseppe—became a favorite with the sailors. Though easily their master at trawling for oysters and swimming through the surf, he yet aroused no envy on their part. His blue eyes had such a friendly warmth in their depths. And his voice, whether in speech or in song, vibrated with such an understanding sympathy.

And he knew so much more than they did. His schooling, to be sure, was no better than their own; but he had read ever so many more books. History, philosophy, poetry. Especially poetry. How pleasant to while away the silent hours of the night listening to that golden voice as it recited the poems of Foscolo or Dante or Voltaire. Or sang the songs of the French revolutionists. Stirring words—he translated them; inspiring music—the music of rebellion needed no translating.

Ten years of singing and sailing and toiling—his hands were as busy as his brain—and Garibaldi had risen from cabin boy to captain. A dangerous career, commanding a ship in the early nineteenth century. He cruised to the Levant, where Turks and Greeks were locked in a struggle to the death; he fought against pirates, who attacked his ship with axes and long knives; he sailed over the seas made famous in Byron's heroic verse. Perils, adventures, aspirations. Battles for freedom. With Byron he came to believe that it was "better to die as a free man than to live as a slave."

And then, word reached him of an Italian who had dared to

die for freedom. Ciro Menotti. This man had tried to unite his disunited country, and to unshackle it from its Austrian bonds. The Austrians had captured and killed him.

But they were unable to kill his spirit of revolt. The spark engendered by Menotti had been fanned into a flame in many an Italian heart. Garibaldi met one of these followers of Menotti—a young Genoese named Cuneo. "Hundreds of our men have been executed," Cuneo informed him. "But the best man of us all is still alive. Mazzini. You ought to meet him some day. This man is like the firebrand of God sent down to avenge our wrongs."

Garibaldi sailed for Marseilles where he met Mazzini, exiled but unbowed. "Columbus was not so happy at the discovery of America," wrote Garibaldi of this meeting, "as I was at the discovery of the redeemer who was to lead our people to the promised land."

The acquaintance between Mazzini and Garibaldi ripened into a lifelong collaboration for freedom. Mazzini, the dreamer of the great dream; Garibaldi, the translator of the dream into even greater deeds.

IV

AT THE OUTSET, the liberation of Italy seemed a hopeless task. As a result of the Unholy Alliance of 1815, Italy lay dismembered like a bleeding corpse. Piedmont and Sardinia had been parceled off to the House of Savoy. Lombardy and Venetia had been reduced to the status of Austrian provinces. Tuscany, Modena, and Parma had been crushed under the heel of the Austrian Grand Dukes. Rome, Umbria, and Romagna had succumbed to the papal rule, supported by a French army. Naples and Sicily had been cast to the untender mercies of the Bourbons. "Italy in 1815," remarked the sardonic Metternich, Father of the Unholy Alliance, "is no longer a nation; it is merely a geographical name."

To transform a lifeless name into a living nation, this was the job of the two inspired young men. Garibaldi threw himself heart and soul into this job. Assuming the name of *Borel,* he tried to organize a rebellion among the sailors of the Genoese royal fleet. Betrayed by a treacherous "fellow rebel," he escaped to Marseilles, there to find his name printed on a number of circulars. The Piedmontese government had set a price on his head.

No time to tarry in Italy. But across the Atlantic, in South America, there were other revolutions to be fought, other tyrannies to be overthrown.

He sailed, together with a company of devoted followers, to South America. There, for twelve years (1836–1848), he led his guerrilla band of consecrated Redshirts to the emancipation of two countries, Rio Grande and Uruguay.

Stranger than a tale out of the Arabian Nights, this South American adventure of Garibaldi's. At first he set out as a buccaneer, a Robin Hood of the Sea, against "the enemies of freedom and the oppressors of their fellow men." But after a few months of sea roving he gave up the boat for the saddle. See him now galloping at the head of his troops over the pampas. His handful of Italians have been joined by a group of South American *gauchos.* The best riders in the world, these centaurs of the Rio Grande seem to be as one with their horses. Strange mythical creatures, half men and half beasts, flying over the fields and brandishing a lance in the one hand and a lasso in the other.

Before many months, Garibaldi had become the most expert of them all. A wild leader of a wild band, harassing the enemy, striking with the suddenness of a thunderbolt, driving their cattle along with them for food, killing what they needed and roasting it over their campfires, submitting to torture when captured without a groan, and dying on the battlefield with laughter on their lips.

And they died in great numbers, always to be replaced by still greater numbers. For they were drawn as by a magnet to that miracle of a leader. Nothing seemed able to hurt or to stop him. Once he was captured by an enemy officer. In an effort to draw some information from him, his captor had him whipped and then suspended by his thumbs for two hours in his cell. "It was an agony not to be described," wrote Garibaldi. Yet not a word escaped from his lips.

An amazing fighter. And an amazing lover. One day in 1839, having left the saddle for a while to take command of a ship, he was examining the shore through a spyglass. "By chance I cast my eyes . . . upon a high hill . . . where a few simple and picturesque houses were visible. Outside of one of these . . . I espied a young woman, and forthwith gave orders for the boat to be got out, as I wished to go ashore. I landed . . . and, making for the houses where I expected to find this young woman, I had just given up hope of seeing her again when . . . an acquaintance invited me to take coffee in his house. We entered, and the first person who met my eyes was the damsel who had attracted me ashore . . . We both remained enraptured and gazed on each other in silence . . . At last I greeted her by saying 'Tu devi esser mia' (You ought to be mine)."

And his she became. Her name was Anita Ribera. Though but eighteen years old, she defied her father's objections—he had plighted her to another man—and surrendered herself to the "magnetic insolence" of her country's liberator. That night she met him on shipboard, and they sailed away together to a union of great happiness, many hardships and—as we shall see—final tragedy. Together they "ploughed the seas and galloped over the pampas," fighting side by side and protecting each other from the enemy's blows. In one of the battles she was taken captive. Believing that Garibaldi had fallen in that battle, she received permission to search for his body. Accompanied by an escort of two enemy soldiers, she walked amidst her slain comrades and turned the face of every one of them toward the light. Finally she eluded her guards, leaped upon a horse she had secured from a peasant, and vanished into the tropical forest.

Four days of galloping through the jungle and swimming rapid rivers, with no food and with hardly a moment's rest—and then she found Garibaldi.

And gave birth to a child. They named it Menotti, after the hero of the first Italian revolution.

V

GARIBALDI was a man's man. And a ladies' man. Always susceptible to new pastures, new enticements. Yet at all times he was devoted, if not at all times faithful, to Anita. Once, to appease her jealousy, he clipped his gold-brown hair to the roots. "Now, for a while, the women will stop running after me."

A shorn Samson. But, unlike Samson, still possessed of his strength to fight the Philistines. Having finished his work in South America, he returned to Italy. Great enthusiasm at his arrival. The fires of rebellion had been kept alive during his absence. "And now, to fan them into a devastating flame!"

He gathered his forces—a mere handful—and marched upon Rome, to rid that city of its French army. One thousand against thirty thousand. "Only a miracle can save his men from being chewed up and spewed out by the French."

And the miracle happened. By a series of bold maneuvers— "one never knows just where or how he will strike next"—the "Tiger of Montevideo" routed the army of General Oudinot. He declared Rome (1849) a free Republic—a government "without prisons, without trials, without violence."

A perfect Utopia, of all-too-brief duration. New forces were gathering against it on all sides. New tactics, and new treachery. General Oudinot proclaimed a truce; and then, relying upon the "simple naïveté" of Garibaldi, made a surprise attack before the truce was over.

The treachery worked. Garibaldi's Roman garrison was massacred; but Garibaldi, with a bullet wound in his side, managed to escape. Anita, once more with child, escaped along with him. And also with him went the broken remnant of his army. "Let those who wish to continue the war against the stranger come with me. I offer neither pay nor quarters nor provisions. I offer hunger, thirst, forced marches, battles, and death. Let him who loves his country in his heart, and not with his lips, follow me."

A battered, bedraggled, hunger-driven and hunted little band. But a great inspiration drove them on—the courage of their wounded leader and his stricken wife. He implored her to remain behind—"the enemy will do no violence to a woman in your plight"—but she was determined to share her husband's perils. "At the first house we came to," wrote Garibaldi, "having asked a woman to cut off her hair, she put on men's clothing and mounted a horse."

An epic retreat. Hiding by day and marching by night, they eluded the pursuing enemy whose numbers had now been increased to seventy-five thousand. Time and again they seemed to be surrounded, only to escape from the net when it was about to be drawn. Always Garibaldi had the uncanny intuition to march along the one path left unguarded by the enemy.

And always he was driven on by an undying hope. But a great grief had now come to distract that hope. The dangerous illness of his wife. When finally the little band had reached the coast town of Cesenatico—"beyond lie the boats that will carry us to freedom"—Anita was on the verge of death.

They boarded the boats and sailed away. No food, no water. A full moon—"lovelier than I had ever seen her before"—overhead; a woman with fever-parched lips underneath. "No matter what happens to me, Giuseppe, go on with your work."

An attack by the enemy fleet. All of Garibaldi's boats were captured, with the exception of three. In one of these three boats sat Garibaldi, with the dying Anita in his arms.

Daybreak, and a deserted coast near Ravenna. Garibaldi carried his wife ashore; and there, on a sand dune, he saw the death-look in her face. "I felt her wrist—there was no pulse."

He dug a grave for Anita on the seashore, and went on.

VI

THROUGHOUT HIS LIFE, Garibaldi had but a single motto—*Avanti* (Forward). He tried for a while to settle in the United States, where he worked in a candle factory. He then took command of a ship that sailed to the Orient. "Enough of adventuring, Giuseppe. Return to Italy and retire. You are getting old."

To Caprera, a small island off Sardinia, he went. There he bought a hut where he felt resigned to end his days in quiet solitude.

But the cry of the oppressed reached him across the waters, and once more he felt the old restlessness in his heart. Italy, under the political inspiration of Cavour, was trying to throw off the Austrian yoke. That same old dream again—an Italy united and free. Garibaldi left Caprera and joined the forces of Cavour. A new stream of youthful vigor in those old veins again. Once more at war, once more in love. He met a girl of nineteen, the Marchesina Rakmondi, laid a brief and impetuous siege to her heart, and married her (January, 1860).

A wintry marriage that ended in a sudden storm. A few days after the wedding he left her because he heard that she was still attached to a lover with whom she had had a former affair.

And now back to the battlefield. Greater activity than ever for that old brave heart. The liberation of Sicily; the emancipation of Naples; and finally, the overthrow of the Austrian yoke and the realization of Garibaldi's greatest dream—Italy united under a single sovereign, King Victor Emmanuel of the House of Savoy.

And the king's gratitude to Garibaldi for the outstanding part he had played in the unification of Italy? On October 26, 1860, Victor Emmanuel met Garibaldi and his little band of consecrated revolutionists. A cold and damp morning, a cold and damp greeting. After a condescending handshake the king rode by, followed by his royal troops in a pompous parade. Garibaldi and his soldiers, who had borne the brunt of the battles, were obliged to look upon this procession as outsiders. An English friend of his, Jessie White, was standing near him. "Jessie," remarked Garibaldi with a wry smile, "they are sending us to the rear!"

Always to the front in a fight. Always to the rear when the fight was over. "In worldly affairs," wrote the historian Michelet, "this man, loftier than fortune, had the divine stupidity of a hero."

KARL MARX

Important Dates in Life of Karl Marx

1818—Born in Germany.
1824—Baptized as Protestant.
1841—Received degree of Doctor of Philosophy.
1843—Married Jenny von Westphalen.
1847—Wrote, with Engels, the Communist Manifesto.
1849—Expelled from Prussia. Expelled from Paris, went to London.

1859—Published Zur Kritik der politischen Oekonomie.
1864—Became head of the International Workingmen's Association.
1867—Published first volume of Das Kapital.
1881—Death of wife.
1883—Death of Karl Marx in London.

Karl Marx

1818–1883

KARL (HEINRICH) MARX was born in Trier, on May 5, 1818.
Both on his father's side and on his mother's, he was descended
from a long line of Jewish rabbis. His father, however, a "very
learned, very industrious, and very conscientious lawyer," had
turned from Judaism to Free Thought and from Free Thought to
Christianity. He had himself and his family baptized (1824) and
accepted into the national evangelical church. He wanted to save
his children from a tragic life, he said, by severing them from the
persecuted Jewish race.

But his precaution was in vain. He couldn't sever his children
from the persecuted *human* race. Two of his sons and two of his
daughters died prematurely of tuberculosis; and his third and
favorite son, Karl, survived to become the hero in one of the
saddest stories of the nineteenth century. A genius to the world,
perhaps; but to his mother, a disgrace. "If Karl had only *made*
capital," she complained in her old age, "instead of merely *mock-
ing* at it!"

II

YOUNG KARL was a brilliant scholar and impractical dreamer. As a high school student he dedicated his life to the least profitable of the professions—fellow-service. The least profitable but the most palatable. "If we choose the career in which we can do humanity the most good, burdens cannot overwhelm us, since they are nothing but sacrifices for the benefit of all . . . Experience rates him as the happiest who has made the greatest number happy; and religion itself teaches us the ideal for which we all strive—to sacrifice ourselves for humanity."

To please his father, he became a disinterested student of law; but to please himself, he became an interested student of justice.

Yet there was nothing of the ascetic in him. He liked his card games, his drinks, and his duels.

And his *wunderschöne Loreleis*. Especially Jenny von Westphalen, the prettiest and the most brilliant of them all. Preposterous for the Jewish young student of eighteen to have fallen in love with "the princess of the Trier aristocracy." But even more preposterous, the "princess" had fallen in love with Karl Marx. They were married after a courtship of seven years. And for the next thirty-eight years, until the day of Jenny's death, they ate together "the bread of affliction"—very often there was no other bread in the house—and drank it down with the wine of an undying love. In spite of their sufferings, they were passionately devoted to each other to the very end.

In 1841, Karl Marx received his doctorate at the University of Jena. Whereupon he tried to get a position as a teacher of law. But everywhere he was turned down. "Too radical." He had written a thesis on the materialistic philosophy of Epicurus. No room for free thinkers in Prussia. Nor for *any* thinkers, ancient or modern. One of the men responsible for the rejection of Karl Marx's application for a teaching job was also responsible for the suppression of the publication of Dante's *Divine Comedy* in German. "No comedy," declared this censor, "should be made of divine things."

Unable to be a teacher, Karl Marx became an agitator. Possessing a keen mind and a literary style that lashed like a flail, he threw himself heart and soul into the revolutionary movement of the day. And within a few months he rose to the leadership of radical thought. "You will be delighted," wrote the historian Moses Hess to the novelist, Berthold Auerbach, "to meet Karl Marx—the greatest, perhaps the *only real* philosopher now living . . . Though still a young man—only twenty-four at most—he combines the most profound philosophical earnestness with the most biting wit. Think of Rousseau, Voltaire, Holbach, Heine and Hegel fused into one—I say *fused,* not just lumped together —and you have Dr. Karl Marx."

Under the leadership of Karl Marx, the German intelligentsia had progressed from an aesthetic into a social rebellion. They were no longer satisfied with revolutionizing the rhythms of their poems and the plots of their dramas. They were now trying to bring about a revolution in the plot of life itself. The literary protest of Goethe had developed into the economic protest of Karl Marx.

In order to interpret this economic protest to the workers, Marx began to write a series of articles on the new social awakening. The paper in which these articles appeared was promptly suppressed, but Marx was not discouraged. He went to Paris and continued his barrage of anti-despotic and anti-theocratic essays and pamphlets. Already, in these early writings of his, we see the germs of his later philosophy. "Religion"—that is, the promise of heavenly reward for earthly privation—"is the opiate of the people." "Where the monarchical principle is in the majority, human beings are in the minority; where no one challenges the monarchical principle, there are no men at all." "Philosophers have done nothing more than interpret the world . . . Our business is to change it."

But Marx's desire to change the world clashed with the desire of the upper classes who were anxious to keep the world jogging along in its old leisurely and—to them—very satisfactory way. The German government charged him with high treason, and this charge divorced him automatically from his native land. To return to Trier, or to any other part of Germany, meant arrest and, possibly, death. His exile from Germany was followed by a decree of the French government that he must leave Paris. He went to Brussels, where he continued to educate the workers, to acquaint them with their rights, and to point out to them how they might best attain these rights. Man, he said, is the product of his environment. But he is also, if only he would realize it, the *producer* of his environment. History makes man, but man can also make history. In other words, we are the creators, as well as the creatures, of evolution.

This conception of man as being both the passive instrument and the active partner in the evolutionary process became the corner-stone of Marx's materialistic conception of history. In accordance with this conception, we can hasten the progress of the world by turning *evolution* into *revolution* whenever, in our judgment, this step becomes necessary.

The most important of all revolutions, according to Karl Marx, is the *social* revolution—that is, the uprising of the working class "which has to bear all the burdens of society without enjoying any of its advantages."

All the earlier philosophers had dealt with the ultimate question of God. Karl Marx busied himself with the more immediate problem of the proletarian (the propertyless workingman— literally, the man who has many children). All history, he said, is a class struggle between the *haves* and the *have-nots,* the possessors and the dispossessed, the exploiters and the toilers, the masters and the slaves. "From time to time the workers are victorious, though their victory is fleeting." Yet their organization is constantly growing stronger. Through the common (or *com-*

munist) interests of the workers of the world, national lines are broken down and the movement becomes international. "The communists everywhere support every revolutionary movement against extant social and political conditions . . . Communists scorn to hide their views and aims. They openly declare that their purpose can only be achieved by the forcible overthrow of the whole extant social order. Let the ruling classes tremble at the prospect of a communist revolution. Proletarians have nothing to lose but their chains. They have a world to win.

"Workers of the world, unite!"

III

THUS FAR the social theory of Karl Marx had much in common with that of the Italian liberator, Mazzini. Both of them advocated a world revolution in order to bring about the liberation of the masses. The *Communist Manifesto,* in which the idea of Marx receives its clearest and most vigorous interpretation, might easily have served as the rallying cry of Young Italy or of Young Europe. The chief difference between Mazzini and Marx was that Mazzini preached the gospel of freedom in accordance with the providential will of God, and Marx preached it in accordance with the providential design of destiny. For evolution is nothing but destiny cut into a scientific pattern.

Yet at this time Marx was still too much of a revolutionist to be a thoroughgoing scientist. His *Communist Manifesto,* written at a time (1848) when all Europe was in a turmoil of insurrection, was a flaming call to arms rather than a cold philosophical treatise. Marx had not as yet learned to base his philosophy of history upon a foundation of economics. His chief interest thus far was to stir up, rather than to educate, the workers of the world.

But the rulers of Europe wanted to keep the workers down. They looked upon Karl Marx as a disturber of the (autocratic and capitalistic) peace. Accordingly they tossed him about from one country to another, until finally Marx found himself banished to England. This was in 1849.

England, the most liberal of the European countries, was called "the mother of the exiles." Free from despotism, she was equally free from the fear of revolution. She could therefore afford to give a home to the homeless outcasts of the other nations. This impartial hospitality of the English government marks one of the most beautiful episodes in the history of the nineteenth century.

When Marx arrived in London, he was penniless. Advocating the proletariat cause, he was himself a typical proletarian. Though hardly able to support himself, he was already blessed with three children—and a fourth was expected within a few weeks.

Let us for a moment glance at this prophet of the proletariat as he steps off the ship into his adopted country where he is destined to undergo so many sufferings. He is thirty-one years old at this time. "He has a thick crop of black hair, a huge round beard, hairy hands, an overcoat buttoned awry; but he appears like one endowed with the right and the power demanding respect, however he may look and whatever he may do. His movements are awkward, yet bold and self-confident. His manners conflict sharply with the ordinary conventions of social life. He is proud, somewhat contemptuous, and his harsh voice, with a metallic ring, is admirably suited to his revolutionary opinions about persons and things."

He is arrogant, conceited and irritable. He treats with sarcastic intolerance all those whose opinions are different from his own. His nerves are almost always on edge. Yet when he is able to relax, he becomes "unpretentious, gentle, tender, cordial, self-sacrificing and kind."

His irritability was due to his constant suffering. "The family of six"—we are quoting from Otto Ruhle's *Karl Marx*—"was packed into two small rooms, not knowing from day to day whether they would get food on the next. Clothing and shoes had been pawned. Marx had to keep in the house, for lack of a coat to go out in, and had no meat for dinner, as the butcher had refused further credit."

On Easter Day, 1852, one of his children died. "Our poor little Francisca fell ill with severe bronchitis," writes her mother. "For three days the poor child struggled with death. She suffered so terribly. When it was over, her little body rested in the small back room. At night, we lay down on the floor . . . The dear child's death happened at a time when we were in the direst need . . . A French refugee gave me two pounds. With this sum I was able to buy the coffin in which my poor child now lies at peace. She had no cradle when she came into the world, and for a long time it was difficult to find a box for her last resting place."

Poverty, hunger and disease had become the incessant visitors at the home of Karl Marx. Although he was one of the greatest writers of the century, he was unable to make a living by the pen. For he had a new religion to sell, and the invention of new religions is the most thankless business in the world. Very few were willing to read his iconoclastic ideas, and even fewer were ready to pay for them.

No prophet should ever marry. He who chooses to bear the cross has no right to lay his heavy burden upon the shoulders of little children. The whole family of Karl Marx would have gone under, were it not for the patient generosity of Friedrich Engels. Employed as a bookkeeper in his father's factory, and making but a scanty living himself, he poured his money again and again into the bottomless sieve of Marx's desperate needs. The whole-hearted sacrifice of Engels for the sake of Karl Marx and his family is one of the golden pages in the history of the human race. Throughout their long friendship there was an endless stream of pitiable appeals from Marx to Engels, and an endless, though slender, stream of funds from Engels to Marx. There was never a word of impatience, never a refusal. "I would rather cut off my thumb than ask you again for help," writes

Marx in one of his letters. And Engels replies, as usual, with a check for ten pounds, another check for fifteen pounds, a Christmas present of twenty-five pounds, and so on, and on, and on.

For Engels regarded his friendship with Marx as a business partnership for the liberation of humanity. Engels supplied the funds to keep Marx alive, and Marx worked on his great "Bible of the Proletariat"—*Das Kapital*. The publication of this book fell like a bombshell into the conventional circles of economic theory. What are the central ideas of Marx's revolutionary philosophy? We shall state them briefly.

IV

THE invention of machinery had brought into the world a new era—the Industrial Age. Money had become King. A new aristocracy of bankers, manufacturers and shop-keepers—the *Bourgeoisie*—had risen to the dominant position in the state. The old Landlord had given way to the modern Bond-baron, or Capitalist; and the vassals of the Feudal Age had been replaced by the wage slaves of the Industrial Age.

Now Ricardo, before Marx, had pointed out the fact that capitalism is based upon the exploitation of labor. He did not, however, explain the cause of this exploitation, nor did he offer any remedy for it. Karl Marx did both.

Labor, he said, is a commodity; and the purchaser of labor (that is, the employer), like the purchaser of any other commodity, tries to get it as cheaply as he can. The value of a commodity is measured by the cost of its production, and the value of labor is measured by the minimum amount of money necessary to keep the laborer alive and in working condition.

The capitalist's profit depends upon getting his labor as cheaply as possible. The difference between what the laborer produces and what he gets is the surplus value of labor—that is, the profit of the capitalist.

For to the capitalist—asserted Marx—labor is an impersonal

thing. The laborer is not a human being, but a *hand*. He is to be bought as cheaply as possible, and his product is to be sold as dearly as possible. This is a condition for which you cannot blame the capitalist any more than you can blame the laborer. Both of them are the tools of economic laws over which they have no control.

The laborer, then, gives more than he receives. He produces more than he consumes. And this inequality results in a peculiar state of affairs. There are more things made in the world than the makers are able to buy. These things keep on accumulating for several years, until finally it becomes necessary to put a stop to further production in order to allow the surplus commodities to be used up. Since no further goods are to be produced for the time being, the worker loses his job, his purchasing power diminishes, the accumulated goods cannot be sold, the overfilled storehouses cannot be emptied, *and the laborer starves because there is too much food in the world.*

This—declared Marx—is the tragic absurdity to which the capitalistic system has brought us! Unless we change this system, we are certain to experience a financial crisis once in every ten years. And it is interesting, though not a bit pleasant, to note that the prediction of Karl Marx was realized with uncanny regularity down to the tragic depression of the nineteen-thirties.

Fortunately, however, as Marx pointed out, the remedy lies in the nature of the disease itself. The development of bigger and ever bigger machinery brings about the concentration of capital in a few hands. "Let the workers take over the machinery and *work for themselves* . . . In this way, the many will no longer suffer because of the greed of the few." Whether we like it or not—he concludes—the concentration of capitalism is slowly but surely paving the way toward the realization of socialism, and the anarchy of the present system is but a necessary transition from the Feudalism of the past to the Coöperative Commonwealth of the Future.

Karl Marx laid his finger on the diseased spot in the present economic system; very few will deny this fact. Whether or not he found the true remedy, it is impossible as yet to say. Let it be noted in passing, however, that Karl Marx was practically alone in predicting (1877) that the social revolution would come first in Russia—"that tsarist colossus with feet of clay." Nobody at that time realized how true a prophet he was. Today his economic doctrine is the accepted bible of the Russian Union of Socialist Soviet Republics.

V

KARL MARX lived to see the first volume of his great work published. But before he could send the second and the third volumes to the press, "death struck the pen from his hand." For many years he had suffered, like Job, from virulent abscesses and carbuncles that attacked every part of his body. These were followed, in the last few years of his life, by excruciating headaches. In the fall of 1881 he suffered an attack of pleurisy. His wife was in another room, dying of cancer. He managed to get on his feet again, and went in to see her for the last time. Writing to a friend about this meeting, his daughter said: "Mother was in bed in the big front room, and Mohr (the family pet-name for Karl Marx) in the back room. These two, whose lives had been so closely intertwined, could no longer be together. Mohr got over his illness. I shall never forget the morning when he felt strong enough to go into mother's room. It was as if they had been quite young again—she a loving girl and he a loving youth, entering upon life together, instead of an old man ravaged by illness, and a dying old woman, taking leave of one another forever."

Frau Marx died on December 2, 1881. Fifteen months later he followed her.

Garibaldi

Karl Marx

SUN YAT–SEN

Important Dates in Life of Sun Yat-sen

1866—Born.

1892—Graduated at Hongkong Medical School.

1895—Led unsuccessful uprising against Manchus. Fled to America to carry on agitation.

1911—Successfully completed Chinese Revolution.

1912—Became first President of Chinese Republic. Resigned same year.

1918—Organized the Kuomintang.

1921—Became head of the Canton government.

1922—Wrote The International Development in China.

1925—Died.

Sun Yat-sen

1866–1925

A NEW "BOY-MOUTH" was born (1866) in Choy Hung, the Village of the Blue Valley. His parents named him Sun Wen—Descendant of Wisdom. But as he grew older, they changed his name to Sun Yat-sen—Descendant of Immortal Leisure. It was so rare a blessing in China, this gift of leisure among the children of the poor. "May our child grow up to be a man of great learning and may he be blessed with a little time for play."

But there was precious little playtime for the growing child. Seven days of schooling; and for relaxation, unceasing drudgery on his father's farm. "Perhaps when he is older," said his father, "he will go in a ship to that land of the Ocean-Men called America. And he will make money there, and come back to the Village of the Blue Valley and live at ease."

But Sun Wen's aunt, an old lady who lived with his parents, cautioned him against the Ocean-Men. "They are strange folk. They wear the queerest clothes, and they have no queues on their heads, and when they eat they stick sharp metal prongs instead of chopsticks into their mouths. Keep away from those barbarous people, Sun Wen."

And Sun Wen, when he heard these words, became curious to

know these Ocean-Men. "They may be barbarous, but they must be very interesting." There lived in the Village of the Blue Valley three brothers who had recently returned from the land of the Ocean-Men. They had worked in the gold mines there, and they now had much more money than anybody else in the village. They had taken a fancy to Sun Wen, and they told him many tales about the people from across the sea. "These people are not ruled like us by a Manchu King, but they choose their own ruler whom they call President. And this President has no power to arrest his people when they are honest, or to take away their money or their homes."

And one day these words were brought dramatically home to Sun Wen. A company of Manchu soldiers swooped down upon the estate of the three brothers and carried them off.

"What do you think has happened to these men?" Sun Wen asked his father.

"They've had their heads cut off."

"For what crime?"

"For no crime at all."

"Then why did the Manchus do it?"

"For a very simple reason. The Son of Heaven, our Manchu King, wanted the estate of these rich brothers, and so he killed them to get them out of the way."

Sun Wen took these words to heart. It was so different, the way they did things here and in the land of the Ocean-Men. Some day he would like to meet these Ocean-Men, and to learn their ways. Perhaps they were not such barbarians after all.

II

AT THIRTEEN, Sun Wen had his chance to meet the Ocean-Men. His older brother, Da Ko, had sailed several years earlier to Honolulu. There he had set himself up in business; the business had prospered; and now Da Ko invited Sun Wen to come to Honolulu as his assistant.

A new and exciting life for Sun Wen! A missionary school in the morning, and clerking in his brother's store in the afternoon. And contacts with those mysterious Ocean-Men, the white folk of the West. No barbarians at all, but men who possessed a gift unknown in his own country—freedom under the law. If only that precious gift could be brought to the people of China!

An exciting life, yet the excitement was not always on the pleasant side. The Hawaiian boys at the missionary school had taken to tormenting him because of his pigtail. Several of the older boys among them had got into the habit of pulling it when he passed by. For several days he endured their rowdiness, and then he challenged them to a fight. "Great fun!" thought the young hoodlums. He looked so quiet, so gentle, so weak. They would simply wipe up the dust with him.

But when the fight began, they found that this apparent weakling had muscles of steel. And an energy that was like a flame. His years of labor in the fields of the Blue Valley had turned him into a fighting machine. When the scuffle was over, it was not Sun Wen but his tormentors who were compelled to bite the dust.

The hoodlums were not through with him, however. Humiliated over their defeat, they decided upon the more cowardly but less dangerous method of passing the game of pigtail-pulling along to the smaller boys of the school. This time Sun Wen suffered his humiliation and his pain without raising a hand—until finally the youngsters got sick of their savage game and left him alone.

This episode tended to bring out two of the most salient features in Sun Wen's character. Fearless opposition to the strong, patient gentleness with the weak. "When my young brother grows up," said Da Ko, "I believe he will be a man to be reckoned with."

And Sun Wen was hardly sixteen when he entered upon his career as a full-grown man. His three years of schooling in Honolulu had given him a perfect command of English, a facility in mathematics, and a mature understanding of history. Upon his graduation he received a special prize for his excellence in studies.

And a special warning against his proneness to rebellion. "You are becoming too Westernized," said his brother, "for a respectable China-Man."

"The trouble with us China-Men," retorted Sun Wen, "is that we have been too respectable too long. Under the guise of respectability, the Manchus have been holding a whip over us for several centuries. 'Do this,' they tell us, 'and don't do that. Otherwise you're not a nice man.' I'm heartily sick of seeing China a country of nice men. I want to see it a country of *free* men!"

"This is dangerous talk, my brother. You want to change the course of centuries. You are fighting against our Chinese traditions. Tradition, you know, is a sacred thing."

"There is nothing sacred about traditional tyranny."

Da Ko shook his head. His brother had divorced himself from what the Chinese considered the greatest of their virtues—submission to their fate. "You have imbibed too deeply of the white men's brew of impatience. You have become too restless. I think you had better go back to the quietude of our father's farm in Choy Hung."

Sun Wen took his brother's advice and returned to his native village. But not to a quiet life.

III

EIGHTEEN YEARS OLD, and Sun Wen was now a full-fledged rebel. He went among the people and roused them from their sleep of a thousand years. He urged them to break loose from the chains with which their emperor held them tied down. "This man calls himself the Son of Heaven . . . I tell you he is the Son of Hell . . . He commands you to pay him your taxes and to bow your heads . . . But where does your tax money go? To build schools and bridges and roads for you, his people? No. It goes to enrich the coffers of the emperor, to encourage him in his debaucheries and to pay his mercenaries who keep you down."

"Blasphemous talk!" muttered the upholders of the old Chinese traditions. But Sun Wen went bravely ahead with his mission to rouse his people out of their ignorance. Whenever possible, he tried to bring home his point by a concrete illustration. Taking a copper coin out of his pocket, he would ask: "Who makes this money?"

"The ruler of China."

"And who is the ruler of China?"

"The Son of Heaven."

"Is he one of us?"

"Of course. Who but one of us can be fit to be the Son of Heaven?"

And then Sun Wen would hold up the copper coin. "Look at the words inscribed upon this coin. Are they Chinese?"

"No."

"No, indeed. They are Manchu. Foreign words. China is ruled by a foreigner."

Strange news! The majority of the common people were so ignorant they were not even aware of the fact that their emperor was a foreigner, a usurper. They began to listen to Sun Wen and to nod an occasional assent to his words.

But for the most part, Sun Wen's words were too strong for them. For he fought not only against the Son of Heaven but against Heaven itself. He tried to stir them into rebellion against their gods. In the village temple there were three idols—The King of the Northern Star, the Queen of Heaven, and the Mother Goddess. To these three idols the inhabitants of Choy Hung came with constant offerings and prayers. Otherwise the idols would bring them bad luck. It was a worship not of adoration but of fear—a superstition stemming out of an ignorant past and barring the way toward an enlightened future. Sun Wen had dedicated himself to the task of breaking this superstition. "These painted images, set up in every part of China, must first be destroyed before China can become a progressive nation."

He decided to begin with the destruction of the images in his own village. One day, gathering a group of young men about him, he went to the temple and stopped before the idol of the King of the Northern Star. Several of his companions prostrated themselves and began to pray. Sun Wen ordered them to stand up. "Listen, friends, to what I have to say. This god is in no position to help any of you. Why, he has no power even to help himself."

Saying this, he seized one of the fingers of the wooden god and wrenched it off. "See, he does nothing to prevent me. He does not strike me dead. He does not even send terror into my heart. He just keeps on grinning idiotically as before."

His companions were horrified at the spectacle. News of the sacrilege spread like wildfire through the village. Parents warned their children to keep away from this "mad image-breaker." They implored Sun Wen's family to send him away from the village. "If he remains here, he will bring bad luck to us all."

And so, one morning at dawn, "the sinful son of a virtuous father" left the Village of the Blue Valley. "May you some day return humble and contrite, an honor to your ancient family and to the ancient wise ways of China."

But Sun Wen had other ambitions in his heart. He was determined to prove to his family, and to all China, the wisdom of the New Way.

IV

HE BOARDED A SHIP for Hong Kong. Here he resumed his interrupted studies and his rebellious teachings. He entered Queen's College and graduated first in his class. And then he took up surgery at the Canton Medical School. The right profession for a revolutionist. By the drastic excisions of the diseased spots, he would cleanse the body and the soul of China. Though he worked hard at his studies, he found plenty of time for his political activities. With the help of a classmate, Cheng Se Liang, he organized a group of students into a fraternity dedicated to the proposition of a free China. These young men called themselves Dare-to-

Dies; and true to their name, they were ready to lay down their lives in their struggle against the Manchus.

It was a small and ineffective group at the start. Yet under the leadership of Sun Wen—he had now set himself up as a surgeon at Canton—they grew in numbers and power until finally (1895) they launched an uprising against the Manchu rulers of China.

The uprising failed. The Manchus put a price upon Sun's head; but he succeeded in making his escape. He went to Hawaii, and from there to America—agitating, planning, lecturing, collecting funds for another attempt at freedom. Of his ultimate victory he hadn't the slightest doubt. "One of these days China is bound to move. And when China moves"—quoting the words of Napoleon—"she will move the world."

It was a dangerous mission upon which he was embarked. For the Chinese consulates in the various cities of America—emissaries of the Manchus—had received orders to put him out of the way. But he always managed to keep a step ahead of his enemies—"the man is a flying ghost"—inured to hardship, fearless of torture, a Dare-to-Die consecrated to the fulfillment of a dream.

His mission in America completed, he went to England. Here his enemies caught up with him. The Chinese legation in London had him kidnaped. "An end to him at last, and to all those pernicious attempts at a Chinese republic."

But again he managed to escape. "The flying ghost has vanished into thin air." Impossible to keep up with the rapidity of his motions. "Never was a gun quick enough to get Sun Yat-sen," wrote one of his followers. And never was a danger frightful enough to interrupt him in his work. "Sun doesn't understand the meaning of the word *fear*."

And he inspired in his followers a measure of his own fearlessness and his own speed. Realizing the weakness of his little company of devoted rebels as measured against the strength of the Manchus, he adopted for his tactics the method of the ancient Chinese wrestlers. "Make the strength of your enemy prove his undoing. Consider yourself as the leverage to break his bones . . .

[*191*]

Do not actively resist your adversary. Let him apply his entire force against you. Then, by an adroit gesture of passivity, let him crack his bones on the obstacle of your own change of balance. His force is the sledge-hammer; your force is the anvil. Your adversary breaks himself between his hammer and your anvil."

With his method of wrestling—physical, moral, social, political —the Chinese David settled down to overthrow the Goliath of the Manchu power. He established his headquarters in Japan (1899), only a stone's throw away from the Chinese consulate at Yokohama. This was both a daring and a clever move. Daring, because every time he stepped out of his office, the Manchu henchmen might pick him off with a shotgun. Clever, because any such attempt upon his life would precipitate the Chinese revolution, so popular had he now become among the masses. From this vantage point he entered upon the patient process of undermining the power of the Manchus. "The emperor has no divine right to rule the people. The people have a divine right to rule themselves. Let all the people disobey the emperor, and he will die of his own impotence."

The emperor has no divine right. With this sharp and simple weapon he kept pricking at the pretensions of the Manchus—day after day, month after month, year after year—until the masses began to believe it, the retainers of the Manchus began to believe it, even the Manchus themselves began to believe it. They felt the earth quaking under their feet; and when they appealed to their courtiers for rescue, they found that these men were courting the good will of Sun Yat-sen. "Those who are deserted by their friends will soon be deserted by the gods." The growing strength of Sun Yat-sen's "army of liberation" threw them into a panic of in-activity. Everywhere, in the tea-houses, in the market-places, in the fields, there sprang up groups of eager young men ready to march to victory. A thousand streams of destruction began to flow from every quarter down upon the palace of the Son of Heaven. Again and again and yet again Sun Yat-sen attempted to strike the final blow—and at every failure came nearer to success. Ten times he tried to proclaim the Chinese Republic, only to find that the day had not as yet arrived. But the Manchus realized that the reckoning was not far off.

And then came that historic day in September, 1911. Sun Yat-sen was traveling in America, collecting funds for the cause. Picking up a newspaper in Denver, Colorado, he saw a headline that made his heart leap:

Wuchang Occupied by Revolutionists

His dream had been realized. The Manchu power was over. China was on the verge of freedom at last.

V

ON JANUARY 1, 1912, Sun Yat-sen was inaugurated as the first President of the Chinese Republic. At that time there was studying at the Wesleyan College, in Georgia, a Chinese young lady by the name of Chingling. She was a member of the famous Soong family and a sister of Mayling, who was later to become the wife of Chiang Kai-shek. The success of the Chinese Revolution inspired Chingling to write an article for her school paper. "One of the greatest events of the century . . . is the liberation of China . . . It means the emancipation of four hundred million souls from the thralldom of an absolute monarchy, which has been in existence for over four thousand years, and under whose rule 'life, liberty, and the pursuit of happiness' have been denied . . .

"The entire world looked doubtfully upon our dreams for a Chinese Republic. To some, even the promise of an early constitutional government was received with skepticism. But deep down in the heart of every patriotic Chinese, were he a politician or a laborer, there was the anti-Manchu spirit."

And the conviction of final victory under the leadership of Sun Yat-sen. When this Leader was inaugurated as the President of China, Chingling celebrated the occasion by unfurling out of her dormitory window the new five-barred Flag of the Republic.

Upon her graduation from Wesleyan (1913), she wrote to one of her teachers: "I shall soon be on my way home. I am taking a box of California fruit to Dr. Sun from his admirers here, and I am also the proud bearer of a private letter to him."

And the humble bearer of her heart. She met her hero, became his secretary, and shortly thereafter his wife. Sun Yat-sen had been married before—an unhappy experience. This second marriage was as happy as it was permanent.

But it was not all happiness for Sun Yat-sen. Having conquered his enemies, he was now betrayed by his friends. Distrustful of his own ability as an administrator, he relinquished the Presidency to Yuan Shih-kai. This man, a former official in the imperial government, had persuaded the Manchus to abdicate. He had done this, however, not to advance the cause of the republic but to further his own ambition. No sooner had he been appointed President than he began to assume dictatorial powers. Too late Sun Yat-sen recognized that Yuan Shih-kai was aiming to become the new emperor of China. Sun Yat-sen set himself against this ambitious upstart. But Yuan Shih-kai had seized control of the army. He declared Sun Yat-sen an outlaw, and set a price upon his head.

Once more, flight to Japan and a regathering of forces for the liberation of China. In the meantime (1915) Yuan Shih-kai had declared himself emperor.

An unhappy cycle had now been completed in Sun Yat-sen's life. From failure, to success, back to failure again. Yuan Shih-kai died shortly after his ascension to the throne, but a dozen adventurers had inherited his ambition and his arrogance. China was now a cauldron of Civil War. A momentary victory, and then once more defeat.

And thus, fighting to regain for his nation the freedom that had once been within its grasp, Sun Yat-sen spent the last ten years of his life.

But he never gave up hope. Not even in 1925 when he knew that he was dying. For in the ranks of his consecrated fighters was a young man in whom he had the most implicit faith. Chiang Kai-shek. "I am departing from the scene, my friend," said Sun Yat-sen when the end drew near. "But I am leaving you to carry on. And some day, through your devotion, China shall yet be free."

LENIN

Important Dates in Life of Lenin

1870—Born at Simbirsk.
1887—Entered Kazan University. Expelled same year for revolutionary activities.
1891—Passed law examinations at St. Petersburg University.
1894—Began propaganda work at St. Petersburg.
1895—Arrested.
1897—Exiled to Siberia.
1898—Married his fellow exile, N. K. Krupskaya.
1900—Freed from Siberia. Started paper Iskra (The Spark).
1903—Became leader of Bolsheviks.

1905—Played prominent part in (unsuccessful) revolution against Czar.
1907—Left Russia.
1907-14—Agitated for the "coming revolution."
1914—Denounced the "imperialistic character" of the World War.
1917—October 25, Lenin seized the supreme power of Russia, "in behalf of the Proletariat."
1918—Wounded in attempt to assassinate him.
1918-21—Fought against the counter-revolutionists.
1921—Defeated them.
1922-24—Ill from overwork.
1924—Died January 21.

Nikolai Lenin
(Vladimir Ilyich Ulianov)
1870–1924

NOVEMBER 7, 1917. For several months now Russia has staggered under a political earthquake. The Czar, having relied upon violence, has been violently overthrown. The Russian people are heartily sick of the war. They believe that there is no further reason for them to fight, now that the Czar is dead. But Kerensky, the president of the new Russian Republic, has made not the slightest move to stop the war. The Russians feel that they have been cheated. The war has sapped their strength to the point of exhaustion. The allowance of bread has fallen to a quarter-pound a day. On many a day there has been no bread at all. In Petrograd, more than half of the babies have had no milk for weeks. At the front, the soldiers are gaunt, hungry and bootless. They have sent a delegation to Petrograd to beg for peace. "Comrades, we are starving in the trenches. We are stiff with cold. We are dying for no reason. We hoped the Kerensky Revolution would bring us peace. But now the government forbids us even talk of such things . . ."

Peace, land to the poor, and bread to the hungry—this is the dream of the soldiers and the civilians alike. In answer to this dream, the reactionary papers have urged a general massacre of all the Russian "radicals, pacifists and Jews."

At last the soldiers have decided to take matters into their own hands. They have been joined by the workers and the peasants. "Enough of tyranny, enough of starvation, enough of war!" They are gathered in an assembly to proclaim their demands. A cloud of tobacco smoke almost thick enough to be cut with a knife. A pandemonium of rasping shouts. The stench of poverty bundled in rags. Clenched fists. White faces ravaged with hunger and disease. Feverish eyes aflame with hatred and hope.

And the flaming words of the agitators who, one after another, insist upon a new way of life. Trotsky, in a staccato of phrases like the bullets of a repeating rifle, announces the "end of imperialistic capitalism" throughout the world. Zinoviev, in a voice quivering with emotion, proclaims this day as the day of reckoning for all oppressors, especially for "Kaiser Wilhelm, the Executioner." A representative of the soldiers calls upon the nations to put a stop to this "senseless murder called war . . ."

And now the preliminary speeches are over. The entire assembly is on its feet, singing the *Internationale:*

> " 'Tis the final conflict; let each stand in his place,
> The International Party shall be the human race!"

Now at last, the principal speaker. Nikolai Lenin. A squat, baldheaded, homely and insignificant little man, with a shabby coat and with baggy trousers that are too long for him. As he rises to his feet, the audience becomes galvanized into an assembly of worshipers. "A grizzled old soldier is sobbing like a child." Men weep and laugh and shout and embrace in a frenzy of unprecedented joy. And Lenin, his hands gripping the edge of the reading stand and his beady winking eyes traveling over the crowd, stands quietly and waits for the ovation to subside.

Silence now. Everybody is on tiptoe. The Workers' and Peasants' Messiah begins his speech. His voice is matter-of-fact, like that of a schoolmaster opening an ordinary daily session in the classroom. "We shall now proceed to construct the Social Order."

And thus begins the final tremor of the earthquake in which the bottom of humanity is to surge to the top.

II

FEW MEN in history have been loved as Lenin was loved. "I have seen Lenin speak to his followers," writes Walter Duranty. "A small, busy, thickset man . . . greeted by applause like thunder . . . I turned around, and their faces were shining, like men who looked on God."

He was so deeply venerated because he was so astonishingly simple. He placed his powerful intellect at the service of his fellows. He explained the most difficult ideas in the most elementary words. He expressed exactly what he thought. His style had nothing of the "diplomatic phraseology" which says one thing and means another. Honest in his dealings, he could well afford to be candid in his speech. If ever he made a mistake, he was the first to admit it. But, on the other hand, he was relentless in exposing the mistakes—and especially the hypocrisies—of others. Having discovered, in the archives of the imperial government, the secret treaties which had brought about the war of 1914, he promptly published them and called down upon himself the enmity of all the dishonest statesmen in the world.

Throughout his life he had but a single purpose—to bring about a social organization in which there would be no tyranny, no exploitation, no unemployment, no international intrigues, and no war. To this one purpose he sacrificed every personal ambition. Born (1870) into a middle class atmosphere—his father was a school inspector and his mother was the daughter of a physician—he grew up amidst the conversational fireworks of the Russian intelligentsia. His native city was Simbirsk, once a center of revolutionary activity. As a child he thrilled to the exploits of Stenka Razin, the Russian Robin Hood who had plundered the rich to help the poor. Storming out of the steppes, this Cossack "liberator" had sailed up the Volga, calling upon the workers and the peasants and the serfs to rebel against their tyrants. He had captured the governor of the district and had hurled him from the tower of Astrakhan to his death. He had lashed the tax collectors with the knout, and broken the aristocrats on the wheel. Finally he had been arrested at Simbirsk and hanged in the public square. A great folk-hero, the subject of legend and song. "Some day"—this was spoken in whispers, for fear that the agents of the Czar might be prowling around—"some day another Stenka Razin will arise, and *his* rebellion will *not* fail!"

Another Stenka Razin, to come out of the city of Simbirsk. Little Vladimir's cheeks flamed up when he heard these words. The new Savior of Russia, the son of educators and doctors—so ran the old Russian legend. Maybe he was the one . . . Some day, perhaps . . .

But his parents cautioned him against such thoughts. They were dangerous under the Czar. Let him grow up into a respectable member of the Russian bourgeoisie. *That* would be the safest and the most practical course.

They sent him to the Simbirsk High School, whose headmaster, Kerensky, had a little boy of about his own age. Young Kerensky, too, was a dreamer. Yet there was a difference in their dreams. Both of them wanted to see justice established in Russia. But while Kerensky was willing to *wait* for it, Vladimir was anxious to *work* for it.

For, young as he was, the seeds of rebellion had already taken root in his heart. Secretly he read the revolutionary pamphlets of Hertzen. "From every corner of our enormous land, from the Don and the Ural, from the Volga and the Dnieper, a moan is growing, a grumbling is rising . . . *Vnarod*. To the people!"

To the people! This was the cry of the intellectuals, even of high school age. Help the masses, and educate them to appreciate your help when you bring it. There was so little appreciation among the masses—so little understanding of your motives. One day a philanthropic landowner by the name of Petrachevsky had built a number of model houses for the peasants. But the peasants, suspecting that he was concocting some sinister plot against them —"why should a rich man want to help us poor folk?"—set the houses on fire.

Poor, misguided, persecuted, unawakened souls! You had to treat them and teach them like children. Human creatures who must be made to understand. A dangerous mission. To the rulers of Russia the peasants were not human creatures but beasts of burden, fit only for plowing the land when they were alive and fertilizing it when they were dead.

Away with the rulers who trampled their subjects into the dust! In 1886, a group of university students plotted to assassinate the Czar. The plot was discovered, and the students were executed. One of the executed young men was Alexander Ulianov, Vladimir's oldest brother.

The death of Alexander made a profound impression upon Vladimir. He had just finished his high school studies at the head of his class. "Very gifted"—so ran his final report—"consistently painstaking and regular in his attendance." Well, from now on he would dedicate his extraordinary gifts and his painstaking consistency to the revolutionary cause. He had a brother's death to avenge, and a nation's soul to retrieve. The course of his life was clear.

III

HIS COURSE was clear, but full of difficulty and danger. As the brother of a "condemned terrorist," he was a marked man. "Watch him, and at the first sign of nonsense put him out of the way." He entered the University of Kazan in the fall of 1887. Before Christmas of that year he was expelled. "A bad influence upon his fellow students."

He continued his studies in private, however, and four years later he successfully passed the entrance examinations to the St. Petersburg Law School. Admitted to the bar at twenty-three, he enjoyed but a brief interlude of legal practice and then he was exiled to Siberia as a dangerous character. "The Russian worker," he had written in a pamphlet, "will overthrow absolutism and lead the Russian proletariat along the direct road . . . to the Communist Revolution." Prophetic words. Had the Russian government realized their true significance, Vladimir would have been sent not to Siberia but like his brother Alexander to the gallows.

He took his exile, as he would have taken his death, with a quiet heroism. There was about him nothing of the hysterical fanaticism that kept so many of his comrades spinning around in a perpetual whirlwind of futility. His was a rebellion of the mind rather than of the heart. He planned every step of his work with the precision of a scientist resolving an equation, or of a lawyer preparing a brief. A good place, Siberia, for the maturing of his political philosophy and for the elaboration of his economic formula. From feudalism to capitalism, from capitalism to communism; from aristocracy to monarchy, from monarchy to democracy; from the "divine right" of the few to the human right of the many, from the tyranny of the prince to the dictatorship of the proletariat. Serenely he spent his exile in laying the foundations for the future state—the Commonwealth of the Forgotten Man.

And he had a faithful companion to help him in this work. Nadezhda Konstantinova Krupskaya. He had met her in his revolutionary activity at St. Petersburg. And now he found her again, a fellow exile in Siberia. She was his collaborator and his secretary, and finally she became his wife. Together they discussed and wrote *The Development of Capitalism in Russia*— a book that served as the New Testament of communism after the Old Testament of Karl Marx.

Shortly after the publication of his book, his Siberian exile was over (February, 1900). Unable, however, to return to Russia, he went to Munich where he launched a revolutionary paper, *Iskra* —*The Spark*. "From the Spark will come the Flame." Already, at 30, he was recognized as the leader of the Russian radicals.

And, the Berlin officials began to suspect, of the German radicals, too. They drove him out of Germany. From that time on, his days were spent in perpetual wandering. And planning. And fighting. He now had a double fight on his hands—against the Russian government on the one side, against the Russian revolutionists on the other. "For every honest man (in the revolution)," he said, "we find 39 scoundrels and 69 fools." With the scoundrels it was comparatively easy to cope. At least there was method to their madness. But not so with the fools. Either they were anxious to start the revolution too early, or else they were willing to delay until it would be too late. "Between the firebrands and the ashes, I am afraid we shall come to a bad end." Especially irritable were the ashes that stifled the ambition of the workers. All that they hoped for, he complained, was a little better job. But this would only mean a better *little* job. What they needed, and what Lenin was determined to get for them, was a better *big* job. The ownership of the tools of production. The acquisition of the entire industrial system of Russia.

But they must be patient, and wary. They must wait for the right moment. That moment, he declared, would come when Russia was at war. "Give the country a number of exhausting battles for an unjust cause, and the soldiers will be ready to come over to our side."

The occasion for this military revolution seemed to arise in the Russo-Japanese War. Owing to the mismanagement of their officers, the soldiers had suffered a series of defeats. The morale of the army was low; that of the civil population, not much higher. The people asked for a constitution. The Czar turned their request into a joke. He gave them an assembly with full power to speak but with no power to act. The people were frantic. A severe winter, no fuel, no food, scanty rags, incessant toil. Sunday, January 22, 1905. A procession of workers, with their wives and their children, marched to the Palace of the Czar. At the head of the procession was the Orthodox priest, Father Gapon. It was an army of peace. Instead of weapons, they carried ikons in their hands. All they asked for was bread from their "little Father"—the name by which they addressed the Czar.

The Little Father gives them bullets instead of bread. A company of soldiers, at the order of the Czar, fires into the procession. The workers disperse in panic. A squadron of Cossacks gallops into their midst, their nagaikas (metal-tipped whips) whistling over bodies and faces and heads. Fifteen hundred dead are left on the palace ground.

The crisis is coming to a head. There is a mutiny of the sailors on the battleship *Potyemkin*. Has the day of reckoning arrived? Lenin waits expectantly, poised for the strike. He has returned to Russia now, ready to take the reins into his hands.

But no, the time is not yet. A false dawn. "The watchman hath said, 'Lo the day is here, but it is still night.' " The Czar concludes peace with Japan; and the revolution, for want of further fuel, dies out.

Many of the leaders of the revolution were now in jail. But Lenin had managed to make his escape. "A slippery man, hard to get into your clutches." Again an exile without a home, hunted from one place to another, always a step ahead of the police—agitating, writing, dreaming, planning for the day "when there will no longer be any need for violence, for the subjection of one man to another, of one section of society to another." Like St. Francis, he had dedicated himself to poverty and suffering in order that suffering and poverty might disappear from the world. And throughout his exile, his wife and comrade shared in his hardships and helped him in his work.

He was grateful for her devotion, and he repaid it with an equal devotion of his own.

And he gave his full heart's devotion to one other woman—his mother. Busy as he was with his revolutionary activities, he always found time to cheer her with a tender word. "Please do not send me any money," he wrote to her when he was on the point of starvation. "I beg of you, my darling, not to sacrifice anything for me out of your pension." "Please do not worry about me," he wrote on another occasion. "I embrace you, my darling, and wish you good health." Again, "My best thoughts, darling, are always with you."

A rare combination, the character of Lenin. A tender heart and a tough mind. He hated nobody. His quarrel was not with persons but with ideas. By nature a poet, he had schooled himself to become a prophet. He loved music. "I know nothing more beautiful than Beethoven's *Appassionata*," he said to Gorky. "It is marvelous, unearthly music. I could hear it every day." But he had dedicated himself to something other than song. "If I listen to music too often, I want to say amiable stupidities and to stroke the heads of the people who can create such beauty in a filthy hell." The world is too full of discord. Time now to harmonize the *body* of mankind. And then you will be able to listen to the harmony of the *soul*.

And so, "this is not the day to stroke people's heads. Today hands must descend to split skulls open, split them open ruthlessly, although opposition to all violence is our ultimate ideal."

Lenin's attitude toward music was similar to his attitude toward religion. He was not, at heart, opposed to religion, but "this is not the day for it." Instead of soothing people with the dream of heaven—he declared—we must extricate them from their nightmare of hell on earth. And this nightmare, he believed, had been brought upon the people through the emissaries of the Czar who acted hand in glove with the representatives of the (Russian Orthodox) Church. If you want to be free, he preached to the masses, you must overthrow your autocratic Czar and his theocratic faith. Like Buddha, he was a mystic and an atheist at the same time. Paraphrasing that other religious rebel, Mohammed, he might have said, "There is no God, and Lenin is his prophet."

IV

WHEN the World War broke out in 1914, Lenin sensed at once that the "Great Day" for Russia was not far off. He was not interested in the issues of the war. "The ambitions of the various countries are but the ambitions of the competing capitalists of those countries." Let these capitalists knock their heads together, he said, and out of the crash would come the Communist Revolution.

And so he waited patiently for the opportune moment. Insensitive to the ordinary feelings of patriotism—"My compatriots," he said, "are the workers of the world"—he looked complacently upon the rising tide of Russian defeats. "This tide will sweep the Czar and his entire regime into oblivion." From his foreign observation post—he was now living at Zurich—he watched the rapid disintegration of the Russian arms and the Russian state. The final gasp came in February, 1917. A group of soldiers at the front disobeyed their officer's command to fire upon their rebelling comrades. The news spread throughout the army. Millions of men in revolt. "Enough of wars and enough of Czars!" Nicholas was compelled to abdicate. The Socialist Revolution was on.

But not Lenin's Revolution. With all his careful watching, he had been caught unprepared. He had not expected so speedy a collapse of the Czarist regime. The reins of the government fell into the hands of Kerensky, who issued the challenge: "The war must go on!"

This was Lenin's opportunity. He replied with the counter-challenge: "The war must stop!"

Lenin's proved to be the popular course. The soldiers and the civilians were sick of the war. Perched upon the top of an armored car, Lenin rode through the streets of Petrograd repeating again and again his offer of an immediate peace. "The people need peace, the people need bread, the people need land. And they give you war, hunger, no bread, and they leave the landlords on the land."

Kerensky's associates advised the arrest of Lenin. "Let him be," replied Kerensky. "He's cracked." Instead of attending to Lenin, Kerensky thought it his business to attend to the army.

He ordered the commander-in-chief to persist in his "defensive and offensive activity" against the Germans. But the soldiers, and even many of the officers, refused to obey. A new cry now: "Enough of war, enough of Kerensky!"

Lenin had won the day. Kerensky was compelled to flee—as Lenin picturesquely expressed it—"into the rubbish can of history." And now Lenin was ready to proceed with the construction of the Social Order.

V

IT WAS a difficult and at times seemingly hopeless task. Lenin was obliged not only to build from the bottom up, but to waste a great part of his revolutionary force against the armies sent into Russia at the instigation of the Allied Powers. They were determined, out of a desire for self-protection, to kill the revolution in Russia before it would gather enough momentum to spread to the rest of the world. But Lenin succeeded in warding off the enemy, and managed to begin the rebuilding of Russia. He was a popular leader who got the coöperation of the masses. Nothing of the Oriental splendor of the Czar about Comrade Lenin. His rooms in the Kremlin were as sparsely furnished as his lodgings at Zurich. His food was the simple fare of the peasants. One day a visitor arrived while Lenin was at supper with his wife. Black bread, butter, cheese, and tea. "Nadezhda," said Lenin to his wife, "try to find something sweet for our guest." After a careful search in the cupboard, she unearthed a little glass jar of preserved currants.

A new phenomenon in history—a dictator with simple tastes. And with an honest heart. Finding that some of his communistic ideas could not work, he frankly abandoned them in favor of capitalistic ideas that *could* work. He was an impartial experimenter in the laboratory of decent government. He had his preconceived notions, he admitted, as to what he wanted to find. But he was ready to accept any formula for justice that the test-tube of his experiments would bring to light. "We shall make thousands of mistakes, but we shall ultimately discover the one true course."

A simple honest scientist of a dictator who knew how to work, and to laugh. At a meeting of the Soviet Congress in Moscow (July, 1918), the highly emotional leader of the Social Revolutionaries, Maria Spiridanova, delivered a scathing attack against him. "I accuse you," she cried, "of betraying the peasants, of exploiting them for your own ends . . . In your philosophy, the peasants are only dung—only manure . . . If you persist in this course," her voice had now risen to a shriek, "you will find in my hand a pistol ready to assassinate . . ." Her last words were drowned out in the pandemonium that had broken out in the hall. "Down with Lenin! Down with the enemy of the peasants! Long live Spiridanova!"

Lenin stood up. He went over to Spiridanova and patted her on the shoulder. Then he turned to the shouting audience and began to laugh. He just held the lapels of his coat and laughed. A quiet, amused, indulgent laughter. Five minutes passed, and then he raised his hand. A dead silence had fallen over the audience. Lenin began to speak. "Comrades, let us forget what Maria Spiridanova has just said in her excitement. Let us go on with our work."

He sat down amidst a thunder of applause. "Lenin is right! He is always in the right! Long live Lenin!"

The magic of Lenin's laughter. Everybody who came into contact with him declared that this was his outstanding characteristic. Some people thought that there was in it a note of cruelty. Others found in it nothing but good nature and a joyous acceptance of his role in the shaping of history. Still others gave it up as an enigma that would never be solved. Yet the solution, it seems to us, is very simple. Lenin laughed not because he was cruel or joyous, but because he was sad. He laughed so heartily because he had suffered so deeply. In spite of his earnest efforts to change the human drama, he felt that it was nothing but a cosmic farce. His laughter was like the laughter of Swift, of Heine, of Mark

Twain. He had sacrificed himself for humanity, and yet he knew that humanity was not worth the sacrifice. "Pretty low trash, the two-legged beast called man." Like Virgil, he had probed down to the depth of human stupidity and human sadness. He, too, understood the Latin poet's *lachrimae rerum.* There were tears in Lenin's laughter.

VI

LENIN'S SUFFERINGS ended only with the end of his life. "Dying is such a long and painful process!" An attack of cerebral sclerosis —a hardening of the blood vessels in the brain—but he kept on working. A hemorrhage, a brief vacation, and he went back to his work. A paralytic stroke, only partial recovery, and once more he chained himself down to his desk. A second hemorrhage, and a third, and finally he was compelled to lay down his task. On January 21, 1924, he closed his eyes with the faint flicker of a smile on his face. The Soviet Congress honored him with a declaration which was almost like an apotheosis. "His vision was colossal. His intelligence in organizing the masses was beyond belief. He was the supreme leader of all countries, of all times, of all peoples. He was the lord of the new humanity, the savior of the world."

They brought his body to Moscow and laid it in the Hall of Columns. Outside, the temperature was thirty below zero. But they lit great fires in the open square to warm the thousands of pilgrims who had come from every corner of Russia to pay homage to their "beloved Lenin." And many of them, as they passed the body, crossed themselves with a prayer on their lips. The man whose life had been devoted to "ungodly disbelief" was now in death becoming consecrated as a God.

MARCONI

Important Dates in Life of Marconi

1874—*Born at Bologna.*

1895—*Began experiments with electromagnetic waves.*

1896—*Took out, in England, first patent for wireless telegraphy.*

1897—*Established wireless communication from land to sea.*

Organized Wireless Telegraph company.

1898—*Established wireless communication across the English Channel.*

1899—*First sea rescue (of East Goodwin Lightship) through wireless.*

1901—*Established wireless communication across the Atlantic.*

1902—*Patented the magnetic detector.*

1905—*Patented the horizontal aerial.*

1909—*Received Nobel Prize for physics.*

1912—*Introduced the "timed spark system."*

1918—*Sent first message from England to Australia.*

1937—*Died.*

Sun Yat=sen

Lenin

Guglielmo Marconi

1874—1937

C̲H̲E̲ orecchi grandi ha"—"What large ears he has!" exclaimed a relative as she saw the newborn babe.

"With these ears," said his music-loving mother, "he'll be able to intercept the still small voices of the air."

And from infancy Guglielmo grew up to be a studious, introspective and dreamy child. From his Irish mother he inherited his imaginative mind; and from his Italian father, his restless hands. And with these restless hands he was able to transmute his dreams into realities.

He was born (April 25, 1874) at Bologna. "This city," said an ancient oracle, "will enrich the world with two great gifts—one for the palate, and one for the mind." His prophecy turned out to be true. For it was a Bolognese butcher who invented the sausage—named *bologna* after the city of its origin; and it was a Bolognese scientist whom Destiny was now educating for the invention of the wireless.

Marconi received his entire education from private tutors. His father, an expert and wealthy agriculturist, was unwilling to entrust his delicate child to the public schools. Curled up in the library of his father's estate at Pontecchio, near Bologna, Guglielmo devoured hundreds of books upon all sorts of subjects. He was especially fond of reading about steam engines and electricity and chemistry. And always he tried to put his reading to the test. "Yes, that's what they say. But how will I know until I try it for myself?" In one of the attics he fixed up a little laboratory—"a magician's workroom." And one day he became attracted to the larger laboratory of the outdoors. He tried to extract nitrate from the atmosphere. This experiment resulted in failure, but it turned his attention to the treasure-house of the air. There were so many sounds that rippled over the air-waves—his large ears were unusually sensitive—such a labyrinth of syllables that waited to be captured and disentangled and rearranged into a definite sense. What happened to all the words that people were uttering, casting them into the air like so many pebbles into a lake? Were these words forever lost, or did they keep floating over the earth, just waiting for some instrument to recapture them?

And once, as he turned these thoughts over in his mind, he read an article about the experiments of the German physicist, Heinrich Hertz. His heart leaped up within him. Here at last was a clue to the mystery! Professor Hertz had invented an electric oscillator which could throw a spark from one end of a room to another without any visible connecting link. How did this spark travel across the room? Over an air-wave apparently, like a piece of wood floating over a water-wave in a lake. If this should prove to be true, wouldn't it be possible to direct a sound from one spot to another, just as a boy might direct a piece of wood over the surface of the water? And if an electric spark or a sound could be made to leap across a room, couldn't it also be made to leap across a field, a city, a country, a continent, perhaps even an ocean? The distance that a sound could travel over the air would depend upon the power of the electrical push, just as the distance that a piece of wood could travel over a lake would depend upon the power of the boy's hand-push.

The thought was terrifying in its simplicity. "It was so elementary, so obvious in logic," remarked Marconi years later, "that it seemed difficult to believe no one else had thought of putting it into practice. I argued, there must be more mature scientists who had followed the same line of thought and arrived at almost similar conclusions. From the first the idea was so real to me, I did not realize that to others the theory might appear quite fantastic."

A vivid dream. And the boy inventor—he was only twenty at the time—proceeded to see whether he couldn't make it real. Impulsively he rushed in where the greybeard professors feared to tread. Together with his brother, Alfonso, he built a crude apparatus with which he tried to ensnare the elusive Hertzian spark. But in vain. Again and again he rebuilt his instruments, and rearranged them, but always with the same negative results. "The greybeards must be right, after all."

He had grown pale and drawn in his efforts. His father begged him to desist from his "crazy" dreams and to settle down to a "practical" job. Even his mother warned him that he was headed for a nervous breakdown. As for the friends of the family, they looked upon him and shook their heads. "Most likely he will land in the insane asylum."

"Ma non mi persi di coraggio"—"But I did not lose my courage." He went right ahead with his "insane and useless experimentations"—and one day he announced that he had a surprise for his parents. Inviting them into his attic workroom, he pressed a button whereupon a bell buzzed in the living room two stories below.

"But how did you do it?" asked his mother. "There are no connecting wires."

"That's just it. I have invented the wireless transmission of sound."

"God bless you!" exclaimed his mother as she embraced him with tears in her eyes. But his father merely turned away with a contemptuous shrug. "So you've invented wireless," he said. "So what?"

II

SIGNOR MARCONI was skeptical about his son's work. Yet his generosity got the better of his skepticism. He contributed a sum of 5,000 lire (about $1,000) for his son's further experimentations with that "crazy contraption of his." Guglielmo was elated. "With this sort of encouragement, I shall encircle the world with my voice."

"See that it enables you to encircle your body with your rags," smiled Signor Marconi. "Your invention seems to me of no practical value whatsoever."

"Maybe so. But we shall see." And Guglielmo went resolutely ahead with his experiments.

It was a time (1892–1895) of great scientific expectation. The leading physicists felt that they had arrived at the borderland of revolutionary discoveries. Especially in the medium of electricity. The opaque was becoming transparent. An electric ray could be made to pierce through a granite rock or a solid wall. "Here," wrote the eminent English scientist, Sir William Crookes, "is unfolded to us a new and astonishing world . . . Here is revealed the bewildering possibility of telegraphy without wires . . . This is no mere dream of a visionary philosopher. All the requisites needed to bring it within grasp of daily life are well within the possibilities of discovery, and are so reasonable and so clearly in the path of researches . . . that we may any day expect to hear that they have emerged from the realms of speculation to those of sober fact."

This prophecy, made by an Englishman, was first fulfilled in England. The Italian government had refused to encourage Marconi in his experiments; and so the twenty-two-year-old inventor, accompanied by his mother, set out for London. Here he found a sympathetic ear, and a public amazed at his wizardry. "What," asked a reporter, pointing to Marconi's instruments, "do you propose to do with them?"

"I propose to send signals over the air."

"Even through a fog?"

"Yes."

"Do you mean to tell us that your signals will penetrate anything and everything?"

"I am forced, as a result of my experiments, to believe so."

And he went on to prove the validity of his belief. At first he sent his messages over a distance of 100 yards; then, by "pumping" more and more power into the transmitter, he extended the distance to three miles, eight miles, eighteen miles. And then, on March 27, 1899, Marconi pressed the sending-key of a wireless which he had set up at Wimereux, a village on the west coast of France. Across the channel, at Dover, an assistant was "listening in." A few moments of tense silence, and then a return signal over the wireless from Dover to Wimereux: "Your message received. Perfect."

The bystanders overwhelmed Marconi with their congratulations. But the young inventor brushed them aside. He was too busy for all these superficialities. "Now that we have conquered the channel," he said simply, "our next job is to tackle the sea."

III

THE ENGLISH GOVERNMENT issued patents to Marconi; and a group of English businessmen organized for him a Wireless Telegraph and Signal Company, with a capitalization of 100,000 pounds. Thus encouraged, Marconi went on with his experiments. He established a series of stations along the coastline of England, and he equipped a number of vessels with broadcasting instruments. In this way he made it possible for the vessels to report their positions from time to time and to call, whenever necessary, for help. Even the skeptics were now becoming slowly convinced. "There's something in this wireless after all."

And one foggy night in April, 1899, came the first real test as to the value of wireless telegraphy. In the heavy darkness the steamer *R. F. Matthews* collided with the *East Goodwin Lightship*. A frantic signal into the air, and the miracle happened. The signal was intercepted, lifeboats were sent to the stricken vessel, and the entire crew was saved.

Thus far, however, Marconi had succeeded only in short-range communications. To be sure, he had dreamed of spanning the Atlantic with his wireless. But such dreams, believed the sober-minded academicians, were preposterous. When S. S. McClure printed in his magazine an article about the achievements and the expectations of Marconi, a professor at Clark University called the publisher to task for "foisting such absurdities upon the public." It was impossible, insisted the professor, for wireless telegraphy to travel over long stretches of the earth's surface. "The laws of physics are against it." The earth is round; but the Hertzian waves, maintained the professor, lead straight up into the air, or at most travel off at a tangent away from the curvature of the earth. Thus a wireless message, broadcast—let us say —from New York, might travel to Jersey City, or even to Newark; but beyond that point, it would trail away from the earth on a tangent into infinity.

Such were the cocksure theories of the academicians. But the experiments of Marconi knocked these theories into a cocked hat. They demonstrated a very strange and very important property of the Hertzian waves. *These waves flow over the ocean of the atmosphere in a curve that is parallel to the curvature of the earth.* "The Hertzian waves, therefore," insisted Marconi, "will eventually carry a message, just as the ocean waves can carry a ship, all the way around the earth."

And he proceeded with his experiments to transmute *that* dream into a reality. Little by little he extended the range of his wireless to twenty-five miles, fifty miles, seventy-five miles. He was invited to America to report by wireless the international boat race between the *Columbia* and the *Shamrock*. The report was a sensational success; but to Marconi, it was merely a relaxation that fitted him for further efforts. His fixed purpose now was to span the Atlantic with his wireless. "Do you really think this is possible?" asked a reporter.

"I cannot think otherwise," replied Marconi. "All we have to do is to build a transmitter powerful enough to hurl the waves across the sea."

IV

THURSDAY, December 12, 1901. Marconi, frail, sad, keen-eyed, thin-lipped, is sitting at a desk in the John Cabot Memorial Building—a bleak tower upon a bleak hill on the Newfoundland coast. He holds a telephone receiver close to his ear and gazes through the window over the thundering Atlantic. The waves are too blustery today. Will he be able to intercept the wireless that is about to be flashed across for the first time from England to America? For a moment he takes his eyes off the horizon and looks up into the air. A kite, driven by a heavy wind, is tugging violently at a copper antenna that holds it fastened to a pole. Will the slender wire stand up against the fury of the storm? On several previous experiments the kite had been torn away from its mooring. But this must not happen today. Two continents are awaiting the outcome of *this* experiment—and almost universally with an attitude of cynical disbelief. *"Of course it can't be done!"*

Marconi waited and wondered. *He* knew that it *could* be done. And yet . . .

The signals in England were to begin at 3 o'clock English time —that is, at 11:30 Newfoundland time.

Half-past eleven. Twelve. Twelve-fifteen. Marconi sits glued to the earphone. No sound other than the lashing of the wind. Perhaps he was wrong after all? Perhaps the skeptical public was right?

Twelve-twenty. Twelve-twenty-five. Twelve-twenty-nine. How slowly the minutes dragged! It looked as if the whole thing would be a fiasco after all. Wouldn't the public have a good laugh over it? Another pseudo-scientist with his crazy dreams . . . Oh, well . . .

Twelve-thirty. Marconi grew suddenly tense. Were his senses deceiving him? No, there they were. Three clicks, faint but unmistakable. The signal agreed upon—the Morse code for the letter *S*.

Marconi went back to his hotel, but spoke to no one about the amazing news. He first wanted to verify the experiment on the next day, and on the day after that—he had arranged with his assistant in England to repeat the signal on three successive days. On every one of these occasions the experiment was crowned with equal success.

He was now ready to make his statement to the press. On December 15 the *New York Times* featured the historic words: "Guglielmo Marconi announces . . . the most wonderful scientific development of recent times. He states that he has received electric signals across the Atlantic Ocean . . ."

And while the world thundered its praise, Marconi went quietly on with his work.

V

In MARCH, 1905, Marconi took a vacation from his work. He married an Irish noblewoman, Beatrice O'Brien, daughter of Lord Inchiquin. A brief enchanted honeymoon, followed by nineteen years of disenchantment. Marconi was not the domestic type. He belonged too much to the world to cultivate the patient intimacies of a happy marriage. Though the union resulted in three children, it was finally dissolved (1924). A second marriage (1927), this time to a beautiful Italian, the Countess Maria Cristina Bezzi-Scali, proved to be more successful. Marconi had learned to play as he grew older—he bought a yacht, the *Elettra*, which served him both as a laboratory and as a pleasure palace—and his newly acquired ability to relax resulted in quieter nerves and a less irritable temper.

The rest of his life was a continual process of growing young. "Science," he said, "keeps one forever youthful. I cannot understand the savant who grows bowed and yellowed in a workroom.

MARCONI

I like to be out in the open looking at the universe, asking it questions, letting the mystery of it soak right into the mind, admiring the wonderful beauty of it all, and then think my way to the truth of things." He lost his right eye in an automobile accident, and remained unbowed. He won the Nobel Prize—the highest of awards—in physics, and remained unspoiled. And it was in this courageous and unassuming pursuit of his experiments the perfection of the wireless and the conception of its even greater offspring, the radio—dreams to encircle the globe, to reach the ear of someone listening in upon another planet ("even *this* may some day be possible, who knows?")—that death overtook him on the *Elettra* (July 20, 1937). "And he embarked upon another ship to continue his explorations in another sea."

ENRICO CARUSO

Important Dates in Life of Enrico Caruso

1873—Born at Naples.

1884—Began to sing in choir.

1894—Made his début at Teatro Novo, in Naples.

1898—Achieved first triumph at Milan.

1899–1903—Sang in Europe and in South America.

1903—First appeared at Metropolitan Opera House, New York.

1903–21—Leading tenor at the Metropolitan.

1921—Died, August 2, in Italy.

Enrico Caruso

1873–1921

DUSK, and a drab Neapolitan street. Along the narrow sidewalk hurries a small boy. He staggers beneath a burden too large for his thin frame. "It is the treasure of Marcellino's household," whispers a shawled figure.

"Of a certainty," answers another, "it is little Errico Caruso."

Into a lightless chamber trudges the boy. Dumping the bundle, he kneels by a bedside. A thin hand reaches out and clasps his own. "See, Mamma, I have brought firewood. And five soldi."

"Did you sing well, Errico mio?"

"Yes, Mamma. But not at first."

"So?"

"I was angry, and threw my medals at Father Bronzetti's feet. Pappa made me kiss the Father's hands and feet. Then I was happy and sang well."

A pat on the black curls rewarded the confession. With competence born of long practice, the child lit a lamp and began preparation of the evening meal. A thin cry arrested his activities.

"A baby sister," the woman smiled feebly.

"May she live long," he whispered.

"And not be taken by God like the seventeen others," she said, crossing herself. "Where is your father now, Errico?"

"He takes himself to the wineshop, as usual, Mamma."

A long sigh. "Only eight, Carissimo, and already you are the man of the family."

Only eight! And already the soft contralto voice is charming all listeners. In choirs and at carnivals, it is Errico that the crowds clamor for. At school he is industrious and painstaking. Father Bronzetti has refused to accept tuition for this bright scholar. His teacher in penmanship recognizes and encourages a talent for portraiture.

At ten, having outgrown Bronzetti, Errico is earning money. Is learning opera arias. Everywhere he is in demand. Confident, he asks for a larger remuneration. Refused, he enters the establishment of a maker of fountains. At night he sings and serenades. But the jingling coins quickly find their way through a hole in his pocket. Even in childhood, Errico possesses the open hand.

Slapped by a teacher for his use of Neapolitan slang, he played hooky, haunting the railroad yards. From this wonderland of noise and dirt, his father took him to work with him.

Days he worked. But nights were given to music. Yet with all these activities he found time to nurse his mother who, after the birth of her last child, never regained her health. The bonds of affection between the two strengthened with the years. Her wise counsel guided him through many trials.

"Tonight they said I sang like an angel, Mamma."

"Then remember it is God who gives angel voices, and no doing of yours. You must work hard, Errico, and never get the swelled head."

"Yes, Mamma, I will work. And I will sing for you."

Sensitive and considerate, Errico wins friends easily. The bright Neapolitan sun smiles down. The sunny, cherub-faced lad smiles back. It is a good world. Good, too, to have a voice that can earn money and give pleasure.

May Festival. All Naples is agog. Gay crowds throng to hear

the beautiful choir. Errico is inspired, and dedicates his singing to the finest of mothers.

But wait! A gentle tap on his shoulder. A sympathetic voice whispers in his ear. "Be brave, Errico, your mother is dead." Kind hands support the stunned boy, and lead him home. Saddened by his bereavement, he is not to sing again for many days.

II

TIME, the healer, performed her wonted miracle. Once more the youth lifted his voice in song. But time had wrought another change as well. The sweet contralto was now a tenor voice. In the Caruso home, too, there was change. Pappa Marcellino had taken to himself a second wife. This woman loved his three children. But above all, she adored the warmhearted Errico— an adoration which he returned in full.

A fellow musician speaks of further lessons. "But I have not the money," explains Errico.

" 'Tis no matter, you have the fine voice. Come with me to Vergine." Vergine listens, lips pouting. He ponders. "It is a small voice," he decides, "like wind whistling through a window." Nevertheless he draws a contract whereby Errico is to repay the master from future earnings. Hard work begins under this teacher, whose first lesson is humility. How well the youth applies himself! Vergine comes to regard this hardworking protégé with tender admiration. But a shadow falls. Errico is called to military service. Sadly he parts from his family, bids farewell to music, to the bright cafés and gay card games.

Now it is Easter morn. The Caruso family looks up from breakfast, startled to see a dusty Errico entering the door. He sports a silky black mustache, and swaggers. Discharged!

What is this, only thirty days a soldier? "The Major objected to my practicing," he tells them.

"Who wouldn't?" Marcellino emphasizes the question with his shoulders.

"You cannot be a soldier and a singer, the Major said." Errico enjoyed the suspense he was arousing. "So now the Major arranges for brother Giovanni to take my place, and I devote myself to music."

"So. And who pays for this?" asks Marcellino, frowning.

"It is of no importance," replies Errico. "I have the voice, I will make the career."

Vergine welcomes back his favorite pupil. More work, and much harder. At twenty-one he is playful and convivial. But his fondness for wine and women does not interfere with serious work.

Hard work brings reward. Vergine has asked Daspuro, impresario of the La Scala Opera, to give audition to the boy.

"Only twenty-two," Daspuro frowns. "It is unheard of in opera."

"But the voice, it is of a liquid gold, Padrone!"

"Well, then, we listen," Daspuro agrees.

La Scala! Errico is dazzled by vistas that he dare not let his imagination traverse. A single electric bulb pierces the gloom of the vast stage. Into the small circle of light walks the bewitched youth, every sensitive nerve aquiver to the significance of this opportunity. The music starts, Errico advances, arms extended, offering to the world its own glory. A few wild, meaningless gestures. A few cracked, sour notes—then silence and dizziness. Vergine leaps over the footlights and embraces the tottering form. Outside Errico orients himself. Wildly he weeps on the old shoulder. "I have failed, Maestro. Never will I sing."

"No, no, Little One. It was because you are the true artist, this fiasco. Vergine asked that of you for which you were not ready."

"This is true?" Errico's eyes beg confirmation.

"Truly, Amico." Vergine's eyes glow. "We make our climb more slow. And some day—why, some day La Scala will come to us."

III

It is as Vergine foretold, Errico thinks. A small success here, a larger one there. And now a whole season's contract. And clothes! "Per Dio! How these associates will envy me my wardrobe. Such color! Such variety!"

A contract to sing in Cairo. This Egypt is gorgeous. How the somber Egyptians stare! Life is a feast of fun. How funny it was last night. In *Manon Lescaut* one forgot the score, then propped it against the back of Manon. So that the dying beauty must expire in upright rigidity. And today! Tumbling into the Nile was not so good. A little embarrassing, too, when no cab driver would allow all that mud on his precious cushions. But riding home on a donkey, wonderful! How they gaped!

Home again. A gradual rise, one rung of the ladder at a time. Setbacks, yes. But they have their good side, too. One learns to work harder, to be more careful in selecting friends.

Still the voice is not matured. Nor is the man a finished singer. An offer of the tenor role in *I Puritan* must be refused. "My voice is too short," Errico explains. "Those high A's and B flats are the bête noire."

"I will make the voice longer," promises the great Lombardi. Under his tutelage the voice grows strong and true. The high notes pour forth in a stream of velvet richness.

Season follows season; and Errico's climb, though not meteoric, is steady. He has long outdistanced the young tenors, is now taking his place among the established favorites. The great Puccini himself has asked him to create the role of Rodolfo in *La Bohême*. An auspicious début this. Errico soars to new heights, for inspiration stands by his side. Ada Giachetti, the vivacious soprano, has come into his life. This experienced singer guides him through the labyrinths of opera intrigue. Their association ripens into love. And for many years she is to fill his life.

St. Petersburg! In the company of the famous. All members

of this troupe have arrived. No petty jealousies here, but cama-
raderie instead. All are artists, and each has a helping hand for
the other. Czar Nicholas II commands a performance. And for
Errico a gift from royalty. Gold cuff links, diamond studded.
How his fellow countrymen will appreciate him now!

But in Italy the anticipated ovation is not forthcoming. At
home he must combat the rumor that in Russia he has lost his
voice. Many times in his career is he to meet this same vicious
whispering campaign. Always it fills him with despair and fury.
It is so hard for a great soul to understand the envy of little souls.

South America. The Latins melt like snow before the warm
sunshine of his music.

This time there is much to make his return joyous. His fame
has preceded him, and Italy awaits her celebrated son with open
arms. Even fonder arms await him. Ada Giachetti has presented
him with a son. They name the child Rodolfo, in honor of their
meeting in *La Bohême*. With this new gladness in his heart,
Errico rises to even greater success.

IV

LA SCALA? Why, now La Scala comes for Caruso. Into this
début he puts his entire soul. The formidable goal of all opera
singers, this is the crucial rung of the ladder. To succeed here is
to have an assured reputation. Failure here, oblivion. The début
is not so brilliant as Caruso could have wished. But he has won
for himself a secure place. "The voice is immature, but of a
golden purity," declares Toscanini, whose baton has waved him
to success.

"He has the true fire," agrees the impresario Gatti-Casazza,
"and some day all the world will acclaim this Caruso."

Buenos Aires—Monte Carlo—Naples, his own beloved city.
But here disaster waits. Prince di Castagneto dominates a clique
that can make or break a singer. Those who kowtow to this petty
dictator receive approbation—woe to the others. Caruso, true

democrat, insists on winning his laurels through his art alone. The Prince's cohorts all but drown his efforts with hisses. The press, too cowardly to flout the Prince, gives only lukewarm notices. "Never will I sing in Naples again," declares Caruso. "If I come here, it will be only to eat a dish of spaghetti."

England calls—England, the terror of every artist. Those English can be as chilling as their own continual rains. At Covent Garden the managers were like a group of housewives determining the worth of a watermelon. "They wished to feel if I was ripe enough to buy," he said. "But I was confident of my own red ripeness." His confidence was justified. The jammed hall responded with an enthusiasm unsurpassed by any Latin audience. The English skies shone their bluest, and Caruso answered with his best.

Now he could turn his eyes toward America. "My Star of the North can now rise."

Confidence has given swagger to his gait. Luxurious living has given volume to his contour. Wealth has given flamboyance to his wardrobe. He is a man of substance now, and such a man must have a villa. Near Florence he purchases the Villa alle Panche. There he installs the Giachetti and their son Rodolfo, along with the art treasures he has begun to collect. Many frown at his vulgar display. Who is this Neapolitan nobody, who sets himself up with such airs? Not yet thirty, and he places himself amongst the world's elect.

They will soon see who Caruso is. Taking Ada, he sails for America, to conquer a new continent.

V

CARUSO adores America. The crowds, the lights, the comforts—above all, the order and the efficiency which prevail at the Metropolitan Opera. And the audiences adore Caruso. More slow to respond are the critics. They find his voice good, but his acting indifferent. The élite find him plebeian, his stoutness and his awkwardness displeasing after the aristocratic Jean de Reszke, for whose crown he is contending. Caruso frets under continual comparison with his predecessor. "Yes, a beautiful voice," he mocks, "velvet, everything that is to be expected from an Italian voice, but—Jean!" Patience, Enrico. They are giving way. And soon all the world will proclaim that Caruso is incomparable.

He does not like American cooking; and in his own home, himself prepares spaghetti for his many friends—the plump be-ringed hands delicately heaping large platterfuls of the aromatic dish.

He feeds his friends, and showers gifts upon them. The faster his money pours into his pocket, the faster it pours out through the ever widening hole of his reckless generosity.

His personal expenses, too, are mounting. There is a second son now. And Caruso is ambitious for his boys. The constant shuttling back and forth over the Atlantic seems little more than a ferry trip, so many times has it been made. On both sides of the ocean, ever rising tribute, ever increasing success. His villas are aglitter with treasures gathered from every part of the world. And everywhere, titles—decorations—royal gifts. Fate has smiled upon Enrico. On his way to London now, whither Ada and his two sons have preceded him. It is a soberer, clean shaven Caruso who paces the deck with a friend. Dignity has replaced the swagger. "Are you royalty," he jests, "that you are the only one aboard who receives a cablegram?" No answer. Caruso stops and looks at the companion, who avoids his eyes. "Let me see the cablegram." He snatches the paper. "Madonna mia. My father is dead!" Weeping wildly, he is led to his stateroom—there to finish the trip in a state of collapse.

But in London he hopes to find solace in the arms of his beloved. He hurries to the house. His glad cries bring no re-sponse. Rushing about from room to room, he finds . . . empti-ness. Ada is gone—this woman who, for eleven years, has been a part of himself. In stunned silence, he sits. As darkness falls he refuses light or food. "What opera shall I announce tomorrow?" inquires Tosti, seeking to rally him. "Cancel all engagements," Caruso answers. "The faithless one has taken not only my joy, but my voice as well."

"You must sing, the houses are sold out."

"Then let it be *Pagliacci*. For am I not a betrayed clown?"

As never before, the golden notes of Pagliacci's grief poured forth. The audience went mad with delight. If the clown's face was deathly white, they could not know it wasn't make-up. Nor could they know that the heartbreak which inspired their idol was all too real.

A sad summer that passed slowly. Possessions and pleasures could not fill the great emptiness. Nor could warm companionships and gay parties still the gnawing hunger that possessed him. Gratefully he welcomed autumn and work.

VI

It is a changed Caruso that the world welcomes back. The eyes still twinkle, but with a cynical gleam. Bitter lines draw down the once cherubic mouth. Violent headaches are etching lines in the brow. Grief has given restraint to his gestures. And the voice. Per Dio, it is not a voice but a miracle! Sorrow has brought maturity. The golden velvet ripples with an ease that is almost divine.

But Caruso is not well. The headaches are past enduring. He is forced to miss one performance after another. A serious matter —something must be done about it. There will have to be an operation upon a vocal cord. To Italy, then, and after the operation, a long anxious convalescence.

And on top of it all, still another anxiety. The clouds of war (1914) are gathering and darkening. Worried over the situation, Caruso cannot gain strength. Now that Germany has declared war, what will Italy do?

A slow and fretful recovery. It seems as though he will never be well. But there is work to do—relief for the Italians stranded in Germany. Forgetting his own troubles, Caruso lends his voice in the cause of his unfortunate compatriots.

And then another call to America.

Onward march the years, and ever higher ascends his North Star. Caruso stands alone, on a pinnacle never before attained by a singer. Playful still—but his play is now gentler. The practical jokes that once delighted the audiences, but embarrassed his fellow artists, have given way to a kindly humor. He is more than ever ready to lend a helping hand. To Chaliapin, nonplused by Toscanini's temper, Caruso observes, "He is like the barking dog who never bites." And of Caruso Chaliapin relates, "His face is full of sweetness. He has the voice I have waited all my life to hear."

Caruso takes his work more seriously than ever. "It is not enough that I act and sing," he says, "I must *live* that man which the author meant."

Serene years now. Italy had joined the Allies, had fought side by side with his second homeland, America. And then, peace.

But in Caruso's heart there is a new restlessness. Forty-five, and he is in love with an American girl—Dorothy Benjamin. His friends are aghast. An American girl for Enrico! It is not fitting. The Benjamin family, too, have set obstacles in the pathway of romance. They demand a financial settlement humiliating to the pair. Enrico and Dorothy are married in secret, with only a few close friends present.

Now it is Caruso's twenty-fifth Jubilee. White and nervous, he receives homage on the stage of the Metropolitan.

"It is not the glory of your voice I have in mind," declares Otto Kahn, "though it is the most glorious voice of a generation . . . but in your case we admire the voice, the art, the man."

Trembling with emotion, Caruso clutches the flag of New York City, presented by the Mayor. Supported by his secretary, he is barely able to thank his admirers.

VII

CARUSO'S ENTHUSIASMS are as keen as ever. But the gestures are less vehement. Gone are the buoyancy and the exuberance that were once his outstanding characteristics. He is growing thin, and the headaches now torture him with hardly a letup. Adverse reviews worry him, shaking his self confidence. To Gatti-Casazza he confides his fears, saying that he wishes to resign.

"These reviewers," Casazza retorts, "they must make themselves important. Take my advice and don't read them."

Caruso shakes his head. "So long as I feel I cannot please, I must read them. If I sing as those critics say I sing, it is time I appeared no more."

"Tonight you sing Samson—you will see then," Gatti-Casazza assures him. After the performance, head in hands, he awaits the verdict. Glorious! The North Star still glitters as brightly as ever. Yet doubt plagues him. His nervousness increases.

But there is one spot where he finds release from his nervous tension. It is home, where his toddling daughter Gloria waits. Each passing month casts her more surely in the image of her father. The same imp-cherub face is hers. For hours they romp together. He delights in the nicknames she invents for him.

And now there are so many engagements to fill, so many demands on his time. Worry and insufficient rest have exacted their toll. Weakened, Caruso takes a chill. Spitting and coughing, with a pain racking his left side, he is ordered to bed. "No, I cannot do it. I cannot disappoint my public."

VIII

ONCE MORE it is *Pagliacci*. Before the mimic theater stands Caruso, in his clown's suit. The audience thrills as he swings into the famous aria. The golden voice swells, filling the remotest

[237]

corners of the huge Opera House. A blinding pain stabs his left side. The high note ends in a cracked scream. Clutching at the curtains of the mock theater, he staggers back, to fall sobbing into the arms of his secretary. "My voice—I thought—it was gone."

Impatiently he brushes aside suggestions that he discontinue. Upon the stage again—a coughing spell interrupts the singing. From the wings, handkerchiefs are passed by trembling hands. They come away from his mouth crimson. A hemorrhage! Now all his objections are of no avail. The curtain is rung down, the frightened audience dismissed.

Followed anxious days. Heroically he strove to keep the seriousness of his condition from his family. Loyally they joined his game of pretense. But a frightened hush pervaded the house. A few days before Christmas, Casazza held a conference with the doctor. They listened to his singing. "There is nothing wrong with his voice," decided the doctor. "He can go back to his work."

Casazza turned to Caruso. "This is a matter for you alone to decide, Amico."

"I will sing, Padrone."

On Christmas Eve his admirers heard, for the last time, the inimitable voice—poured forth in the music of La Juive. Next day, in the bath, his piercing screams brought the household running. Physicians, hastily summoned, looked grave. A contracted left lung, and paralysis of the right hand.

Long months of slow convalescence; and gradually, life returning to the hand. Then Sorrento, where sunshine brings returning strength. Once more father and daughter romp in the garden, laughter again fills the rooms. But there is still one thing to be discovered. A few chords on the piano, a little tentative vocalizing—then confidence and ease. The glorious songs of La Bohême fill the room, while the assembled household weeps with joy.

A crashing exultant chord. Caruso turns to his family. "Madonna mia, it is a miracle! Tomorrow we journey to Pompeii, and there we give thanks to Our Lady."

IX

Before the shrine of Our Lady of Pompeii the family knelt; while Caruso, weeping, offered prayers of gratitude. Their rejoicing, however, was premature. The trip had proved too great a strain. Returning from his devotions, Caruso collapsed in the hotel. Examining physicians pronounced an abscess of the left lung—Rome and an immediate operation his only chance. But Caruso was too weak to be moved. Through the night and late into the next day he lingered, for the most part with mind wandering. In rational moments he clung to his wife's hand, pleading feebly: "Doro, don't let me die."

Toward noon, a gentle smile spread over his features, erasing the lines of recent pain and stress. The same cherubic smile that had been his childhood charm. The Neapolitan choir boy had joined the eternal choir.

PADEREWSKI

Important Dates in Life of Paderewski

1860—Born at Podolia.

1876–77—Made first concert tour.

1879–81—Taught piano at Warsaw Conservatory.

1887—First public appearance in Vienna.

1890—First public appearance in London.

1891—Toured the United States.

1895—Founded Paderewski Fund for musical education.

1914–18—Worked in behalf of Polish freedom.

1919—Became premier of Poland.

1921—Abandoned politics for music.

1939—Reëntered politics as President of Polish Parliament in Exile.

1941—Died in New York City.

Ignace Jan Paderewski

1860–1941

"HIS IMPERIAL MAJESTY is pleased that the world's most eminent musician is a Russian." With these words Czar Nicholas II invited Paderewski, the artist, to give a command performance. It was Paderewski, the patriot, who replied: "His Majesty is mistaken, I am a Pole."

In 1860, Poland was writhing under the yoke of Russian oppression. On November 6 of that year, Ignace Jan Paderewski was born. With his first breath he inhaled the love of freedom.

And of music. Every life has its tempo. That of the young Ignace Jan was rapid and strong, like the waltzes and the mazurkas that expressed the yearning of the Polish people. A people habituated to tragedy. At three, the sensitive child watched his father taken prisoner as the Cossacks burned Polodia and killed most of the inhabitants. The memory of that day was never quite erased from his impressionable mind.

His studies began under an itinerant instructor. It was not long before he exhausted the knowledge of this man. But from him he had learned hard work and self-discipline. At twelve he was quite certain as to what he wanted to do. Music was the essence of his being, and the piano his chosen instrument.

He met with disappointment, however, when he entered the Warsaw Conservatory. His small hands, they told him, were not suited for the mastering of the keyboard. "Better try the flute, where strong lungs will serve you well."

He listened politely—and stuck to the piano. With that capacity for work which was to characterize his every undertaking, he soon overmastered the handicap of his small hands.

A child full of music and full of play. Twice expelled for his pranks, often he went supperless to bed. Great privation to an active boy. Already he was tall, with a shock of auburn hair above a thin poetic face. His striking appearance, as well as his unvarying good nature, won him devotion at every turn.

Especially from Kerntopf, friend of the Paderewskis and patron of the arts. Recognizing the youngster's genius, Kerntopf took him into his home. Here food was plentiful and life gay. In Kerntopf's company, Paderewski thrilled to the glories of the opera and made the acquaintance of the musical great.

A contagious atmosphere. Ambition seized the sixteen-year-old pianist. With another Jan, violinist, he toured the provinces in violation of the Conservatory rules. From this venture the two virtuosos earned little money, but considerable experience. They had learned how much there was still to learn. And, re-instated at the Conservatory, they worked the harder.

Jan's eighteenth year, an eventful occasion. He fell in love. The girl was Antonina Korsak, his fellow student. Appointed to an instructorship at the Conservatory, he married Antonina. Though their income was meager, and their home but a single room—he had refused a proffered dowry—their union was extremely happy. Antonina's faith in his genius, her great love and her constant help inspired him to heights seldom reached by one so young. His happiness was too complete. He had a terrible foreboding that it wouldn't last.

II

"MUSIC is the only art that lives," he said. He had now begun to live in earnest. After the day's practice, he gave concerts and private lessons; and for relaxation, he composed. His *Impromptu in F Major* saw publication in his nineteenth year. Its success was immediate, but it didn't turn his head. Always there was work, practice, self-criticism—and further work. And always, the radiant presence of Antonina.

And then tragedy singled him out for the testing of his soul. Antonina died in childbirth, leaving behind a sickly son. On her deathbed she had urged that Paderewski take the dowry offered by her parents for the first-born. Paderewski must continue his own studies, she insisted. "Some day you will repay this sum a hundredfold."

Widowed at twenty, he turned his back upon the past, facing courageously an undecided future. "I am grown . . . out of that which saddens me," he said, adopting his father's motto— "Majesty unbroken by misfortune."

A year of study in Berlin. Here he plays for Rubenstein, who holds out to him friendly encouragement. From Berlin to the Tatra Mountain region; and thence to Vienna, mecca of musicians. He longs to study under the great Lechetitsky, but indecision halts his steps.

In the lovely mountain district, he composed the *Tatra Album* —a collection of haunting folk melodies. Here, too, he met the famous Modjeska, and the soft-eyed Madame Gorska. "He looks like a Botticelli angel," Modjeska said, adding that he hypnotized his listeners because he himself was hypnotized.

The friendship of this great woman proved more than inspirational. It included the practical. Advising him to go on with his concert work, Modjeska assisted in the raising of funds for the continuance of his study.

At last, a pupil of Lechetitsky—most exacting of masters. With great relish Paderewski attacked the grueling labors assigned him. An offer of professorship at the Strasbourg Conservatory came to him as a great surprise. He still looked upon himself as a student. One reluctant year of teaching at Strasbourg, and then he was back with the master, laboring with almost more than human energy.

At last Lechetitsky presented his "finished product" to the public. Ignace Jan Paderewski, age twenty-six—a miracle of sublime beauty that electrified the musical world. Ecstasy, adoration, fame.

And a sublime doubt. If an artist be truly gifted, he is truly humble before his gift. It is his, that he may share it with the world. Paderewski felt exalted, and afraid. The sensation of his début impelled him to question. Was this but a freak of fate, or had he real genius? And questioning, he found within himself the answer. His the divine spark but to tend, to fan into a flame that would burn ever more brightly. More work and harder.

Paris—still greater triumph. The critics declare they cannot do justice to this genius, having exhausted all superlatives. "With the suddenness of a lightning stroke . . . an inspired poet took possession of the keyboard," one of them wrote. But neither acclamation nor social success could turn the head of this giant with the iron will and the impishness of a small boy.

The English were slower to respond. Four concerts were arranged for London. The first was poorly attended, the reception cold. One critic said he expected the piano to break down under Paderewski's pounding. And another: "The result of his labors may be marvelous, but it is not music." George Bernard Shaw alone hailed him.

Paderewski remained stubbornly undismayed. With his innate sense of artistic responsibility, he fulfilled the engagement. The fourth concert sold out. But the critics were still unconvinced.

Paderewski accepted the challenge presented by the reserved British temperament. Overruling his manager's objections, he insisted that the advance notices in the Provinces contain all the

Marconi

Enrico Caruso

adverse criticisms. This psychological gambit proved his knowledge of men. The Provinces went wild with enthusiasm.

Once more in London, he found himself the darling of a nation. Received by the Queen, courted by the great, besieged by autograph hunters for the signature of that magical hand, he remained through it all gracious, whimsical and unspoiled. Still that mischievous genius of a child.

He was invited to America. Here his reception was without precedent. Carnegie Hall could not hold the crowds that wrestled to fight their way in. His first appearance established a custom that was to endure for the forty years of his returns. At the conclusion of the concert, the audience rushed to the stage and refused to leave until the master had played encore after encore.

Yet Paderewski disliked crowds. He was one of those rich rare spirits who could best commune with himself. His most beloved "holy place of communion" during his residence in New York was the "wilderness" of Prospect Park. There he "roamed unbeaten by-paths, knocking his head against the stars."

Though he loathed the adulation of the insincere rabble, he loved the appreciation of those who really thrilled to his playing. Even if they happened to be musically uninformed. A mathematical knowlege of notes does not necessarily mean a sensitive ear. His manager had hired a special train for his prolonged trips across the United States. In his private car he practiced daily, the railroad men gathering around him to listen. "Gosh," remarked one of them, "the man plays like they must play in Heaven!"

A master musician, with a master chef. It was one of his own countrymen who presided over the cuisine. Cooking to Paderewski was one of the fine arts—an art to which neither the British nor the Americans had been able to attain.

His chef catered to him as to a child. He adored this "angel-child" entrusted to his care. Such an impractical and gentle and generous soul! Too generous by far. One day he instructed his chef to feed any tramps who might come to ask for food. The word having been passed around the hobo "jungles," there thronged to Paderewski's door so great a horde of hungry bellies that the guardian of the larder was compelled to rescind the order—without, of course, the knowledge of Paderewski.

III

A GENIUS with a personality of many facets, he shed benediction like a rainbow upon all manner of persons and things. Oftentimes his sympathetic universality led him into strange situations. Once, while on tour, his sympathies were enlisted in behalf of a Polish woman on the city streets, prostrate and alone. Speaking no English, she could not explain her plight. Hastening to her side, Paderewski acted as interpreter. He learned that she was ill, had her removed to a hospital at his own expense, and found time for daily visits to her.

Yet this generosity of Paderewski's was not altogether of the selfless type. If he was kind to others, he insisted that others be fair to him. While he was touring the western states, a couple of overenthusiastic young men persuaded him to perform in a small town, guaranteeing him $2000. The performance over, the youngsters found that their receipts were insufficient to cover Paderewski's fee. They came to him with their dilemma, and waited fearfully for his verdict.

The Maestro assumed a serious air. Reminding them that their responsibilities must be met, he suggested a practical way out of the difficulty. They were to pay all expenses; and then, having deducted a percentage for their own efforts, they were to give him what was left. This "justice tempered with mercy" secured not only two friends for Paderewski, but one friend for Poland. For one of these boys was Herbert Hoover, who many years later (1917–1918) was to minister so valiantly to the starving millions in Paderewski's native land.

IV

MORE TOURS, more concerts, more triumphs—and over it all hung the shadow of his son's illness. The Baroness do Rosen— Madame Gorska—had long loved and mothered the motherless boy. After her marriage to Paderewski (in 1899), the three had become a closely-knit and happy family. Though confined to a wheelchair, the boy played an interesting part in the brilliant gatherings about him. He had developed an early talent for satirical writing, and often he amused the company with his clever sketches of their foibles.

Yet his days, his father knew, were numbered. Having heard of an Augsburg specialist who might be of help, he sent his son to that city.

On the way, the boy caught a chill which developed into pneumonia. He died at nineteen. This second bereavement left an emptiness in Paderewski's heart. "Get away from life, Jan. Leave the clatter and the chatter of the world and submerge yourself for a while completely in your music and your thoughts."

He rented a villa at Morges, in the lake country of Switzerland. Here, surrounded by historic ruins, he tended his flowers and brooded upon the mystery of life and death. The sinking of a seed in the ground, the decay, the resurgence into a thing of beauty in the upper air. Was not this a symbol of all existence? It was as if God had said: "Here in the syllables of the flowers, I teach you the story of man." Death is but the rebirth into greater fulfillment, the fragrant final flowering of the seed of life.

There was something prophetic in Paderewski's choice of a home—Switzerland, the eternal abode of freedom. Two years after he had settled there, he made his first important address to the Polish people. A call to rebellion, yet delivered in veiled words. For no man of Poland could freely speak his mind. Patriotic expression, even in the medium of fiction and poetry, was drastically banned. Paderewski's audience, accustomed to interpreting the double entendre, understood the message hidden in his speech. Reverberations of his call—a battlecry for the resumption of hope—reached the tiniest village of Poland. Russia's police, alarmed, forbade publication of the speech. But too late. Already thousands of copies were being secretly distributed throughout the land. The Poles were hailing Paderewski as their new prophet.

A prophet at the keyboard. A master of the two languages that most closely interpreted the aspirations of the human heart—salvation and song. He had dedicated his life to an unenslaved and singing Poland, an unenslaved and singing world.

Tours, lectures, compositions—and a great growing fatigue. He suffered now from frequent attacks of neuritis. Oftentimes he was compelled to cancel engagements. A reminder of his mortality. "Be humble, little man. With all your greatness, you have but an instrument of clay to interpret a soul of fire."

More and more he directed the fire of his soul toward the struggles of his homeland. At the Chopin Panegyric he besought his countrymen: "Let us brace our hearts to fresh endurance . . . the nation cannot perish that has a spirit so great and immortal."

V

NINETEEN-FOURTEEN, at Sarajevo, the rash impulse of a student rocks the world. To Paderewski, familiar with the political setup and the net of intrigue that crisscrosses all Europe, the outcome is inevitable. In the midst of a festival for his name day, he recalls the words of the poet Mickiewicz: "For the universal war of human liberation, O God, we beseech thee."

Amid the merriment a whispered message from his secretary. Soberly Paderewski relays to his guests the portentous words. Germany has declared a "condition of danger of war." Not one present but knows the significance of this announcement. Quickly and quietly the revelers depart.

Five o'clock the next afternoon. War has been officially declared. For the first time the beloved piano waits untouched as he reviews the situation of Poland. Will she rise to the occasion? And how, surrounded on all sides by belligerents, can she defend herself?

The next few weeks, a whirlwind of tragic events. Belgian and Polish neutrality are violated. The French and the English take arms. Russia proclaims a re-united Poland—a diplomatic move, designed to enlist the Polish fighting forces. And now Paderewski watches his homeland torn asunder, as Pole wars against Pole under Austrian, German and Russian colors. Sadly he speaks of this savagery, "sweeping away every sign of civilization."

The only music at Morges now is the crackling staccato of the guns, laying waste a continent. Converting the villa into a relief center with Madame Paderewska and his sister Antonina as his assistants, he worked tirelessly. A floodtide of civilian refugees and wounded soldiers kept pouring into Switzerland. Paderewski's magic fingers were now busy with something other than the making of music. "Like the touch of an angel—that cool, white, delicate hand of his."

The work had expanded beyond his means. Leaving Morges in the care of his sister, he sought help from the French and the British. He tried to interest them in the problem of the refugees, but more especially in the cause of Polish freedom. He distrusted the Czarist Russian "protection" of Poland. "The ball-bearings of that steam-roller are of wood, and its chauffeurs hail from Germany."

From England he went to America. Here he found his work already anticipated by Madame Sembrich and by other loyal Poles. He threw himself into the colossal task of uniting the Poles, both in America and abroad. And he set himself to win for Poland Allied recognition. Soon his speeches were applauded with as great acclaim as his concerts.

And then—1917—the Russian Revolution and the "liberation" of Poland. But this spectacle afforded him no joy. For Russia had made peace with the Kaiser, and both Russia and Poland lay crushed underneath the German heel.

Paderewski was now the unofficial ambassador of Polish aspiration to the United States. A familiar daily sight to New Yorkers, this tall magnetic man, striding through Central Park. Atop the lion's mane, a derby hat; and all around him, his fellow-patriots, with whom he pleads and gesticulates like a conductor leading an orchestra to a grand finale.

His ambition now is to reach the ear of Woodrow Wilson. This he accomplishes through Colonel House, Wilson's "other self." The dream of his life is about to be fulfilled. He has met "the one man his country needs. The hand of freedom is about to be extended to a nation struggling to be free."

VI

MORE DISAPPOINTMENT. Asking for a loan of a million dollars, Paderewski met with a flat refusal. "The United States cannot lend money to a committee."

"The United States," he replied fiercely, "can do anything!"

And now at last, his work is bringing desired results. On November 6, his birthday, he announces Polish independence from Germany. His country has become a world power. Hopefully he waits for America to espouse the Polish cause. For Colonel House has assured him that Wilson is sympathetic. Soon the first shot will be fired, House tells him.

The American Poles, united, have voted him plenipotentiary. Wilson has declared New Year's Day as Polish Day.

Triumphant, Paderewski takes a vacation from his politics. He starts upon a concert tour of the United States. While appearing in the West, he hears the echo of that promised first shot. Addressing the Senate, Woodrow Wilson has declared: "Statesmen everywhere are agreed that there should be a united, independent and autonomous Poland." The Union of Polish Falcons has voted an army of Kosciuszko, to fight side by side with the army of the United States.

Paderewski wired his manager: "Cancel tour. All my time is needed for Poland." At a previous concert he had said: "I declare that I will never play again until Poland is free." He continued to compose, from time to time. But the piano remained silent, except for one occasion. Aboard the *Concord*, Danzig bound, he played for hours upon an instrument so old and battered that many keys were missing. But to the assembled ship's company who listened enthralled, this did not matter. The great master had played for them alone.

Arrived at Danzig on Christmas Day, he was met with a great ovation. And with a sharp warning. For here he found himself beyond the protection of the Allies. Danger lay ahead in German-occupied territory. Staging a prearranged riot during a demonstration, the Germans aimed at the life of this man now recognized as the leader of Poland. But the young Poles, overcoming the guards and securing machine guns, quickly occupied the hotel where Paderewski was staying. A battle of three days, resulting in the death of many men on both sides. But the national hero remained unscathed.

Poland was a nation now; she had allies in arms. But internally she was a caldron of conflicting passions. No one better than Paderewski knew the stupendous task ahead. His the job to reconcile the divergent factions, and to create unity within the borders. But he was not afraid. From childhood he had been trained to manipulate difficult chords. His aide said of him, "His confidence is absolute . . . he never for an instant questions whether he will conquer."

And conquer he did. Conservative himself, he won the Radical Pilsudski and his followers over to a coalition government. When the new cabinet was formed (1919), Paderewski was appointed Premier and Minister of Foreign Affairs.

· VII

PADEREWSKI as Premier was a colorful picture. His physical daring was equal to his idealism. One day against the advice of his followers, he walked from a hotel lobby into the midst of a mob that was demonstrating against him. The courage of this tall old man, his whitening hair uncovered, startled the rioters into quiet. The simplicity and the sincerity of his words soon brought cries of "Paderewski, Viva!" The near riot turned into a triumphal march.

But Paderewski had no time for triumphs. There was work to be done. Though America had already recognized his new government, there were other countries still to be won. So on to Paris and the Council of Ten. To all who met him at this time, Paderewski's selfless idealism was his outstanding trait. He appeared as the champion not only of Poland, but of every bruised and persecuted group throughout the world.

Sixty now, with a little less spring to his walk. An ever so slight stoop to the shoulder. But his eyes are still atwinkle and his impishness is as rampant as ever. He has struck up an ardent friendship with Lloyd George, in spite of the Welshman's anti-Polish sentiments. Owing to the resemblance between the two, they are often mistaken for each other. A pair of grey-headed, mischievous gamins, tramping together through the streets of Paris and giggling over the pranks they have played upon the populace.

At last the friendship of England has been assured. Home now to harder work—and heartbreak. His enemies have concocted a bitter brew for him. He is accused of anti-Semitic activities. This slur against him has reached even across the seas; and America, his second home, has hearkened to the cry. Throwing open the doors of his house—and of his heart—he invites Morgenthau and others to investigate. He is exonerated of all charges, but the scar remains.

Paderewski

Mustapha Kemal Ataturk

And there is more strife on the wing. Pilsudski has become restive again, and his followers are in a maelstrom of revolt. Desiring, above all, peace for his country, Paderewski resigned. A time of tumult—strikes, riots, famine. At last, unable to stand idly by and wait for Pilsudski to act, Paderewski formed a new cabinet. He attended the first meeting—sad but hopeful. Sad, not because he was Premier no longer, but because Poland in her hour of freedom was unable to co-ordinate her forces. Hopeful, because he felt that the will of the people—a passionate will for peace—must triumph in the end.

Without bitterness, he removed his belongings from the Zamek. With his own funds he paid off his staff. On a bleak day in January, one year after his arrival, he departed from Warsaw. Deep devotion from his people. Home to Morges, from there to watch sadly Pilsudski's march upon Kiev, and his disastrous retreat.

Attending the League of Nations, and winning there a measure of Allied support, he returns to Morges. Without funds—this patron who has given so freely to his country. Without activity— this genius who has filled his every moment with work. Once again he opens his beloved piano. The world waits with bated breath.

VIII

STRONG AND SURE, his mastery returned. And once again the Villa by the Lake was filled with music. Jubilantly his friends flocked about him, as genius once more made magic on the keyboard.

Paderewski himself was a bit nervous about his "new début." Crossing the Rubicon, he called it. On November, 1922, the crossing is achieved in triumph. Admirers battle their way into Carnegie Hall. They refuse to leave even after lights out. Again and again the master plays. A flood of music, so long pent up, sweeps out from his finger tips. The crowd is beside itself. "Viva, Paderewski! The Maestro is greater than ever!"

In Minnesota, he appeared with the Symphony Orchestra,

playing his own *Symphony in B Minor*. Onto the stage marched six officers from the Reserve Corps, bearing American and Polish flags. As one man, the audience rose and cheered, while Paderewski stood with bowed head. Perhaps at that moment he recalled Modjeska's words: "Poland needs you—not only as a statesman, but as a musician."

New audiences—new triumphs. Then back to Europe. In England, the queen leaves the bedside of the sick king to attend his concert.

In his seventies now. The lion's mane is snow-white; his shoulders, more stooped; but his heart, as vital and energetic as ever. The eyes are still aflame with that mischievous glint.

In 1933, New York University bestows upon him a Doctorate of Music. The delegation finds him in sickbed; yet even there he will not deprive himself of his joke. "Gentlemen, you have come to a sick man to make a doctor of him."

He recovered from his sickness. But death, in passing him by, claimed now for the third time the one dearest to him—Madame Paderewska. For thirty-five years she had been his constant companion and devoted co-worker. Wayworn and alone, he wound up his business in America and returned to Switzerland. "Time to retire, old heart!"

Yet one more adventure awaited him—the leading role in a British film, *Moonlight Sonata*. To this venture he brought all the gusto that had marked his other undertakings.

In slippers and dressing gown now. Ready for the final lights out. But wait, a last word to be spoken. A word of warning. And from Switzerland he broadcasts his warning to his countrymen in Poland: "Beware of the rising threat of Fascism!"

IX

ONCE AGAIN Prussian poison had been poured into Poland. And Paderewski was compelled to look from afar upon the tragedy of Polish blood spilled for that pathway to the sea called the Polish

Corridor. With all the strength left in him, he implored his countrymen to resist to the end.

And now it was necessary to flee Europe, in order to escape from the Nazi hordes that reached their octopus tentacles into every corner of the continent. Denied a Spanish visa, braving innumerable dangers, and suffering untold hardships, Paderewski at length arrived at Lisbon. And there, accompanied by his sister and a secretary, he secured passage for America. The home of his adoption, the shrine where his genius had received its highest worship, offered him now much more than a home. It was a haven and a refuge in a world gone mad.

He spent his last days in the city of New York. There, in order to drown out the death-dealing crash of the German guns across the sea, he went frequently to listen to the music at Carnegie Hall. Harmonies that calmed the soul and brought new hope to an aching heart. A world at peace, growing out of the discords of a dying age.

MUSTAPHA KEMAL ATATURK

Important Dates in Life of Mustapha Kemal Ataturk

1881—Born at Salonika.
1890—Lost father.
1898—Entered Military College.
1904—Commissioned captain in Turkish army.
Caught in revolutionary activities, sent to prison.
1905—Released.
1908—Took active part in Young Turk revolution.
1910—Studied military maneuvers in France.

1915—Defended the Dardenelles against the British.
1922—Drove invading Greek army out of Anatolia. Began modernization of Turkey.
1923—Established Turkish Republic.
1928—Reformed Turkish alphabet.
1928-38—Continued reforms.
1938—Died.

Mustapha Kemal Ataturk

1881–1938

Gallipoli. For days, for weeks, for months the Turkish soldiers have been lying in their trenches, rotting and starving slowly to death. It is late afternoon. Two of the soldiers, having completed their prayer to Allah the Merciful, are talking to each other in whispers.

"Do you see him up there in the front?"

"The *Komandan?* Of course I see him. He's always in the front-line trench."

"He's watching the *Inglis* with those glasses that bring far things near."

"I wonder what he sees?"

"Probably sees them eating a nice hot supper."

"Must make his mouth water, just like the rest of us."

"Yes, he too is nothing but skin and bones."

The bark of a gun from the English side. A startled look on the faces of the Turkish soldiers. For Mustapha Kemal was still sitting exposed on the parapet of the foremost trench.

"Down, *Komandan!* Please take shelter below!"

But the Commander only shook his head. He persisted in watching the enemy through his field glass.

Another shot. This time the shell burst on the edge of the parapet. But Kemal still sat unperturbed in his place.

A third shot. The shell struck twenty yards nearer. The English gunners were getting Kemal's range. "Under cover, *Komandan! For our* sake!"

Kemal turned his head and shouted to the frightened soldiers. "For *your* sake, men, I stay here. Can't show you a bad example, you know."

He lit a cigarette and continued to watch the enemy.

A fourth shot. A blinding flash. This time their beloved *Komandan* must surely have been hit! The smoke cleared away. Mustapha Kemal was still sitting in his place, calmly puffing at his cigarette.

"A miracle! Allah has preserved him!"

"Yes. Saved his life so he can set us free."

II

ANKARA. Mustapha Kemal is now the President of Turkey. His closest friend, Colonel Chopal Osman, has been appointed Commander of the Lifeguard. Osman is worried about his President, whose enemies are plotting to assassinate him. They have been organized under a dangerous leader. Something must be done to nip their conspiracy in the bud.

Osman hits upon a good old Turkish plan. He invites the leader of the conspiracy to dinner. A splendid repast. For dessert, a rope is slipped around the leader's neck, and he is strangled to death.

Osman sends word to Kemal that all's well. He expects a splendid reward from the President for his loyalty. But Kemal dispatches a squad of soldiers, instead, to put Colonel Osman under arrest.

"Arrest for what? For sending a mangy dog to hell?"

"No. The charge is first degree murder of a Turkish citizen."

"But he was your enemy!"

"In the New Turkey we don't kill our enemies. We kill their *enmity,* by turning them into our friends."

III

MUSTAPHA was the amazing son of an amazing father. A revenue collector for the Sultan of Turkey, Ali Riza was an object of astonishment, and of ridicule, to his neighbors at Salonika. All the other officials of the government—"the Turkish Caliphate is a four-thousand-headed monster of corruption"—were good Mohammedans and dishonest scoundrels. Ali Riza, on the other hand, was a bad Mohammedan and an honest man. "How can a tax collector, with the money of the Province passing through his hands, refrain from putting a little paste on his fingers now and then?" A servant of the Sultan untainted with *bakshish* (graft) was a new phenomenon under the Turkish sun.

Ali Riza was not only a new phenomenon, but he harbored a secret longing for a new world. A world without sultans and savageries and bribes. He kept his thoughts to himself, however. Too risky to speak of such matters to his neighbors. Now and then he would partially unburden himself to his wife, Zubeida, who was too old to accept new ideas, and to his son, Mustapha, who was too young to understand them.

Some day, however, Mustapha would understand. The child was already a little rebel at heart. To be sure, he adhered to the customs of the Turkish home—never wept in the presence of his parents, kissed his father's hand when he entered the house, remained standing until he was asked to be seated, and never spoke until his elders had had their say. But all this was because he loved and respected his parents. In school it was altogether different. He neither loved nor respected his teacher, Hafiz. This man was so vain of his position, so stupid in his authority. "The teacher commands, the pupil obeys."

"But suppose a pupil has ideas of his own?"

"A pupil is not supposed to have any ideas."

[*263*]

What could you do with such a man? One day Mustapha had a fight with a fellow pupil. Hafiz happened to come along at the time. He turned upon Mustapha. "Why do you beat this boy?"

"Because he insulted me."

For answer, Hafiz tore Mustapha away from his opponent and belabored him with an unmerciful thrashing. "It's only what you deserve," he cried. "An eye for an eye, a tooth for a tooth."

"No, it isn't an eye for an eye," returned little Mustapha, his voice trembling with rage. "You see, sir, the fellow I was fighting was my size. But you're not."

With eyes blazing—"even as a child he had the grey eyes of a wolf"—Mustapha walked out of the room. He never came back to that school.

A great problem to his mother. She was a widow now, Ali Riza having died the early death of those whom the gods love. What was she to do with her rebellious youngster? "Let him go to work for me," suggested an uncle who was a farmer. And so, for a time, young Mustapha put his hand to the pitchfork and the plow. A great life, this farming. Some day he would have his own piece of land—a master who would take orders from none.

Tilling the soil, grazing the sheep—a time for work, a time for thought. And he did much thinking as he lay under the stars watching his uncle's sheep. Good to be a farmer. And yet, this sort of thing would mean living only for yourself. Wouldn't it be more fun trying to live for others? Or to die for others? The life of a soldier—ah, *that* would be something! A course in a military academy, and then a commission in the Turkish army.

Reluctantly his mother consented to his urging that she send him to a military academy. Here he became the model pupil. He loved the scientific precision of his studies at this school. Especially of mathematics. A subject with logic to it! So different from the illogical nightmare of his Salonika grammar school days.

And his master, though a strict disciplinarian, was so different from the teacher of his grammar school days. No fighting for *him* against anybody less than his own size. A great believer in fair play, this man, just like himself. And his name, too, was like his own—Mustapha. One day the teacher spoke to his favorite pupil about this similarity of their names. "Rather confusing, isn't it? Suppose we make a distinction between us. From now on, we shall call you Mustapha Kemal."

Mustapha the Excellent. A great name. Well, from now on he would try to live up to this new name. He would try to be a great man.

IV

A STRANGE FELLOW, the young graduate from the military academy. Trousers pressed, head uplifted, eyes alert—so European in bearing, so unlike the careless slouch of the other Turkish officers. The only thing about his appearance that betrayed his Tartar origin was the prominence of his cheek bones.

An Oriental face with an Occidental restlessness in his heart. An eagerness to tear down, and to rebuild. "He is a born rebel," observed his mother as she sadly shook her head. She had married a rich man, largely for Mustapha's sake. She was anxious to set him up in life. But Mustapha refused to be set up, refused his stepfather's help. "I will carve out my own career in my own way."

But this career of his own choosing, his mother feared, would bring him to an early bad end. He organized a secret revolutionary society under the name of *Vatan* (Fatherland)—a word forbidden at the command of the Turkish Sultan. Denounced by a spy who had wormed his way in as a member of the society, Kemal was arrested and sent to prison.

For months nothing was heard of him. His mother in vain tried to get information from her husband's former associates. "Is Mustapha still alive?"

"Who knows?"

"Stabbed in the back, perhaps?"

"Perhaps. That sort of thing frequently happens to political prisoners."

"Or poisoned, maybe?"

"That, too, is possible. You know the ways of the Padisha."

Finally Zubeida received word about her son. Mustapha was still alive, but banished from Constantinople.

V

RELEASE, promotion—Mustapha was now a major—further rebellion against a dishonest régime. A conspiracy to overthrow the government was being plotted in his house. His mother, who lived with him, became aware of the plot. Her heart was torn between two passions—loyalty toward the Sultan, love toward her son. "Give up your strange new ideas, Mustapha. Be like your father, a faithful servant of the Padisha."

But Mustapha refused to be faithful to tyranny. Better the dangers of the battlefield than the safety of a corrupt palace. When the revolution broke out (1908), Mustapha was appointed chief of staff of the Army of Liberation.

Success, and then failure. The officers in the Army of Liberation had become enslaved to their own greed. A wild scramble for the leading posts, the softest jobs, the richest spoils. From all this turmoil Mustapha kept conscientiously away. His was but a single aim—liberty through honest government. And in this objective, for the time being at least, he failed. The forces arrayed against him, both on his own and on the enemy's side, were too powerful. His character needed more leavening, more experience, more time.

And so Mustapha returned to the maturing of his plans while the Sultan swirled once more to the top of the maelstrom.

But there was trouble for the Sultan just beyond the horizon of his triumph. The Balkans declared war on Turkey, they captured Salonika, they pounded at the gates of Constantinople. A clamor arose among the people. "A savior! Give us a savior!"

"And who is to be our savior?"

"Who else but the Excellent One? Mustapha Kemal!"

For a time the Sultan hesitated. It would be a dangerous thing to confer so great a power upon the "chief of the rebels." But the Bulgarian pressure kept growing more and more intense. Turkey was in danger of imminent defeat. Not a bad idea, perhaps, to invite Kemal to a conference—not, of course, with the Sultan's exalted self, but with one of his subordinates. He sent a note to Kemal: "You are to visit the office of the Minister of Foreign Affairs."

And to the Minister of Foreign Affairs the Sultan sent another note: "You are to keep Kemal waiting in the anteroom until his heels are completely cooled off." They needed Kemal—yes—but Kemal needed a stiff lesson. He must be taught to know his place.

Kemal reached the Minister's office at the appointed time. He sent his card in to the Minister. A shout from the Sanctum loud enough for Mustapha to hear. "Tell him to wait!"

Mustapha sat down. Visitor after visitor arrived, and every one of them was immediately admitted into the inner room. One hour, two hours, two and a half hours. Mustapha sent in a reminder.

"Tell him to wait!" came the shout from the inner office.

It was growing toward evening. Almost time to close the office. At last the Minister sent word that he was ready to receive him. Mustapha was talking to the attendant in the anteroom. He turned to the messenger from the inner office and snapped, "Tell the Minister to wait!"

VI

THE revolution failed, and the Sultan went on with his iniquities and his stupidities and his jests. And then (1914), when the Kaiser launched upon the first World War, the Sultan perpetrated the most sorry jest of them all. He joined the Kaiser's side.

As for Kemal, the Sultan had sent him "out of harm's reach" as commander of the Turkish force in the Caucasus. But Kemal, restless as ever, was still planning for the day when Turkey would be free. From fortress to fortress he traveled along the Caucasian front, urging his soldiers to fight not only against aggression from without, but against oppression from within. "The Turkish nation must emerge as a free and indivisible whole . . . If the Imperial Government fails in this mission, a Revolutionary Government must take its place."

Murmurs of approval among the soldiers. "The Grey Wolf"— Kemal had received a new sobriquet—"speaks words of truth!" But mutterings also of anger and fear. "He would have us rebel against the sacredness of our Caliph-Pasha!"

The Caliph-Pasha, Sultan Mohammed VI, ordered Kemal's arrest. But the soldiers refused to surrender their beloved *Komandan*. The British embarked upon their campaign against Gallipoli, and the *Komandan* saved the day for Turkey. And then, armistice and peace, and once more the *Komandan* came to Turkey's aid. In order to enforce her terms against Turkey, England sent a ship with two battalions on board to Samsun, the only Turkish outlet to the Black Sea. The commander of the Turkish troops at Samsun was Colonel Refat. He had a mere handful of men under him, but a trump card hidden up his sleeve.

Summoned by the British commander, Refat came obediently to his headquarters. He listened in silence while the Englishman expatiated upon his two battalions of brave men. When the Englishman was through, the Turkish officer smilingly pointed to the window. The eyes of the Englishman almost popped out of his head. Column after column of Turkish troops, lusty young fellows in smart uniforms and with glittering arms, kept marching past the window. Good lord, would there be no end to them?

"Well," smiled Refat, as his men kept marching on and on, "do you still intend to occupy Samsun with your pitiable little two battalions?"

"Let the Devil occupy Samsun!" exclaimed the Englishman. That night he steamed away from the harbor, with all his troops on board.

"How did you manage to display so big an army?" asked a reporter later on.

[268]

"It was an idea of Mustapha Kemal's. There were only a few men in the column. But I had ordered them, when they reached a certain point, to double around a block of houses and to fall in again at the rear. What the Englishman actually saw was the same group of soldiers marching past him over and over and over again."

VII

THE entire Turkish army, the entire Turkish nation was now behind Mustapha Kemal. The Sultan, terrified at the rising tide of the rebellion, remained a virtual prisoner in his palace at Constantinople. The city on the Bosporus had now become a capital without a state. Kemal had established the new Turkish capital in the city of Ankara. Thatched hovels gave way to towers of granite and marble. Ankara was becoming one of the most beautiful cities in the East, when a Greek invasion put a sudden halt to the rebuilding of Turkey. The Greeks, always eager to extend their power within the borders of Anatolia, saw now in the political turmoil of Turkey their golden opportunity. From Smyrna they launched an invasion of 200,000 fresh troops against the battletorn remnants of the Turkish army. The Turkish defenders were wiped out. The Greeks called upon Kemal to negotiate for terms of peace. Kemal's reply was: "No negotiation. We shall have either freedom or death."

Feverishly he set to work building a new army—barefoot men in rags and with obsolete rifles in their hands, but with the unconquerable weapon of determination in their hearts.

The army, hopelessly outnumbered and out-equipped by the Greeks, was drawn up for battle on the slopes of the Black Mountain. A few days before the battle, Mustapha Kemal fell off his horse and broke a rib. The doctors ordered him to a hospital in Ankara. An evil omen for the impending struggle.

The Greeks begin their attack. Slowly, stubbornly, foot by foot, the Turks give way. Their losses are appalling. It is only a matter of time before they will be completely annihilated.

And then, suddenly, a miracle! Their stricken commander, pale, emaciated, his lips drawn in pain, rides into their midst. "Allah be praised, the *Komandan* is back!"

But hush! The *Komandan* is speaking. Nothing pale or sickly about that glorious voice of his. "A sign from above! Here, where I broke my rib, we will break the enemy's back."

With such a spirit to lead them—Kemal's fractured rib had penetrated a lung—how could his soldiers help but win the fight? For forty days the battle hung in the balance, and then word reached Kemal at his headquarters: "Our army has captured Chal-Dagh!"

The strategic height of the Black Mountain. The Turks had conquered the foe!

The story of David and Goliath, retold once more on that sacred hill. And the David of that new epic received an appropriate honor from his countrymen. They named him Kemal Ataturk—The Excellent One, Father of the Turkish nation.

VIII

THE SULTAN had been banished from Constantinople. Kemal was now complete master of Turkey. His countrymen implored him again and again to become their new Sultan. But Kemal emphatically refused the title of sovereign power. "The day of imperialism in our country is at an end. From now on, we live in the Turkish Republic."

They elected him President. By nature a man of peace, he was glad to discard his military uniform and to settle down to the rebuilding of his native land. His policy toward the rest of the world was—live and let live. He wanted Turkey to be a country great enough to forego ambition, strong enough to resist oppression. He was a Messiah of the twentieth century.

But a Messiah should never marry. A man who is dedicated to all cannot be devoted to one. Kemal tried the experiment, and failed. He married his secretary. A whirlwind of passion for a

George Bernard Shaw

Winston Churchill

while; then a clash of two strong temperaments; finally a separation. Kemal was obliged—and felt rather relieved—to go on with his pioneering work alone.

Alone he planned to bring medieval Turkey up to the modern tempo of living. He abolished the wearing of the fez—the Turkish headgear symbolical of his nation's enslavement to the past. He threw into the discard the jerseys and the baggy trousers of the Moslems. "We must adopt," he said, "international civilization. This applies to our appearance as well as to our thought. In future we must regard international, civilized dress as the only form worthy of us." He banished the dervishes and the babas and the magicians and the fakirs from the temple courts and the city squares. "Let us free our people from the weavers of spells and the spinners of superstition."

And then he betook himself to the liberation of the women. Here, too, the process must be complete. Away with their antiquated ideas, away with their antiquated veils. A delicate task, but Kemal was equal to it. He decided to lead the crusade in person. Whenever he met a woman in the street, he observed to her that it was a pity to conceal such lovely features with such an ugly cloth. The women took quickly to the idea. They began to come out of their houses unveiled and unafraid. Turkey became a land of powder and lipstick and laughter and gaiety—and hope. Equality of women before their men, equality of men before the law.

All this was but the beginning of Kemal's reforms. He abolished the ancient enslaving laws of Islam and established in their place the modern legal code of Switzerland. He built railroads, airports, harbors; he formed pacts of friendship with foreign states; he introduced the European system of chronology; he drained the marshes; he laid water pipes to irrigate the desert; and he outlined a new method of education to irrigate the human heart.

And the purpose of all this? "A disciplined march to freedom . . . Turkey for the Turks, friendship to the world."

GEORGE BERNARD SHAW

Important Dates in Life of George Bernard Shaw

1856—*July 26, born at Dublin.*
1871—*Got job as clerk.*
1876—*Came to London.*
1876-84—*Tried, unsuccessfully, to succeed as a writer.*
1884—*Joined Fabian (socialist) Society.*
1892—*Finished, in collaboration with William Archer, his first play* (Rhinegold).

1893—*Wrote his first play without collaboration* (The Philanderer).
1898—*Published* Plays Pleasant and Unpleasant.
1923—*Wrote his last important play,* Saint Joan.
1926—*Awarded Nobel Prize for Literature.*

George Bernard Shaw

1856–

I HAVE GOT the tragedian and I have got the buffoon in me, and the buffoon trips me up in the most dreadful way." This confession of G.B.S. is a perfect miniature portrait of his character. Bernard Shaw—he dislikes to be known by his first name—is an idealist with too playful a pen. When he wants to sting people into indignation, he merely tickles them into laughter. He is an angel of vengeance armed with a quiverful of lollipops, a preacher who turns handsprings on the pulpit while delivering the most sacred of his sermons. One day he watched the tomfoolery of Whimsical Walker at the Olympia Circus. After the performance he begged to be introduced to the famous mountebank. "It is very nice of you," said Whimsical, "to shake hands with an old clown." "Not at all," replied Shaw. "It's just one old clown shaking hands with another." Never taking himself seriously, he is yet amazed that nobody else ever takes him seriously. He would like most of all to hear the world say of him, "What a supreme teacher!" All that he ever hears, however, is—"What a clever guy!"

II

His father was a drunkard with a sense of humor. His mother was a humorist with a sense of art. Both of them were interesting characters. "We as children," writes Shaw of himself and of his two sisters, "were obliged to find our way in a household where there was neither hate nor love, fear nor reverence, but always personality."

And he found plenty of personality outside as well as inside of his home. Every day he was taken out by a servant "who was supposed to air me on the banks of the (Dublin) canal." Actually, however, she took him to visit her friends either in the taverns or in the city slums. The "curious child" absorbed the smelly drinks and the soggy food and the sordid misery of the poor, and he grew up with an instinctive hatred of it all.

Every Sunday he was compelled to go to church. He found this experience so distasteful that he never cared to go to church after he grew up. "If you want to commune with God, look for Him out-of-doors. You'll never find him inside on Sundays listening to those insufferable sermons."

At night he recited a prayer of his own composition—not, however, at his *bedside* but *inside* his bed. "God doesn't like cold prayers uttered while kneeling on the floor; he prefers to have them come warm from under the blankets."

Shaw's secular, like his religious, education fell upon a rebellious soil. He learned Latin irregularly from an educated uncle, and forgot it—he tells us—when he began to study it regularly at school. As for arithmetic, he "managed laboriously" to master addition, subtraction and multiplication; but he never could conquer division—"because my teacher kept saying two into four, three into six and so forth." As for doing a problem in four figures—"give me a slate and half an hour's time, and I can produce a wrong answer."

His parents, in the effort to make an educated fool out of him, sent him to one school after another. Finally they gave it up. He left school, and remained for the rest of his life an uneducated wise man.

He detested prescribed study, but he loved impromptu reading. And his reading skirted the entire horizon of the world's literature.

Above all, however, he loved music. His mother was an accomplished musician, and the children grew up to whistle from memory the sonatas of Beethoven and the oratorios of Handel. In his early teens, Shaw learned to play the piano—without a teacher. His mother had now left her erratic husband; and Bernard, as the "head" of the family, felt that maybe he ought to do something about supporting them. He tried clerking in Dublin for a while, made a fairly good living at it, and gave it up in disgust. He then went to London, tried musical criticism, practically starved at it, and loved it. He took an unholy pride—he tells us—in being a burden to his impoverished mother. "I did not throw myself into the struggle for life: I threw my mother into it."

For he had discovered a direction for himself. He had a genius for writing; he was a consecrated artist. "The true artist will let his wife starve, his children go barefoot, his mother drudge for his living at seventy, sooner than work at anything but his art." He allowed his mother to teach music to unmusical pupils until she was ready to drop from exhaustion. He tramped the sidewalks in gaping boots and in trousers with holes—not always mended—in the seat. He shrugged his shoulders when the friends of the family called him a good-for-nothing vagabond. He smiled into his untrimmed gingerbread beard when people pointed to his shambling skeleton of a figure and then pointed to their heads. He knew that everybody regarded him as queer. He *was* queer, different from the general pattern of mankind. He was an artist. Daily he wrote his stint of a thousand words, finished five novels and hundreds of articles, earned a total of £6 (about $30) for the entire labor of ten years, and gradually—at his mother's expense—"made a man of myself instead of a slave."

III

AT 26, HE BECAME a vegetarian—partly for humanitarian reasons, partly for reasons of health. Those who eat flesh, he said, are not only cannibals but walking cemeteries. A diet of vegetables and a glass of water, he maintained, kept him "ten times as well as an ordinary carcass eater." At about the time of his dietary reform, he also became interested in political reform. He had read Karl Marx's *Das Kapital*—a book which he regarded as a revelation. "The reading of that work . . . provided me with a purpose and a mission in life." He became a soap-box orator, preaching the "gospel according to St. Marx" about three times a week for a period of twelve years.

And then he gave up persuading the workers and tried to convert the intellectuals. He joined the Fabian Society—so named after the Roman general, Fabius, whose motto was: "Don't fight until the right moment arrives; but when the right moment arrives, fight like hell." The Fabians believed in socialism as a constructive evolution rather than as a destructive revolution. Their tendency was to emphasize the delay rather than the fight. Bernard Shaw, however, had come to the society fresh from the soap-box. He believed that even in the delay there is a weapon with which you can conquer the enemy. The weapon of the tongue. In his first public address at the Fabian Society (1885), he lashed out at capitalism in a new English style—irony with a Shavian flourish: "It is the desire of the President (of this society) that nothing shall be said that might give pain to particular classes. I am about to refer to a modern class, burglars, and if there is a burglar present I beg him to believe that I cast no reflection upon his profession." And then, continuing this vein of irony, Shaw embarked upon a subtle comparison between the capitalist and the burglar: "I am not unmindful of his (the burglar's) great skill and enterprise, his risks . . . or his abstinence; nor do I overlook his value to the community as an employer on a large scale, in view of the criminal lawyers, police-men, turnkeys, gaolbuilders and sometimes hangmen that owe their livelihoods to his daring undertakings." And then, having established the "respectability" of the burglars, he goes on to assure the capitalists that he regards them as equally respectable: "I hope any shareholders and landlords who may be present will accept my assurance that I have no more desire to hurt their feelings than to give pain to burglars; I merely wish to point out that all three inflict on the community an injury of precisely the same nature."

In this speech Bernard Shaw had discovered both his mission and his livelihood. He would save humanity by appointing him-self as its prophet; and he would enrich his purse by delivering his prophecy as a jest. From now on his life, like one of his most serious plays, *Androcles and the Lion,* was to be "a great religious drama—with leonine relief."

A new sort of play—a new sort of clown. And the world was shocked and tickled at the spectacle of Gabriel disguised in the motley of Punch. "The only reproach with which I became familiar was the everlasting 'Why can you not be serious?' Soon my privileges were enormous and my wealth immense."

His first pulpit was a magazine in which he wrote musical criticisms under the pseudonym of Corno di Bassetto—"an in-strument that gives forth melancholy sounds suitable for a funeral." And then, having laid to rest all the bad music and all the bad musicians in London, he turned his criticism to the stage. For three years he worked as a dramatic critic under the tutelage of Frank Harris, editor of *The Saturday Review.* It was a superb intellectual extravaganza, this spectacle of London's foremost libertine and England's leading ascetic thumbing their noses to-gether at the public, while the public went into paroxysms of laughter. One thing the two men had in common—a dramatic genius for self-praise. Frank Harris pictured the world as a capital "I" surrounded by an ocean of dead fish that stank in his nostrils. As for Bernard Shaw, "I yield to no man"—he wrote—"in the ingenuity and persistence with which I seize every opportunity of puffing myself and my affairs." In both cases, however, this egotistical bunkum was merely the assumption of a false front. Under the mask of their effrontery, both Shaw and Harris were sad and solitary thinkers who saw much to be done in the world but who didn't know how to do it.

The dramatic flair in Harris led him into all sorts of adventures in which Harris was either the hero or the villain. The dramatic flair in Shaw impelled him to write plays in which all the heroes and the villains are mortals created after the image of Bernard Shaw.

His attitude toward his plays, like his attitude toward life, is that of an apostle who tries to save the world with a decalogue of paradoxes. He pokes fun at the motheaten respectabilities of his age, yet he accepts every one of them. He is not an iconoclast—a breaker of images. Instead of *breaking* them, he merely *shakes* them, to the horror of all the bystanders who expect them to crash at any moment—and then, when they are teetering on end, he carefully replaces them upon their pedestals.

Like a mischievous child, he plays at being naughty because, by doing so, he can attract everybody's attention. He builds nearly all of his dramas upon this paradox of pretending to be naughty while really meaning to be nice. He leads his characters—especially his women—into all sorts of compromising situations, and then he leads them safely out again before they are compromised. "How glorious it would be to yield, but how prudent it is to refrain!"

This formula—of rushing close to the fire and then jumping away just in the nick of time—becomes rather monotonous when you find it repeated over and over again in his dramas. Only a few of them are free from the Shavian cliché. And these few plays are—in our opinion—among his best. This is especially true of *Saint Joan*. In this drama about the consecrated Maid of Orleans we penetrate beyond the grinning mask to the tender heart. Here at last Shaw speaks without cap and bells—"the prophet at his best without his silly jest." Here we get the quintessence of Shaw's philosophy—his indignation at man's cruelty, his impatience at his stupidity, his sadness at his suffering. The human animal is a strange admixture of passion and pity—passion when he is powerful to hurt, pity when he is powerless to help. God sends us his prophets, and in our moments of anger we slay them. And then, in our hours of repentance, we sanctify their ashes. Their *ashes,* but not their *persons.* Twenty-five years after the Church had burned the body of Joan of Arc, the selfsame Church rehabilitated her name. "But I will tell you this," observes King Charles to Ladvenu in the epilogue to the play. "If you could bring her back to life, they would burn her again within six months, for all their present adoration of her." And why all this cruelty? Because our human vision is out of focus. "You do not see aright. That is the great thing: you must see." Until that day arrives, "a Christ must perish in torment in every age."

And then comes the final cry from the spirit of Saint Joan, from the innermost heart of Bernard Shaw: "O God that madest this beautiful earth, when will it be ready to receive Thy saints? How long, O Lord, how long?"

IV

MANY THOUGHTFUL PEOPLE, while admiring the prophet in Bernard Shaw, have learned to despise the clown. And foremost among these thoughtful people is Bernard Shaw himself. One evening, at the final curtain of *Arms and the Man,* Shaw took his call as author. There was an outburst of tremendous applause, punctuated suddenly by a solitary *boo.* Shaw held up his hand for silence. And then, turning in the direction of the *boo,* he said: "I quite agree with you, my friend. But what can you and I do against a houseful of the opposite opinion?"

Before the houseful of society, Shaw plays the mummer. In his private life, however, where he doesn't have to put on a show, he is a quiet, friendly, modest gentleman—the word here should be divided into its components, *gentle man*—with an English headful of ideas and an Irish heartful of love. Simply, unobtrusively—many of his closest friends even are unaware of it—he launches all sorts of plans for the betterment of conditions among the poor, and labors for countless hours as a committeeman in an effort to bring these plans to fruition. His chief objective is to see Christianity applied to everyday life. Christian reciprocity through economic socialism—this, in a phrase, embraces the innermost kernel of his philosophy. He has often been called—and at times has called himself—an atheist. Yet the Bible is to him the greatest of books. "You cannot begin to appreciate it until you are sick of the novels and plays and other trash that our grown-up babies feed on." As for his attitude toward Jesus, "I see no way out of the world's misery but the way of Christ"—provided the teachings of Christ are taken out of the cloister and put into practical use. "This man (Jesus) has not been a failure yet; for nobody has ever been sane enough to try his way."

V

IN SPITE OF his mannerisms and his mummeries, Shaw is a Christian Puritan. He is abstemious in his appetites—including even the sexual appetite. In all his long life he has yielded only two or three times to the "illicit intimacies of the flesh." In addition to these few diversions, he has enjoyed two lasting devotions—a passionate love-affair (on paper) with Ellen Terry, and a dispassionate cordiality (in person) with his wife. In his letters to Ellen Terry, "the most enchanting actress who ever graced the stage," he made himself "more fatuous even than Beethoven." Yet in his conduct toward his wife he was the soul of tenderness and fidelity and tact. His "very well-regulated house," wrote Mrs. Patrick Campbell, "came before everything. Whatever might betide, Mrs. Shaw must not be kept waiting ten minutes."

His love-letters, like his dramas, were part of his mummery. They were literary exercises—efforts to show his admirers how

clever he was. He loved to pin down an emotion with an epigram
—even though the emotion might be lacerated in the process.
Often, in his attempt to be witty, he failed to be wise. In his
anxiety to make the telling retort, he would hurt even those who
tried to be friendly to him. Once a beautiful actress—the story
has been wrongly attributed to Isadora Duncan—made him a
proposal. "With your brain and my body," she said, "we would
produce the perfect child." "But suppose," rejoined Shaw, "the
child were to inherit *my* body and *your* brain."

VI

JESTERS, as G. K. Chesterton once observed, are among the most
serious people in the world. They clown in order to attract attention. They flavor the wormwood of truth with the teaser of
molasses. Otherwise the ill-behaved children of the world will
refuse to take the medicine for their spiritual sickness. "If people
didn't laugh at me," wrote Shaw, "they couldn't endure me."

And so, with tongue in his cheek but with sadness in his heart,
he utters the most serious truths with a grin on the face. An ardent
lover of democracy, he selects its vices for ridicule rather than its
virtues for praise. A hater of all tyranny, he is ready to shoot his
epigram at the anti-tyrants if by so doing he can raise a laugh.
"All these anti-Mussolinians," he wrote in 1933, "are idiots."
Horrified at all forms of destruction, he will not forego his merry
quip in favor of the destroyer. "It is unfair," he jested, "to call
Napoleon a wholesale butcher. Any sharpshooter in his army
killed more men than Napoleon." In 1925, when he refused the
Nobel Prize for Literature, he gave a very sensible reason for his
refusal: he didn't need the money. This money (about $35,000),
he said, "is a lifebelt thrown to a swimmer who has already
reached the shore in safety." But, having made this wise observation, he couldn't resist the temptation of spoiling it with a wise-
crack: "I can forgive Alfred Nobel for having invented dynamite.
But only a fiend in human form could have invented the Nobel

Prize." No wonder that a disciple once exclaimed in his perplexity, "Do you mean what you say, Mr. Shaw, or are you saying it just to be mean?"

Of late years, however, Bernard Shaw has spoken clearly and unmistakably on two subjects—the Russian Revolution, and the (second) World War.

In 1931 he visited revolutionary Russia, in company with Lady Astor. He not only found *kasha* (a thick Russian gruel) "the best porridge in the world," but he discovered on the faces of the Russian workers and peasants a buoyancy, a freedom from apprehension, a reflected sense of security such as he had not been able to see anywhere under "capitalist civilization."

Shaw admired Stalin. But he had no sympathy for Trotsky. He was opposed to Trotsky's agitation for the immediate spread of communism to every other country. Nevertheless, he looked upon the Russian experiment with the greatest admiration and the greatest hope. Russia, he believed, need not *force* the rest of the world into socialism. The rest of the world, having seen its success in Russia, would *adopt* it of its own free will.

Shaw admired not only the political but the military organization of Russia. When Germany attacked her in June, 1941, he stood almost alone in predicting a Russian victory. "The news," he said, "is too good to be true . . . It is beyond anything we could have hoped for . . . Germany has not got a dog's chance."

As for his attitude toward the war in general, Shaw had never before the outbreak believed in its possibility. Nobody, he declared, would be mad enough to start it. "Any statesman who is not desperately afraid of starting a cannonade should be sent to a mental hospital." But when Hitler proved himself to be that mad statesman, Bernard Shaw abandoned his pacifism of eighty-three years. "There are now no war aims, and no peace aims, except the aim of winning the fight."

WINSTON CHURCHILL

Important Dates in Life of Winston Churchill

1874—November 30, born at Dublin.

1895—Joined the Fourth Hussars.

1897–98—Served in India.

1898—Served in Egypt.

1899—Served in Boer War.

1900—Elected to House of Commons.

1903—Appointed Under-Secretary of State.

1910—Became Home Secretary.

1911—Became First Lord of the Admiralty.

1915—Relieved of Admiralty post.

1916—Appointed Minister of Munitions.

1919—Appointed Secretary of State.

1924–29—Served as Chancellor of the Exchequer.

1939—Reappointed First Lord of the Admiralty.

1940—Became Prime Minister and leader of England's war efforts.

1945—Churchill government ousted by Labor Party victory.

Winston Churchill

1874—

IN 1900 WINSTON CHURCHILL came to New York for his first American lecture tour. Mark Twain introduced him to the audience in his characteristic fashion: "Ladies and gentlemen, I give you the son of an American mother and an English father—the perfect man!"

What Mark Twain uttered as a jest turned out to be a prophecy. In this world of human imperfection, Winston Churchill comes pretty close to the universal ideal of the perfect man.

Born prematurely (November 30, 1874), he was dubbed, from the hour of his birth, "Young Man in a Hurry." Approaching his seventieth year in the exciting events of 1944, he appeared among all the statesmen of the world as the youngest man in the greatest hurry. "There's work to be done. Let's to it without delay."

As a child he hated the severity of mathematics but he loved the magic of words. He abhorred the lessons assigned to him by his governesses and his teachers. Never would he truckle to the demands of these tyrants who kept on nagging him, "Do this," and "Don't do that." Good Lord, hadn't he a mind of his own? He tried to appeal from their dictatorship to his mother; but she, thoroughbred sportswoman, was too fond of her hunting to pay much attention to him. "She shone for me like the Evening Star I loved her dearly—but at a distance."

At seven he was trundled off to (St. James) School—with fourteen pairs of socks, three half crowns, and two clenched fists. The headmaster handed him a Latin grammar. "You must learn to decline *mensa*."

Winnie looked in perplexity at the various cases until he came to the vocative—*mensa, O table*. "What does this mean, sir?"

"This is the expression you must use when you address a table."

"But, sir, I never address a table."

For answer, the headmaster administered a caning. The boys in his school must be taught their discipline early. But Winnie didn't take lightly to his master's idea of discipline. Snatching the man's hat, he kicked it to pieces. Another beating, another outburst of temper. "The little rascal is going to be hard to handle."

An intractable child. To this day, writes H. G. Wells, "I can think of him as . . . a mischievous little boy, a knee-worthy little boy. Only by thinking of him in that way can I go on liking him."

But his masters at St. James found nothing likable in this tempestuous little roughneck. They requested his removal from their midst. His father transferred him to a school conducted by two elderly ladies at Brighton. "A small red-headed pupil," one of his teachers observed of him, "the naughtiest boy in the class. I used to think him the naughtiest boy in the world."

Still a very poor scholar in Latin and in mathematics. But a good student in French—there are no silly vocatives, *O table*, in this language—and a veritable magician in the use of English words. And a memory in which a poem stuck like a fly alighting on fly-paper. He read a stanza once or twice—and there it was, forever fixed.

His assigned lessons were as distasteful as ever. He was almost grateful for the interruption to these lessons when he came down with an attack of double pneumonia. In those days, double pneumonia was almost always fatal. But Winnie pulled through. "The child," remarked the doctor, "has a charmed life."

Throughout his days, Winston Churchill was to lead a charmed life. Fire cannot burn, nor bullets pierce, the man whom the gods have elected to do their work.

Recovered from his illness, Winston took the examinations for Harrow. He had hoped to be examined in French, poetry and essay-writing—subjects in which he could shine. Instead, he was examined in Latin and in mathematics. He just barely managed to squeeze through.

And just barely squeezed through his entire career at Harrow. True, the headmaster admired his "literary powers" and expressed his belief that young Winston might possibly distinguish himself later in life. But when the final marks were computed for the entire school, Winston Churchill's name stood out—last.

His father, a better than average scholar and a man prominent in public life, was sadly disappointed. "What, my son, do you intend to do with yourself?"

"I shall be a soldier so long as there is any fighting to be done. After that I shall have a shot at politics."

"But first of all, there's Oxford to think of."

"If you don't mind, sir, I had rather go to Sandhurst."

Lord Randolph Churchill did mind. At heart a pacifist, he didn't relish the idea of his son's going to a military school. Winston insisted, however, and Lord Randolph finally consented.

Winston took the examinations for Sandhurst and failed. He took them again, and again failed. He tried a third time—and succeeded through a lucky chance. He knew that one of the assignments at the examination would be the drawing, from memory, of a map of some part of the British Empire. But the British Empire, unlike ancient Gaul, was divided into very many parts. Gambling on a long shot, he threw into his hat several slips of paper, each bearing the name of a British colony or dominion. Then, closing his eyes, he drew one of the paper slips from the hat. New Zealand. This was the map he studied.

At the examination the instructor said, "Gentlemen, you will kindly draw a map of New Zealand."

II

FOR THE FIRST TIME, Churchill finds himself in his element. He tries for a cadetship in the cavalry—and succeeds. You don't have to solve an algebraic equation in order to become a daredevil in the saddle. And Churchill loves the saddle, loves the whistling of the wind through his hair, as he gallops over the drillground. "No hour of life is lost that is spent on horseback," he writes exultantly. "Young men have often been ruined through *owning* horses, or through *backing* horses, but never through *riding* them. Unless, of course, they break their necks, which, taken at a gallop, is a very good death to die."

A steady seat, an old Oriental proverb has it, will often rescue an unsteady head. In spite of his academic deficiencies, young Churchill finished eighth in a class of a hundred and fifty at Sandhurst.

A great triumph, a commission in the Fourth—the Queen's own—Hussars. And a great tragedy, the death of his father. Lord Randolph, Chancellor of the Exchequer, had succumbed to a weak constitution and to the calumnies of his political enemies. Winston stood at his bedside. "The dunce of the family," he vowed, "will take revenge on the whole pack of curs and traitors!" His work, he felt, was mapped out before him. His life was to be a constant campaign—against the enemies of England from without, against the enemies of his father from within.

His campaigning began under his regimental leader, Colonel Brabazon. Rarely were commander and subaltern more closely in accord. Both of them lisped. "The gwass is veddy gween." "Yeth, thir, veddy gween indeed." Both of them were less concerned with authority than with common sense. And both of them concealed, under a formal military gruffness, a very informal love for literature. Their daily duties performed, they could sit together for hours quoting English poetry to one another.

Partly through the influence of Brabazon but largely because of an inner urge, young Churchill began to look for another outlet to his restless energy. He wrote a number of short stories and a novel, *Savrola—The Tale of a Revolution in Laurania*. Not a literary masterpiece, but a penetrating attempt at self-revelation. The hero of the story, Savrola, is a prototype of Winston Churchill —a young man eager to be the honest and intelligent leader of a revolution. "All the other revolutionists throughout the course of history have been either scoundrels or fools." Hiring himself out as a war correspondent to the *Daily Graphic*, Churchill had taken a trip to Cuba, to report a political upheaval in that colony. He had seen, at first hand, enough of the intrigues of the so-called "liberators" to disgust him with that tribe for the rest of his days. "While the members of the old régime are masters of the art of suppressing the truth," he wrote in one of his articles, "the leaders of the new are adepts in inventing falsehoods." And in another article—"I sympathize with the revolution—not with the revolutionaries."

But enough of articles and of stories—for the present. There is fighting to be done. Threats of rebellion in India. Churchill's regiment is ordered to Bombay. A battle against the Mamunds, "a tribe utterly pestilential in their cruelty." In the midst of the battle, Churchill leaps down from his horse and clambers up a hill together with a detachment of infantry. Always where the fighting is thickest! They reach the top of the slope. The forest comes alive. A blaze of bullets from behind every rock and from the branches of every tree. Impossible to stand this fire. The detachment retreats. But not Winnie Churchill. A comrade has been wounded—right eye slashed out by a Hindu dagger. Can't leave him behind to the mercy of the enemy. Churchill tries to carry him down the slope. He finds himself surrounded. Laying down the wounded man, he takes out his revolver. It balks. He snatches up an abandoned rifle. By the Devil, it works! Twenty, thirty, forty rounds. The enemy gives way. Churchill brings his man safely down to camp!

"Nobody but Winnie could have come out of that with a whole skin. A charmed life—what else can it be?"

And a charmed life he carried into his other campaigns—in India, in the Soudan, in South Africa, wherever he served in the line—never behind the line—either as soldier or as war correspondent. Generally he served as both, finding equal activity for his pistol and his pen. Always he sought the center of the fight, and always he came out unscathed. Once he was captured by the Boers, and made use of his captivity to catch up with his reading. Gibbon, Lecky, Carlyle, Stuart Mill, Plato's *Republic*, Aristotle's *Politics*, Winwood Reade's *Martyrdom of Man*. Great men, great thoughts. But enough of them now. There were great deeds to be done. This imprisonment was getting on his nerves. He made his escape, hid himself in a coal mine, found himself packed amidst a shipment of coal bags in a freight car, and finally reached his own lines.

Not only a man with a charmed life, but a daredevil to boot. In his spare time he had trained himself to become a champion polo player. Once, when he was stationed at Hyderabad, the Golcondas, champion polo team of India, challenged his team to a match. "A slaughter," predicted everybody, feeling sorry for poor Churchill and his mates. The match did indeed turn out to be a slaughter—for the other side. Final score: Hussars 9, Golcondas 3. But Churchill, who had led the onslaught at center, almost collapsed at the end. He had played the entire game with a broken shoulder.

A fighting-cock who knew his worth. Nothing of the shrinking violet about him. In one of the articles which he sent as a war correspondent to the *Allahabad Pioneer*, he wrote glowingly about "the courage and the resolution of Lieutenant Winston Churchill, of the Fourth Hussars."

III

HE HAD SERVED as a soldier while there was fighting to be done. And now that the fighting was (temporarily) over, he had his shot at politics. He ran for Parliament (1899) on the same ticket with a labor leader—"the Scion and the Socialist," they were dubbed—and lost. He had received, however, a great deal of publicity during the campaign. "The Youngest Man in Europe," an enthusiast had written of him in the *Daily Mail,* "possesses qualities which make him, almost at will, a great popular leader, a great journalist, or the founder of a great advertising business. What he will become, who can say?"

Least of all, Winston Churchill himself. But he was eager to find out. Another try for Parliament—and this time he was successful. Smiles, handshakes, huzzahs wherever he turned. What a colorful event for England! A Rough Rider in the House of Commons—so gallantly reminiscent of that other Rough Rider across the sea who had just been elected Vice-President of the United States.

But politics is a costly game. To rise in power, he must keep open his purse. A rather lean purse, unfortunately. He decides to fatten it through a lecture tour over England, in Canada, in the United States. Everywhere he electrifies his audiences with the story of his battles, his capture, his breathless escape. He returns with sufficient capital to carry him on to the top.

Back to Parliament and his maiden speech. Here the public sees revealed a new Winston Churchill—a man with a heart. Like Lincoln, he speaks words of charity for his erstwhile enemies, the Boers. "If I were a Boer fighting in the field—and if I were a Boer I *should* be fighting in the field . . ." Liberal words, these. The Conservatives in Parliament shook their heads in disapproval. "He's going to be a hard man to handle . . . Stands against his own light."

But Churchill did nothing of the kind. He knew precisely where he was facing—forward and upward, in order to keep his *country* facing forward and upward. To preserve the Empire—united, righteous and strong.

He advocated a powerful navy. The heart of the British Empire, he pointed out, is an island; for the very flowing of its life-blood it depends upon the channels of the sea. "The Admiralty is the only office strong enough to insure the British Empire."

Strange words for a soldier, this advocacy of a strong navy against a strong army. But what matters the branch of service so long as a man is anxious to serve?

And what matters the party through which a man can attain to service? Parties always meant less than principles to Winston Churchill. Liberal, Conservative, Whig, Tory, Labor—these were but slogans for the rallying of political support. The essential thing was to insure "a Government that will think a little more about the toiler at the bottom of the mine and a little less about the fluctuations of the share market in London . . . a Government and a policy which will think the condition of a slum in an English city is not less worthy of attention of statesmen . . . than the jungle of Somaliland." Political observers often smiled cynically and called him a turncoat. What he actually did was merely to turn his eyes always in the direction of the light.

IV

IN 1905, UNDER the first liberal Minister in a decade, Churchill was appointed Under-Secretary for the Colonies. In this office the "men of all colors and creeds" had a friend who understood them and meant them well. Especially the Boers had reason to be grateful to him. In his effort to solve the Boer problem, he pointed out to Parliament again and again that "we must insure not only British wishes but Boer assent." When the Liberals—the party to which he now belonged—had voted to grant a Constitution to Transvaal, he implored the Conservatives to make the vote unanimous: "With all our majority we can only make the

Constitution the gift of a party. You can make it the gift of England."

From liberalism he turned to radicalism. "Why have I always been kept safe within a hair's breadth of death except to do something for the poor?" But he stopped short of socialism, because of its avowed purpose to put an end to competition. "The existing organization of society is driven by one mainspring—competitive selection. It may be a very imperfect organization of society, but it is all we have got between us and barbarism."

A crusader for justice within the bounds of private enterprise. And in his vigorous fight for justice he felt "as if I could lift the whole world on my shoulders."

And thus, carrying lightly the burden of humanity, he reached his thirty-fourth year (September, 1908) when, to quote his own words, he "married and lived happily ever afterwards."

With the accession of a loving and understanding wife, his ambitions and his achievements grew more rapidly than ever. A little too rapidly, perhaps, for his success tended to make him precipitate. "He is too apt to act first and think afterwards," observed Lord Haldane. Yet "of his courage," Haldane confessed, "one cannot speak too highly."

A man of courage was needed in the Admiralty. For there were too many deadweights who kept the British navy down. And once appointed to that office, Churchill proved to everybody's surprise that he was also endowed with a great measure of wisdom. He was himself impressed, and he tried to impress the Government, with "a sense of ever-present danger." Germany, he was convinced, was constantly on the jump to start a war against England; and it was his habit suddenly to ask the question, "What happens if war with Germany begins today?"

The British navy must be prepared for any eventuality. Battleships, cruisers, destroyers, even seaplanes—this as early as 1913—sprang up under the magic touch of Winston Churchill. His insistence upon a strong navy occasioned a break with the radicals; for most of them were pacifists and believed in reducing, rather than in expanding, the instruments of war. Churchill alone saw the war clouds gathering just above the horizon.

And then the storm broke. Winston Churchill, still under forty, was now First Lord of the Admiralty. Upon his shoulders alone rested the success or the failure of the British navy. And of the British army, too; for it was the navy that must transport the men and the arms to the battlefield on the continent. In the presence of his associates he wore—to quote one of them—"a happy face." But when alone, he had his moments of misgiving. In spite of all his efforts prior to the war—time and again he had worked on a twenty-four hour basis—the pacifists had had their way. England had been caught in 1914 unprepared.

That is, the army had been caught unprepared, but not the navy. When, as a result of the Dardanelles fiasco Churchill was asked to resign from the Admiralty, Lord Kitchener paid him a visit. After he had chatted with him about the latest news, he turned to go. And then, with a sudden impulse, "Well, there is one thing at any rate they cannot take from you. The Fleet was ready."

V

RESIGNATION, but no respite. From the navy he transferred his services to the army. Major Winston Churchill, of the Oxford-shire Yeomanry—a man who, in spite of his setbacks, still appeared to his colleagues to exhibit "great form and tearing spirits."

All quiet on the battlefront. Churchill whiled away his time learning a new art—painting. He enjoyed bright colors, bold strokes—mirror of his own bright and bold personality.

His headquarters were close to the front—too close, thought his superiors who were fond of him, for his safety. His brains were too precious for his body to take too many chances. "Do you realize," said the Commander-in-Chief, "that this is a very dangerous place?" "Yes, sir," replied Churchill, "but after all, this is a very dangerous war."

A brave spirit, and a perfect *confrère* to that other brave spirit, Clemenceau. One day the two stormy petrels met on the battle-field, where Clemenceau was paying a visit to the British troops. There was active fighting going on at the time. "You really ought not to risk your life under fire," said Churchill. Whereupon Clemenceau retorted, *"Mon ami, c'est mon grand plaisir."* ("My friend, it's my great pleasure.")

November, 1918. The end of the war; and the end, it seemed, of Churchill's career. "To keep him out of mischief," they rele-gated him to the post of Minister of Munitions. A meaningless job, now that peace had arrived. Politically he was almost friend-less. Due to his honest habit of sacrificing the expedient for the just, he had become anathema to all the parties. Neither the Conservatives nor the Liberals nor the Laborites could "trust" him as a tool to do their bidding. He had a "peculiar" philosophy of his own—the permanent interest of the entire British Common-wealth. So foreign to the interests of a *party*—that is, a *part*—of England. No significant role for *him* now to play in the politics of the time.

Obscure tasks. Yet he entered upon them, as usual, "in good form, very energetic and very cheerful."

And then, an attack of appendicitis. While he lay convalescing in the hospital, an election for Parliament came up. His wife fought his campaign for him. Two days before the voting he got out of his invalid's chair and addressed his constituents at Dun-dee. Angry faces, shaken fists, muttered threats. At the polls he was overwhelmingly defeated.

VI

TWENTY YEARS of comparative obscurity—writing, lecturing, painting. And always dreaming of the day when he would come back. His critics looked unkindly upon his dream. "Mr. Churchill," wrote H. G. Wells, "believes quite naïvely that he belongs to a peculiarly gifted and privileged class of beings . . .

His imagination is obsessed by dreams of exploits and a career . . . Before all things he desires a dramatic world with villains— and one hero."

This caricature was unfair to Churchill. He had his human share of egotism, to be sure, but his chief interest was the welfare of England. It was of England that he thought when he warned the world (1932) against the advent of Hitler. He was almost alone to see, in the stirring of the Nazi uprising, a threat to all Europe. A prophet in the wilderness. "It is good to live in the wilderness; it gives you time to think." He thought about England's danger, and her weakness in face of it, and he was terrified at the thought. Terrified, and determined to transform England's weakness into England's strength. He spoke of the new menace in modern warfare—the menace of air attack. "This cursed, hellish invention and development of war from the air"—he insisted as far back as 1933—"has revolutionized our position. We are not the same kind of country we used to be when we were an island . . ." He called again and again for "an airforce at least as strong as that of any power that can get at us."

But England only half-listened, and slept. "A fire-eater, doesn't know what he is talking about." Hitler went on with his preparations for the most stupendous adventure of gangsterism in history —and England slept. Slept under Baldwin, slept under Chamberlain—while Hitler collected his tools, and Mussolini launched upon that prelude to international burglary in Ethiopia, and Hitler and Mussolini aided and abetted Franco in the murder of a legally constituted democratic government in Spain. Slept while Hitler robbed nation after nation, and slaughtered their people, and kept gathering and sharpening his tools against England herself. And Churchill looked on with a great rising anger in his heart against a British government "decided only to be undecided, resolved only to be irresolute, adamant for drift, solid for fluidity, all-powerful to be impotent."

Munich and Chamberlain's disgraceful flight in an airplane to lick the dust off Hitler's boots—"Chamberlain crawled to Hitler on all fours," a clever journalist remarked, "at two hundred miles an hour." And still England slept. "No need for alarm," Chamberlain reported. "Herr Hitler is a gentleman. He has promised us peace."

But Churchill knew better. "We have sustained a defeat," he declared, "without a war."

And then, the avalanche. The air attack on England. The threatened defeat of civilization. Almost too late, they called Churchill to the rescue. The Young Man in a Hurry. Great need for hurry now if civilization was to be saved.

Churchill's mood as he undertook the job was realistic, but unafraid. "I have nothing to offer but blood, toil, tears and sweat." Yet out of this blood and toil and tears and sweat, he emphatically declared, would come triumph in the end.

Electric words. Overnight they transformed England into a nation of heroes. Throughout the country, but a single resolve—to *bear* arms, to *make* arms, to *win the victory!* "Victory at all costs, victory in spite of all terror, victory, however long and hard the road may be."

A long and hard road, indeed. But with Churchill leading the way, what other end could there be but victory?

Dark days and nights. The blackout of the world. The drone of Germany's planes over London. "The capital of humanity" in flames. The imminent invasion of England. But Churchill kept on presenting to the world a countenance undismayed. "We shall defend our island, whatever the cost may be, we shall fight on the beaches, we shall fight on the landing grounds, we shall fight in the fields and in the streets, we shall fight in the hills; we shall never surrender."

The old Churchill determination. The old Churchill courage. And the old Churchill defiance. Hitler at last had met his master —the man who could outguess him step by step. June, 1940. Hitler was in possession of the entire coastline of the Continent from the North Cape to the Pyrenees. In his evil hands he wielded two irresistible instruments—an undefeated army and an unlimited air fleet. He was poised for the invasion of England. But there was one man who stood in the way. Churchill, armed with a weapon greater than all the accumulated might of Hitler. A spirit that refused to go down in defeat. He braced his countrymen for their "finest hour," and he hurtled the challenge into Hitler's face: "Come on, we shall easily devour your entire hostile horde!"

Hitler hesitates, and is lost. The invasion of England is "indefinitely postponed." The fighting heart of Churchill—"I shall be a soldier as long as there is fighting to be done"—has saved the day for the human race.

When the fighting was over and the United Nations had won the war, he was "honorably discharged" from his post. His countrymen felt that the new day required a new guide. And so, in the elections of 1945, they replaced the tried warrior with an untried man of peace. Yet in looking forward with their new social leader, Clement Attlee, the voters of England cast a reverent glance upon the fighter who had preserved for them the right to vote him down.